THE
EVERYTHING
SOUP, STEW, & CHILI
COOKBOOK

Dear Reader,

Writing this cookbook has been a happy adventure. Usually, when I share the subject of an in-progress cookbook with family and friends, they demand recipes. Or cooking tips. However, when I told people I was writing *The Everything® Soup, Stew, & Chili Cookbook*, the tables turned. Instead of asking for recipes, everyone wanted to give me recipes. Over and over I heard, "My grandma's chicken soup is the absolute best" or "Here, you've just got to include my rabbit stew" or "My uncle gave me his green chili recipe—you've never tasted anything so good!"

Of course, most of the recipes shared were more like compass points than actual roadmaps. That's because soups, stews, and chilies are among the most flexible and personal of dishes. The same recipe can vary based on the mood of the cook, the availability of fresh ingredients, the amount of liquid added, and the time available for simmering. Having been raised on my mother's heirloom gumbo and fricassee recipes and my father's ever-evolving chili pot, I can attest to the joy of anticipating the nuances of every batch.

In this book you'll find recipes that represent the culinary heart of many different cultures. One cook's strange new curry is another's family comfort food. Follow the recipes as given or use them as a starting point for your own explorations. Either way, my great hope is that you'll find recipes you'll embrace and want to share.

Belinda Hulin

Welcome to the EVERYTHING® Series!

These handy, accessible books give you all you need to tackle a difficult project, gain a new hobby, comprehend a fascinating topic, prepare for an exam, or even brush up on something you learned back in school but have since forgotten.

You can choose to read an *Everything*® book from cover to cover or just pick out the information you want from our four useful boxes: e-questions, e-facts, e-alerts, and e-ssentials.

We give you everything you need to know on the subject, but throw in a lot of fun stuff along the way, too.

We now have more than 400 *Everything*® books in print, spanning such wide-ranging categories as weddings, pregnancy, cooking, music instruction, foreign language, crafts, pets, New Age, and so much more. When you're done reading them all, you can finally say you know *Everything*®!

QUESTION

Answers to
common questions

FACT

Important snippets
of information

ALERT

Urgent
warnings

ESSENTIAL

Quick
handy tips

PUBLISHER Karen Cooper

DIRECTOR OF ACQUISITIONS AND INNOVATION Paula Munier

MANAGING EDITOR, EVERYTHING® SERIES Lisa Laing

COPY CHIEF Casey Ebert

ACQUISITIONS EDITORS Katie McDonough, Katrina Schroeder

SENIOR DEVELOPMENT EDITOR Brett Palana-Shanahan

EDITORIAL ASSISTANT Hillary Thompson

EVERYTHING® SERIES COVER DESIGNER Erin Alexander

LAYOUT DESIGNERS Colleen Cunningham, Elisabeth Lariviere, Ashley Vierra, Denise Wallace

Visit the entire Everything® series at *www.everything.com*

THE

EVERYTHING®

SOUP, STEW, & CHILI COOKBOOK

WITHDRAWN

Belinda Hulin

adamsmedia

Avon, Massachusetts

*To my daughter Sophie and son Dylan, who
never tire of helping me stir the pot.*

An Everything® Series Book.
Everything® and everything.com® are registered trademarks of F+W Media, Inc.

Published by Adams Media, a division of F+W Media, Inc.
57 Littlefield Street, Avon, MA 02322 U.S.A.
www.adamsmedia.com

ISBN 10: 1-60550-044-5
ISBN 13: 978-1-60550-044-7

Printed in the United States of America.

J I H G F E D C B A

Library of Congress Cataloging-in-Publication Data
is available from the publisher.

This publication is designed to provide accurate and authoritative information with regard to the subject matter covered. It is sold with the understanding that the publisher is not engaged in rendering legal, accounting, or other professional advice. If legal advice or other expert assistance is required, the services of a competent professional person should be sought.

—From a *Declaration of Principles* jointly adopted by a Committee of the American Bar Association and a Committee of Publishers and Associations

Many of the designations used by manufacturers and sellers to distinguish their products are claimed as trademarks. Where those designations appear in this book and Adams Media was aware of a trademark claim, the designations have been printed with initial capital letters.

This book is available at quantity discounts for bulk purchases.
For information, please call 1-800-289-0963.

Contents

Acknowledgments

Many thanks to my friends at Adams Media for their encouragement and guidance. In particular, I'd like to thank project editors Katrina Schroeder and Katie McDonough, development editor Brett Palana-Shanahan, copy editor Sheila Elmosleh, and managing editor Lisa Laing. Bob Diforio has been a wonderful advocate, for which I am ever grateful.

Hugs and kisses to my husband, Jim Crissman, who sampled my recipes, listened to me whine, and, when the bubbling pots got to be too much, took the family fishing. The Cast Iron Literary Circle of the Jacksonville Beaches—particularly authors Ruth Chambers and Carol O'Dell—have my devotion for their no-nonsense advice and unfailing moral support. Thanks to Robin Warshaw for sanity checks. And finally, *merci beaucoup* to my mother, Audrey Hulin, whose wonderful gumbo, vegetable soup, and étouffée are forever imprinted on my taste buds.

Introduction

THINK OF IT AS comfort in a bowl. Soups, stews, and chilies certainly provide an economical source of nourishment. But these creations are so much more than the sum of their ingredients. No two batches can be exactly alike because each carries the *terroir*—the flavor signatures—of its components, captured at the moment of preparation. In addition, each version of a soup, stew, or chili recipe is influenced by the whim, the mood, the loving hands of the cook.

A good recipe can ensure a good dish, but it can't predict the grace notes added by time, place, and human expression. A bumper crop of fresh zucchini, a particularly fragrant bunch of basil, a dish of savory leftover pot roast; such variables are what make any slow-simmered jumble of ingredients a wonderful, original work of art.

Anthropologists quibble over where and when the first pot of soup or stew appeared. Some credit the Neanderthals with softening foods in water in a hollowed bit of bark. Others note later evidence that African and European tribes learned to cook meat and plants together in the sealed stomach cavities of animals, while South American tribes used hollowed turtle shells as soup and stew vessels. Purists date the first real soups and stews—and in South America, where peppers were thrown in, chilies—to around 10,000 B.C., when ceramic pots appeared on the scene.

References to soups and stews appear in the earliest surviving cookbooks, including some dating to the third century. By the Middle Ages, sages and essayists were recommending chicken soup as a cure for all manner of infirmities. Early American writings on food trace recipes and soup customs with English, German, and French origins. Added to that early melting pot were offerings from Native Americans featuring tree nuts and wild greens. Journal entries from the colonial period make clear that soup, then as now, was considered a community-building dish that required both generosity and sharing.

Soup became a lifesaving elixir during the Great Depression. Beginning in 1929, churches and charities opened makeshift dining halls serving hot soup and bread to anyone who lined up for a meal. Eventually, soup kitchens cropped up across the U.S., with bean and chicken soups being ladled out in most cities and towns. Many were operated by the Volunteers of America, some by municipal governments and nonprofit groups. Al Capone even opened a soup kitchen in his hometown, Chicago.

Modern households appreciate these ancient dishes for the same reasons as our ancestors; namely, sustenance and satisfaction. However, in addition, we've learned that soups, stews, and chilies can be an easy and accessible way to sample the flavors of other cultures, to expand our own culinary horizons, and to entertain friends. A hearty Louisiana gumbo, a delicate ginger-scented broth, a fiery but rich Thai coconut chicken soup—the varieties of soups, stews, and chilies in the world are limited only by the collective imaginations of cooks.

In *The Everything® Soup, Stew, & Chili Cookbook,* you'll find a broad sampling of both classic and innovative dishes from around the globe. You'll also learn everything you need to create your own unique offerings. The important thing to remember is this: Relax; soups, stews, and chilies are naturally forgiving dishes. Enjoy the process, and your family and friends will love the results.

CHAPTER 1

Bowled Over!

Soups, stews, and chilies are, of necessity, slow food. The process of making stock, selecting and chopping ingredients, braising and simmering can't be rushed. And while the food cooks, the cook has time to reflect, consider, make adjustments. For this reason, every bowl of soup, stew, or chili is a work of art, each as individual as a thumbprint. And yet, every batch reflects the contributions of multiple cultures and has roots in ancient civilizations.

The Evolution of Soups and Stews

The first soups and stews probably originated with the first prehistoric cook who figured out how to soak flora or fauna in water to make it more easily edible. That said, food historians credit the advent of cooking pots—clay or carved stone vessels able to withstand high temperatures—with the arrival of soups and stews that resemble the dishes you know today. Without heat-safe pots, water could not be boiled for extended periods. Very hot water is needed to dissolve meat sinews, break down plant fibers, and extract nutrients from otherwise inedible bones. The flavorful broth would have been a happy side benefit of cooking meats and vegetables in a pot.

The first stews were probably porridges of grain—which boiling would have rendered soft and thick—studded with meats and berries. No doubt, soups left on the fire too long were another source of prehistoric stew.

FACT

Archeological evidence suggests that once animals became domesticated and crops cultivated, soups and stews flourished. Ancient cooks around the Mediterranean in particular, including Southern Europe, Northern Africa, and the Middle East, used soups and stews extensively, boiling their harvest in crockery vessels. Biblical scholars cite references to lentil stew in the tale of brothers Esau and Jacob, and an A.D. 4 Roman cookbook offers instructions for stew making.

Although early recipes and practices passed from country to country via migrations, armies, and trading vessels, the ultimate melting pot for soups and stews was the colonial United States. The British brought their recipes for pea soup, duck soup, and broths; the Germans added potato soups, fruit soups, meaty stews, and dumplings; French settlers added soups thickened with roux, julienned vegetable mélanges, and turtle soup. Strongly flavored soups and stews with tomatoes, peppers, fish, sausages, and beans were the province of the Spanish. African hands stirred the pots with okra, greens, pork, and herbs. The first writings about food from the American colonies mention both subsistence and well-laden tables offering soups and stewed meats.

During the 1800s, home cooks canned soups for year-round use and travelers could reconstitute dried soup mixes while en route from one corner of the United States to another. But the biggest development in the distribution and automation of soup came in 1899, when Joseph Campbell figured out how to make canned, condensed soup in a preserving and canning factory outside Philadelphia. Five years later, the company was selling 16 million cans of condensed soup a year, including Tomato, Vegetable, Chicken, Consommé, and Oxtail varieties. Today, the company sells more than 2.5 billion cans of soup annually, and it is by no means the only major player.

Combine commercial soup sales—including restaurant soups, canned soups, aseptic-pack soups, improved dehydrated soups, and gourmet frozen soups—with the gallons of soups made by home cooks every day, and there's no doubt that soup is one of the world's most beloved dishes.

Old- and New-World Chilies

The New World is actually the Old World where chilies are concerned. Sweet and hot chili (or chile) peppers have been traced back some 10,000 years to South America. There's evidence that ancient peoples of what is now the western United States cultivated peppers, as did tribes in Mexico and Central and South America. Christopher Columbus discovered several varieties of capsicums on his journey of discovery in 1492, and within a couple of years, peppers began turning up in Spain, Portugal, the Caribbean, India, Southeast Asia, the Philippines, and parts of Africa.

Spanish and Portuguese explorers valued dried chilies, which they scraped and powdered, as a substitute for black pepper, which is one of the things that sent them on their voyages of exploration. However, they carried capsicum plants home and to other colonies and quickly discovered how easily they grow. Stews using powdered and fresh chili peppers quickly became part of the local diet wherever the pepper plants took root. Locals added native ingredients and spices to the mix, yielding a vast array of chili-based dishes, which then became part of international cultural exchanges. One of the most interesting cases of this is Indian curry, which was embraced by the British during their Indian colonial period, then spread to other British Commonwealth nations, including the Caribbean Islands, where many Europeans first encountered chili peppers.

The meaty, saucy dish known as chili con carne (chili with meat) in the United States likely originated in San Antonio in the nineteenth century. Poor women of Spanish and Mexican descent used chili peppers to season, stretch, and otherwise make palatable stews of very low-quality beef. They prepared chili con carne for their families, then began to carry pots of chili to the central plaza for sale to soldiers, cattlemen, and railroad workers.

ESSENTIAL

The precursor to chili con carne was probably a "chili brick" stew made by cowboys for cattle drives. The men created pressed-together bricks of dried beef, dried chili, and other desiccated ingredients, which made for a source of protein and sustenance that would not spoil along the trail. The bricks were dropped into pots of boiling water over campfires and simmered until the ingredients softened into a thick stew.

Texas historians note that San Antonio chili was a great equalizer of peoples, with swells and poor immigrants alike lining up next to their favorite chili purveyor's table. The dish, originally made with chili peppers, meat, onions, and a few other seasonings and served with a side of beans, eventually came to be served throughout North America, with each region boasting its own distinctive chili preferences and recipe secrets. Interestingly, the place where chili, the dish, did not really take hold is in the country where everyone assumes it originated. Chili con carne is not a Mexican import.

Types of Soups

Although soup recipes vary from country to country, culture to culture, and household to household, it is still possible to organize soups into three distinct categories.

Clear Soups

Clear soups include any soup that begins with a translucent broth. This includes broths, consommés, most chicken soups with rice or noodles, beef and vegetable soups, bouillabaisses, and tomato broths. It doesn't matter how packed a soup might be with meats, grains, and vegetables; the thing that makes it a clear soup is the presence of a translucent broth.

Cream Soups and Veloutés

Cream soups can be simple broths to which heavy cream or milk has been added, or they can be complicated bisques made from reduced seafood stock, puréed shellfish, and cream. Velouté is a French version of cream soup that begins with a butter-and-flour roux and may or may not include eggs as a thickener. Cream soups can be chunky, like clam chowder, while most veloutés are smooth soups.

Thick Soups

Thick soups include heavy vegetable purees, roux-thickened soups like gumbo, hearty bean soups, and fruit purées. Some chefs also classify cream soups and veloutés as thick soups.

Chili Powders, Fresh Chilies, and Spice Blends

The commercially prepared powdered spice known as chili powder is actually a blend of ingredients, including powders from dried hot peppers, dried garlic, finely ground dried oregano, cumin, and salt. Depending on the brand, chili powders can be made from ancho chilies, cayenne chilies, pasilla chilies, or virtually any other hot pepper. They may also include small amounts of many other spices such as cinnamon, cloves, mace, and onion powder. This is why different brands often taste very different from one another.

Chili purists compose their own chili blends or make sauces using fresh roasted or reconstituted and puréed dried peppers, along with their own preferred quantities of ingredients like cumin and garlic. Increasingly, single-source chili powders have become available in supermarkets. Like cayenne, these peppery powders usually don't have extra ingredients, so you're getting a pure dose of chipotle chili, New Mexico chili, or ancho chili. If your favorite store doesn't stock single-source powders, try a Mexican food market or order online directly from pepper growers.

Asian chili preparations usually take the form of pastes rather than powders. This is because perishable ingredients like lemongrass, galangal root, and Kaffir lime leaves are essential to the flavor of Southeast Asian dishes. These can't easily be powdered, hence the shelf-stable pastes. You can purchase hot Thai chilies or an equivalent chili pepper at many venues, but to get the full from-scratch experience, you'll have to track down an excellent Asian market that handles a range of perishable goods. For convenience, you may want to start by experimenting with different pastes.

FACT

Like chili powders, curry powders and jerk spice blends are recipes based on a popular notion of what should be included in a curry or jerk-seasoned dish. The two seasonings often share ingredients like nutmeg, mace, and cinnamon, but in differing quantities. Jerk powders are usually sweeter and hotter than curry powders.

In a Stew

By definition, a stew is simply a slowly cooked mélange of ingredients simmered together in one pot. The ingredients cook in a moderate amount of liquid, either added to the pot or drawn from the ingredients themselves. The cooking method can be braising or boiling on a stovetop, baking in an oven or on a hearth, or simmering in a slow cooker.

To make a good stew, it's important to respect the recipe ingredients. Meats should be seared—to add caramelized flavor and rich color to the stew—before any liquid is added. Vegetables can be pan roasted before adding or not, but all aromatics—onion, celery, carrots—should be cut into similar-sized pieces so they cook evenly. Seasonings should be added to the browned meat and vegetables before liquids are added. Starches should be added last to keep them from overcooking or sticking.

Seafood stews are delicate affairs. Always cook ingredients that need a lengthy cooking time before adding seafood. Shrimp, clams, mussels, crabs, and lobsters should be cooked just until done, even if that means cooking some ingredients separately and combining a few minutes before serving.

If your stew is all-inclusive—that is, you aren't serving it over rice or another starch—think in terms of a twelve-ounce bowl per serving. One-third to one-half of the plate should be taken up by one or more star ingredients, such as seafood, beef, chicken, game, or pork. Starchy vegetables like potatoes, corn, or beans should occupy one-third of the dish, while sauce and aromatics make up the rest of the serving.

Taking Stock

The best soups and stews, and even some chilies, begin with a flavorful, rich broth. Most cooks have had experience making soups and other dishes with canned broths and many have crumbled a bouillon cube into a pot of boiling water. Soup bases, similar to the kind used in some commercial kitchens, have become increasingly available in supermarkets. These products vary in quality, flavor, and additives and it's important to know how salty or seasoned a prepared broth will be before dumping it into a dish you're spending time and money to prepare.

Only the most curmudgeonly purist—or a cook with plenty of time on her hands—would suggest there's no room for these handy shortcuts. That said, homemade broth is always best. With homemade, the cook controls the ingredients, the seasoning, the length of cooking time, and other variables. There are no unwanted surprises like monosodium glutamate, food coloring, preservatives, and trans fats.

ALERT

In most recipes, the terms "broth" and "stock" are used interchangeably. In commercial-food terms, stock is a liquid made from boiling bones while broth is made from both meat and bones. Chefs make this simple distinction between the two: Stock is an unseasoned liquid that can be added to other ingredients to enhance flavor. Broth is a finished product. It can be added to recipes or it can be consumed as is.

Although homemade broth takes time to prepare, it isn't difficult and doesn't have to be expensive. Get in the habit of preparing broths during stay-at-home days when you can let a stock pot simmer on the stove for several hours. Store broths in the freezer in resealable plastic bags and thaw as needed.

Poultry and Meat Broths

The best poultry and meat broths begin with meaty bones and fatty scraps. Bits of chicken, turkey, duck, beef, veal, lamb, or pork—in the form of trimmings or meat on the bone—flavor the broth and leach nutrients into the liquid. The bones release minerals and gelatin, which gives broth its characteristic body and satiny mouthfeel. Gelatin is also the substance that makes cooled homemade broths congeal.

Raw ingredients, slowly simmered in water for three to six hours, make the most flavorful broths. However, there are two good reasons to use meat and bones leftover from such simple preparations as roasting and poaching. The first is availability. A chicken carcass, baked ham bone, or half-eaten pot roast au jus from Sunday dinner still has plenty of available flavor left and shouldn't go to waste. You may have to cook it longer to get the intensity you want, but that's a small inconvenience. The second reason to use specially cooked bones is to get a dark, roasted broth. Bones that have been caramelized—but never burned—in the oven produce a rich, brown broth with a slightly sweet, roasted essence. Roasted beef broths are essential to classic soups like French onion and consommé.

ESSENTIAL

Make your own broth concentrate. After straining broth, reheat the liquid in a saucepan over medium heat until the broth is reduced by three-fourths. Pour this super-strong broth into ice cube trays, cover, and freeze until solid. Pop the frozen broth cubes into a resealable plastic bag and use as needed for sauces and soups. Two cubes can be diluted to make a cup of broth.

Regardless of whether you start your broth with raw or cooked ingredients, always begin with cold ingredients and cold water. Starting cold and slowly heating the meat and bones helps draw out the nutrients and gives the best taste. A bit of vinegar or lemon juice added early in the cooking process also helps to draw calcium from the bones.

As broths, particularly meat and poultry broths, cook, bits of impurities rise to the surface of the water. Skimming this gray foam from the broth will ensure a more translucent, aesthetically pleasing broth once it's strained.

Vegetable Broths

Vegetable broths have gained popularity in recent years as research has shown the health benefits of antioxidants and phytochemicals in fruits and veggies. Vegetarians and hosts who want to make sure dishes can be enjoyed by all their guests have also been stocking freezers with ready-to-use broths made from aromatic vegetables, root vegetables, and herbs.

As with meat and poultry broths, vegetable broths can begin with raw or roasted ingredients, depending on the flavor and color desired in the finished product. Use onions, carrots, celery, mushrooms—any vegetables you like. That is, with a few caveats. Tomatoes overpower most other flavors in broth. Unless you're specifically looking for a light tomato broth, it's probably best to add tomatoes to the final recipe rather than the broth pot. Cruciferous vegetables such as cabbage, broccoli, and Brussels sprouts give broths a bitter flavor and sulfurous scent and should be avoided. Bell peppers and celery leaves can turn broth bitter and should be used in moderation. Go easy on resinous herbs like rosemary.

Although cooks once used the stock pot to get rid of aging vegetables, peelings, and skins, that's no longer advised. What you put in the pot directly affects what you'll get out of it. So use fresh ingredients, and make sure they are well washed, peeled, or scrubbed to get the best vegetable broth.

Fish and Seafood Broths

Fish broth, or fish fumet as it's known among chefs, is the quickest cooking of all broths. Made properly, it's also one of the most satisfying. Proper fish broth should taste delicate, with a scent that very lightly hints of the ocean. Always use fish bones and gill-removed heads from lean white fish and cut aromatic vegetables, such as leeks and carrots, into small pieces.

Shellfish broth can be made in one of two ways: Either boil clean shrimp or lobster shells or crab claws to extract flavor or strain the cooking liquid from steaming clams, mussels, or lobster and use that. Don't use the liquid from Maryland-style steamed crabs or any other highly seasoned shellfish—the broth will taste more like spice than seafood.

Both fish and seafood broths can be enhanced by the addition of one-half to a cup of dry white wine to the cooking liquid. Add early in the cooking process to allow the alcohol to evaporate, leaving the flavor behind.

The Right Equipment

There's nothing worse than trying to cook with inadequate or poorly constructed equipment. Mishaps such as boiling over and scorching can often be directly attributed to having the wrong size or wrong weight of cooking vessel. Cheap pots with loose handles can lead to a big mess at best, dangerous burns at worst. Dutch ovens that don't have tight-fitting covers, slow cookers that are hard to clean, poorly balanced ladles that fall into or out of the pot—these are all nuisances that can be avoided by smart shopping.

Stock Pots, Soup Pots, and Dutch Ovens

Good cookware is an investment that can last generations. Look for heavy-gauge pots made of anodized aluminum, cast aluminum alloys, or stainless steel with an aluminum core.

Aluminum—like copper and cast iron—is an excellent conductor of heat. However, like copper and cast iron, it is reactive. That means certain ingredients, such as tomatoes and other acidic foods, can pit and discolor the pot. In turn, some metal will leach into the liquid, discoloring the soup or sauce. Anodizing aluminum or adding other metals to cast aluminum mitigates the problem. Stainless steel with an aluminum core captures the conductivity of aluminum while eliminating the reactivity problem altogether. Nonstick interiors have become more durable, but if you choose nonstick pots, recognize that the surface coating will eventually wear or become less effective.

Regardless of the brand you choose, make sure the lids fit tightly and securely and that the handles are big enough for you to comfortably hold with pot holders. Start with a good, tall stock pot of at least eight quarts. For most soup and broth recipes, this will give you plenty of room to include solid and liquid ingredients with a few inches to spare. For braising, stews, and chilies, a Dutch oven that holds seven to nine quarts is a good idea. You'll probably want a five-quart Dutch oven for family use, but a double batch of any recipe will leave the small pot crowded.

Strainers

Colanders and strainers are essential to making broths and some noodle soups. A standard, heat-safe colander with large holes is needed to drain noodles and dumplings and to drain off fat from browned ground meats. However, you'll also need a large, fine-mesh strainer with hooks that can rest on the rim of a large bowl. The fine-mesh strainer will ensure broths that are free of bone fragments and other solids. Shop for stainless steel, aluminum, or enamel-coated implements that will resist rust.

ESSENTIAL

These are the only two strainers you absolutely need. If you're a gadget aficionado, you can always add a China cap strainer (which makes it easy to press the liquid from solid ingredients) to your armory, as well as fine-mesh skimmers to remove foam and fat from bubbling broths.

Slow Cookers

To crock or not to crock? As far as the final product is concerned, it really doesn't matter. Slow cookers with nonstick metal cooking vessels work just as well as those with crockery inserts. In some cases, the crocks look nicer but they also break and chip more easily. Some cooks buy a large nonstick metal slow cooker for meats and stews, but also have a small crock-lined pot to keep sauces and fondues warm.

When shopping for a slow cooker, just make sure you get one that's big enough for the recipes you plan to prepare. Most cooks look for a five- or six-quart model. The unit should have low, medium, and high settings and the cooking vessel should be removable for cleaning. A clear lid that fits inside the lip of the pot will give a tight fit and keep condensation from dripping out of the pot. Slow cookers range in price from under $20 to over $60, and the price difference is usually attributable to bells and whistles like automatic shut-offs, timers, and sensors. Almost any meat dish can sit in a slow cooker on low for an hour or more after it's done with little harm, so don't buy more slow cooker than you need.

Slow cookers are essential appliances for cooks who don't want to tend pots all day. That said, remember that most don't brown meats effectively. If you want a nice caramelized coat on your beef stew cubes, brown them in a skillet before adding to the slow cooker. Also, slow cookers do not allow liquids to evaporate and reduce. Add only the amount of liquid you absolutely need for the dish you're preparing.

FACT

The term Crock-Pot is actually a registered trademark of the Rival Corp., maker of the first automatic cooker with a removable crockery insert. Although the term is often used generically, the original branded product still exists.

The Right Ladle

Picking a ladle is really just a matter of common sense. A ladle that's too short, too shallow, too flimsy, or too heat sensitive invites burns and spills.

For soups, get a metal, enamel, or heat-safe plastic-coated ladle that has a bowl capable of drawing at least one-half cup of soup from the pot. The handle should extend several inches above the rim of your favorite soup pot so the ladle can rest in the pot without sliding below the surface of the soup. A hooked end is nice, but only necessary if you expect the ladle to sit in the pot for long periods. Likewise, the question of whether the handle should be plastic or wood covered to prevent burns is only relevant if the ladle will be in the hot liquid for long periods.

For stews, buy a ladle with a wider, shallower bowl. Being able to see what you're scooping will help distribute the various stew ingredients evenly among diners. A hard metal bowl also makes it easier to scoop meats and vegetables that may have settled to the bottom of the stew pot. Buy a ladle with a long-enough handle, but not too long and not too heavy. When serving from a relatively shallow Dutch oven or deep skillet, a heavy or long-handled ladle will become unbalanced and easily tip out of the pan, making a big mess.

Setting the Table

Soups, stews, and chilies are the refuge of cash-strapped hosts. So does it really matter how these one-pot wonders are presented? Well, yes and no. If you're having a big, casual dinner party with family or close friends, it's perfectly okay to allow guests to serve their own chili from a pot on the stove. But it's also fine—and not at all pretentious—to ladle the chili into a low, inexpensive pottery bowl, sprinkle the top with chopped cilantro and cheese, and set the bowl on a colorful placemat or a fan of folded $1 bandanas. Guests can still serve themselves, but no one has to run back and forth to the kitchen, interrupting the conversation.

There are also dishes and utensils that are designed to accommodate certain types of recipes.

Soup Bowls, Mugs, and Porringers

Wide, low, rimmed soup bowls are the best option if you're only going to own one type of bowl. These dishes, also known as soup plates, usually hold a twelve-ounce serving. They're serviceable for smooth soups, but work particularly well for chunky soups, gumbos, chilies, and stews because the ingredients are spread over a large area. This allows guests to see what they're eating and leaves room for adding garnishes. The rim gives spoons a place to rest and keeps spills to a minimum. This size and shape also gives an appearance of abundance, which is important for main-dish soups and stews.

Double-handled, delicate cream-soup bowls are rarely included in standard place settings these days. But if you find a set you like in an antique or thrift shop, buy them. These little jewels are the perfect vessel for first-coarse bisques and veloutés. Oh, and while you're shopping antiques, look for pewter or silver porringers. These shallow, metal, one-handled bowls were the seventeenth- and eighteenth-century version of a soup or porridge bowl. Households held their porringers dear, and while you probably won't want to serve soup in yours, they're interesting conversation pieces and useful for holding croutons, nuts, and other garnishes.

For a fun splurge, buy kitschy, colorful soup mugs. These oversized coffee cups—with tops a little wider than most coffee mugs—are essential for casual entertaining where guests will be supping on chili or chowder while mingling. They're also useful for cooks who occasionally like to curl up on the couch with a bowl of chicken soup and watch TV.

Any soup served on a table—that is, not in a ladle-and-carry soup mug—should have an under plate to catch spills and keep the hot bowl from sitting directly on the table. When serving Cioppino or another dish with seafood shells, you might want to add saucers for discarded shells.

Proper Flatware

Most households have place spoons included in their stainless or sterling flatware sets. Place spoons look just like teaspoons, only bigger. These have been used as all-purpose soup and stew spoons and work perfectly well—except for children who need smaller utensils.

Soup-specific spoons, sometimes called cream soup spoons, are only a little larger than teaspoons and have a perfectly round bowl. The same spoon in a larger size can be found in some silver patterns, and these are considered gumbo or chowder spoons.

Some Asian cultures avoid eating with metal utensils, believing the cold metal is unpleasant and imparts a metallic taste to the food. Purists use ceramic or plastic spoons with Asian soups. These are easy to find at import stores and can be a fun, authentic addition to a table setting.

ESSENTIAL

Pairing wines with first-course soups isn't as tricky as it might seem. The classic pairings for broths and cream soups is a dry sherry or Madeira. If that seems a bit heavy, consider serving a dry, sparkling white wine with your bisque, chowder, or tortellini in broth. Heartier soups like vegetable beef and chicken and sausage gumbo need something with a little more body, like a light Pinot Noir or Merlot.

Since bread of some sort should be part of your soup course or stew entrée, a knife should always be included in the flatware service. Seafood forks must be available if your offering includes shellfish still in the shell, and standard forks—as well as spoons—should be part of the table setting for any stew served over a starch such as rice or couscous.

Tureens

Soup tureens come in as many whimsical, fanciful, and beautiful designs as cookie jars. These covered ceramic or earthenware dishes keep soup warm and bring it to the table in style. Prices range from $10 for plain white tureens to thousands of dollars for antique silver.

Smart hosts invest in one or two heat-safe tureens that can go into the oven to keep a soup or stew warm, if need be, before bringing it to the table. Shop for a low, wide-mouthed tureen with a notch for a silver or ceramic serving ladle. Your tureen should serve at least six people.

A Word about Safety

Don't use your soup or stew pot to try to revive ingredients you wouldn't want to eat otherwise. Although leftovers make great soups, think in terms of the three-day rule. Add an ingredient to a soup no longer than three days after it has been cooked, and only if it has been properly stored in the refrigerator. If you can't get around to making soup within that window, just freeze the leftovers until you're ready to cook.

Once your chili, stew, soup, or broth has been prepared, allow it to cool to a warm temperature before placing it in the refrigerator. Otherwise, the dish could begin to cool on the outer edges, while the center of the soup or stew remains hot. That sets up a breeding ground for bacteria that could ruin your food. To cool a large batch of soup more quickly, ladle it into smaller containers or just stir the pot periodically to even out the food temperature and allow heat to escape.

Never allow any foods to stand at room temperature for more than two hours. And, serve or freeze your soup, stew, or chili within three days.

CHAPTER 2

A World of Chicken Soup

Basic Chicken Broth

For a more concentrated broth, return the liquid to the pot after straining.
Cook, stirring occasionally, until the broth is reduced by half.

INGREDIENTS | SERVES 6

3 pounds chicken backs and necks
or combination of chicken carcass
and backs
2 ribs celery, coarsely chopped
2 carrots, coarsely chopped
2 medium onions, quartered
1 parsnip, coarsely chopped
1 sprig parsley
1 sprig thyme
2 bay leaves
1 teaspoon kosher salt
10 peppercorns
½ teaspoon Angostura bitters
10 cups cold water

1. In a large soup pot, combine chicken pieces, vegetables, herbs, peppercorns, and bitters; cover with cold water. If water doesn't cover chicken and vegetables add more.

2. Bring water to a boil over high heat. Stir once, then reduce heat to medium. Cook 2 hours, skimming any foam that rises to top of pot. Reduce heat to medium low; continue to cook 4 hours, adding more water if needed. Remove from heat; let stand 20 minutes. Strain broth through a fine sieve; discard solids. Use broth as directed in recipes.

A Taste for Homemade

Homemade chicken broth can be an acquired taste. If you're accustomed to eating broth from a can or made from bouillon cubes, you'll find the homemade version to be much more subtle. Commercial broths have a lot of salt, flavor enhancers, and sometimes coloring added. Until you wean yourself from the store-bought broths, try adding a touch more salt to your homemade version and cooking it down to concentrate flavors.

Asian Chicken Broth

*Soy sauce adds flavor to this broth, but it also adds a bit of caramel color.
If you prefer a clear broth, omit the soy sauce.*

INGREDIENTS | SERVES 6

1 recipe Basic Chicken Broth (Page 18)
1 tablespoon minced fresh ginger root
1 stalk lemongrass, chopped
1 teaspoon soy sauce (optional)
Pinch sugar

1. Place broth in a large soup pot over medium-high heat. Add ginger root. Bruise lemongrass pieces with back of a knife; add to broth. Stir in soy sauce and sugar.

2. Bring broth to a boil. Reduce heat to medium; simmer 20–30 minutes. Remove from heat. Strain broth into a bowl; discard solids. Use in place of regular chicken broth in recipes, as desired.

Chicken, Barley, and Mushroom Soup

Barley is a complex carbohydrate that adds body and texture to soups.

INGREDIENTS | SERVES 6

1 tablespoon butter or chicken fat
8 ounces mushrooms, sliced
2 garlic cloves, minced
8 cups chicken broth
1 rib celery, sliced
1 carrot, sliced
½ cup pearl barley
1½ cups diced or shredded chicken
Salt and pepper to taste
¼ cup minced parsley

1. In a large soup pot, heat butter over medium-high heat. Add mushrooms and garlic; sauté 3 minutes.

2. Pour in broth; add celery and carrot. Bring broth to a boil; stir in barley. Reduce heat to medium. Cover pot; simmer 40 minutes, stirring occasionally. Add chicken and simmer 5 minutes longer.

3. Add salt, pepper, and parsley; remove from heat. Let stand a few minutes before serving.

Mom's Chicken Noodle Soup

*This soup can be prepared with premade broth, leftover chicken, and noodles,
but this is how your mom or grandma probably did it.*

INGREDIENTS | SERVES 6

1 stewing hen, about 5 pounds
Water
1 onion, quartered
1 small bunch parsley, rinsed
1 green onion, halved
3 ribs celery, cut in thirds
3 carrots, cut in thirds
1 rib celery, thinly sliced
1 carrot, thinly sliced
1 cup peas
1 cup medium noodles
¼ cup minced parsley
Salt and pepper to taste

A Hen in the House

Technically, all female chickens are hens
and males are roosters. However, when it
comes to buying and cooking poultry, a
"hen" refers to a bird that is older and
larger than the typical fryer or broiler. Hens
usually weigh 4–6 pounds, in contrast to
the 2½–3 pound average fryer. They're
more flavorful, but also tougher birds, making them perfect for slow-cooked soups
and stews.

1. Rinse hen and remove giblets. Save for another use.
   Place hen in large Dutch oven with enough water to
   almost cover. Add onion, parsley, green onion, celery
   cut in thirds, and carrot cut in thirds. Bring water to a
   boil over high heat; reduce heat to medium low.
   Simmer 2 hours. Remove from heat and allow to cool.

2. Carefully remove chicken from broth. Remove breast
   and thigh meat. Return chicken carcass and skin to
   broth. Cook over medium low heat 6–8 hours.
   Remove from heat. Strain broth through fine sieve.

3. Pour broth into clean soup pot. There should be about
   10 cups. Add sliced celery and sliced carrot. Stir in
   peas. Bring broth to a boil over high heat; add
   noodles, stirring to disperse. Cook, stirring frequently,
   until noodles are tender, about 10 minutes. Reduce
   heat to medium low. Chop or shred reserved chicken
   meat. Add to broth; simmer 10 minutes. Add parsley.
   Season with salt and pepper and serve.

Pennsylvania Dutch Chicken Corn Soup

Rivels—part dumplings, part free-form pasta—
are a favorite addition to Pennsylvania Dutch soups and stews.

INGREDIENTS | SERVES 6–8

1 tablespoon butter
1 medium onion, diced
1 rib celery, sliced
4 cups corn kernels
10 cups chicken broth
1½ cups diced chicken
1 cup flour
1 egg
½ teaspoon water
Salt and pepper to taste

1. In a large soup pot, melt butter over medium-high heat. Add onion and celery; sauté 3 minutes. Add corn; continue to cook, stirring, 5 minutes. Add broth; reduce heat to medium and simmer 30 minutes. Stir chicken pieces into broth.

2. Bring soup to a boil over high heat. Pour flour into a bowl. Beat egg and water; add to flour, stirring into a thin paste. With a fork or medium-gauge sieve, drizzle flour mixture into boiling soup. Reduce heat to medium. Stir gently; cook 10 minutes longer. Season with salt and pepper.

Dutch as in Deutsch

The Pennsylvania Dutch kitchen brings together centuries-old German cooking traditions and the bounties of Pennsylvania agriculture. By religious belief or by custom, the modern descendents of the German settlers of southeastern and central Pennsylvania prize a simple life in which nothing goes to waste. That means canning and pickling fruits and vegetables, using all parts of a slaughtered animal, preserving meats, and finding ways to stretch the harvest by making breads, noodles, pies, and tarts.

Chicken and Sausage Gumbo

Chicken and Sausage Gumbo is a filé gumbo—thickened and flavored with ground sassafras leaves (filé powder) rather than okra.

INGREDIENTS | SERVES 8

10 cups chicken broth
¾ cup vegetable oil
1 cup granulated flour
2 onions, diced
2 bay leaves
1 pound smoked sausage, sliced
1 green bell pepper, cored and diced
2 ribs celery, sliced
3 cloves garlic, pressed
1 teaspoon kosher salt
2 teaspoons Tabasco
½ teaspoon thyme
½ teaspoon sage
½ teaspoon cayenne
½ teaspoon black pepper
3 cups diced chicken
2 green onions, minced
⅓ cup minced parsley
1 tablespoon filé powder

1. In a large soup pot, bring broth to a boil.

2. In a heavy saucepan over medium heat, combine oil and flour; stir to form a smooth paste. Cook, stirring constantly with a wooden spoon, until roux turns a rich, dark brown. Remove from heat; immediately add ½ of onions to roux. Keep stirring until heat from roux fries onions.

3. Very carefully pour roux and onions into boiling broth; stir until roux dissolves in broth. Add bay leaves. Reduce heat to medium; simmer 2 hours, occasionally stirring and checking liquid levels.

4. Add smoked sausage; cook 10 minutes, then remove from heat. Let stand without stirring, allowing fat from sausage to rise to top. Skim fat and any filmy residue at top of gumbo; discard. Return to medium heat; stir well.

5. Add remaining onion, green pepper, celery, and garlic; cook, stirring occasionally, 20 minutes. Add salt, Tabasco, thyme, sage, cayenne, and pepper. Stir in chicken, half of green onions, and half of parsley. Continue cooking 15 minutes.

6. Remove from heat; stir in filé powder, remaining green onion, and parsley. Let stand 10 minutes before serving in bowls with white rice.

Matzo Ball Soup

*Matzo balls can be made in advance and refrigerated overnight.
Just allow more time for the matzo balls to reheat in the broth.*

INGREDIENTS | SERVES 8–10

4 eggs

1 teaspoon salt

½ teaspoon pepper

4 tablespoons chicken fat or oil

⅓ cup club soda

1 tablespoon minced fresh parsley

1 cup matzo meal

10 cups chicken broth

Salt and pepper to taste

Minced fresh dill or parsley

Heavy or Light?

At every Passover Seder, diners debate the merits of heavy versus light matzo balls. Some complain if the dumplings aren't feathery while others prefer leaden orbs. Recipes usually aim for a mid-point. But here's an important tip: Often, the difference between heavy and light isn't in the recipe; it's in the way the dough is handled. Too much rolling and pressing packs the dough, making a heavier ball.

1. Make matzo balls: In a glass or ceramic bowl, whisk eggs until well beaten. Add salt, pepper, rendered chicken fat or oil, club soda, and parsley; whisk until well blended. Add matzo meal; stir until meal is completely moistened. Cover and refrigerate 1–2 hours.

2. Bring a pot of lightly salted water to a rolling boil. With wet fingers, scoop up bits of matzo mixture and lightly roll into small balls, about 1½ in diameter. Drop matzo balls into boiling water. Cover pot, leaving cover slightly off-center to allow steam to escape. Cook 25–30 minutes.

3. In a soup pot, bring broth to a boil over high heat. Add salt and pepper to taste. Reduce heat to medium low. Remove matzo balls from water with a slotted spoon. Drop balls into broth. Keep warm until ready to serve. Sprinkle with dill or parsley.

Kreplach Soup

Once made, kreplach can be added to soup or browned in oil and served as an appetizer.

INGREDIENTS | SERVES 8

2 cups flour

2 eggs

1 tablespoon water

½ teaspoon salt

1¼ cups cooked chicken, chopped

2 tablespoons minced onion

1 garlic clove, minced

1 tablespoon minced fresh parsley

1 tablespoon margarine or chicken fat

¼ teaspoon seasoned salt

10 cups chicken broth

1. Place flour, eggs, water, and salt in a mixer bowl. Mix with a dough hook 5 minutes. Place dough on a floured surface; roll to coat. Wrap in plastic and let rest 20–30 minutes.

2. In a food processor, combine chicken, onion, garlic, parsley, chicken fat, and seasoned salt; pulse until very finely ground. Unwrap dough and cut in half. Roll each half into a thin rectangle on a floured surface. Cut dough into 2 diamonds. Place a small amount of chicken filling on lower half of diamond; fold top over filling to make a triangle. Press dough together to seal.

3. Bring a large pot of salted water to a boil. When all kreplach are formed, drop into boiling water; simmer 20 minutes.

4. While kreplach are cooking, heat broth in another soup pot. Lift cooked kreplach from water with a slotted spoon; drop into broth. Keep warm until ready to serve.

Chicken Rice Soup

If you decide to use brown rice instead of white,
either cook the rice in advance or double the cooking time.

INGREDIENTS | SERVES 6

1 tablespoon olive oil or chicken fat
1 onion, diced
1 rib celery, sliced
1 carrot, sliced
8 cups chicken broth
⅔ cup uncooked white rice
2 garlic cloves, pressed
1 cup peas
1 cup shredded chicken
Salt and pepper to taste
¼ cup minced fresh herbs (parsley, thyme, chervil, dill, etc.)

1. In a large soup pot, heat oil or fat over medium-high heat. Add onion, celery, and carrot; sauté 3 minutes. Pour in broth; bring to a boil. Stir in rice, garlic, and peas.

2. Reduce heat to medium low; cook, stirring often, 25 minutes. Add chicken, salt, pepper, and herbs; simmer 10 minutes longer. Remove from heat.

Rice Is Nice

The average world citizen eats more than 300 pounds of rice a year. This easily digested grass relative first shows up around 4,000 B.C.E. in southeast Asia and now grows on every continent except Antarctica. Long-grain white rice and unpolished brown rice are the most common varieties found in Western kitchens, but basmati, jasmine, sticky rice, pecan rice, and even heirloom black or red rice can be found in some supermarkets and specialty stores.

Chicken Tortilla Soup

If you don't have time to fry your own tortilla strips, just break up a few tortilla chips.

INGREDIENTS | SERVES 8

3 corn tortillas, cut into strips
Vegetable oil
1 tablespoon olive oil
1 sweet onion, diced
1 green bell pepper, cored and diced
2 jalapeño peppers, diced
2 cloves garlic
2 (16-ounce) cans fire-roasted tomatoes
8 cups chicken broth
1½ tablespoons chili powder
1 teaspoon cumin
1 (16-ounce) can black beans
2 cups cut corn
4 chicken breast halves, diced
Salt to taste
¼ cup minced cilantro
¼ cup minced green onion
Shredded Cheddar and Monterey jack cheese
Lime wedges

1. Using a sharp knife or a pizza cutter, cut tortillas into thin strips. Fill a skillet with oil to a depth of 1–2. Over high heat, fry tortilla strips until crispy. Remove to paper towel.

2. In a soup pot, heat olive oil over medium-high heat. Add onion, green pepper, jalapeño peppers, and garlic; sauté 5 minutes. Add tomatoes, broth, chili powder, and cumin. Bring to a boil; reduce heat to medium.

3. Add beans, corn, and chicken breast pieces; simmer 20 minutes. Add salt, cilantro, and green onion. Remove from heat. Serve topped with fried tortilla strips, shredded cheese, and lime wedges.

Gnocchi in Chicken Broth

Homemade gnocchi is delicious but labor intensive.
Try frozen or vacuum-packed gnocchi from the supermarket.

INGREDIENTS | SERVES 4

6 cups chicken broth

⅓ cup minced fennel

2 cloves garlic, pressed

1½ cups prepared gnocchi

Salt and pepper to taste

2 tablespoons minced parsley

Zuppe d'Italiano

There's no such thing as a bland Italian soup. Even clear broth-based Italian soups are full of strong flavors like fennel, cheese, greens, and herbs. If you're fresh out of gnocchi for Gnocchi in Chicken Broth, consider making Stracciatella, the Italian version of Egg Drop Soup. Whisk two eggs with a little Parmesan cheese, salt, and pepper. Slowly pour the mixture into hot broth, stirring until the eggs form ribbons.

1. In a soup pot, combine broth, fennel, and garlic. Bring broth to a boil over high heat. Reduce heat to medium; cover and simmer 15 minutes.

2. Raise heat to high; bring broth to a boil. Add gnocchi; boil 2–3 minutes, stirring gently, until gnocchi rises to top of broth. Remove from heat; add salt, pepper, and parsley. Cover and let stand a few minutes before serving.

Tom Kha Gai (Thai Chicken Soup)

If you don't have access to lemongrass, lime leaves, and galangal, you can still make this soup. Just buy prepared Tom Kha Gai seasoning paste at the supermarket.

INGREDIENTS | **SERVES 4**

4 cups chicken broth

3 stalks lemongrass, white part only

4 Kaffir lime leaves

2 slices galangal root

2 garlic cloves, pressed

3 Thai chili peppers, halved lengthwise

2 tablespoons lime juice

1 tablespoon fish sauce

4 small chicken breast halves, diced

4 ounces white or straw mushrooms, quartered

1 small onion, cut in strips

½ red bell pepper, cut in strips

1 (14-ounce) can coconut milk

Salt and pepper to taste

⅓ cup fresh cilantro leaves

1. Pour broth into a large soup pot. Bruise lemongrass with back of a knife; add to broth with lime leaves, galangal, garlic, and chilies. Bring to a boil over high heat. Reduce heat to medium; cover and simmer 20 minutes. Strain broth.

2. Return broth to soup pot; add lime juice, fish sauce, chicken, mushrooms, onion, and red bell pepper. Simmer over medium heat, stirring often, until chicken is cooked and vegetables are just tender, about 10 minutes. Stir in coconut milk. Add salt and pepper to taste, and cilantro. Simmer 5 minutes. Remove from heat and serve.

Avgolemono Soup

Plan on eating this classic Greek soup immediately. Reheating will likely cause the eggs to curdle.

INGREDIENTS | SERVES 4

6 cups chicken broth
½ cup white rice
6 eggs
½ cup fresh lemon juice
1 cup shredded cooked chicken breast
Pinch dried oregano
2 tablespoons minced fresh parsley
Salt and pepper to taste

Eggs-actly

Eggs can make a sauce or soup thick, rich, and velvety. Mishandled, they can also curdle and make a dish—while still edible—unappetizing. The best way to handle eggs is to temper them by adding a small amount of hot liquid to the beaten raw eggs, whisk quickly, then immediately whisk the warmed eggs into the hot sauce or soup. This causes the eggs to disperse in the dish, rather than sticking together and poaching.

1. In a soup pot, bring broth to a boil over high heat; stir in rice. Reduce heat to medium; cook, stirring frequently, about 20 minutes, or until rice is tender.

2. In a bowl, whisk together eggs and lemon juice until well beaten. Ladle some of hot broth into eggs, whisking constantly. Pour egg mixture into soup; whisk quickly. Remove soup from heat.

3. Add chicken, oregano, and parsley to soup. Season with salt and pepper to taste. Serve in shallow bowls.

Italian Wedding Soup

The mini meatballs should be very tightly rolled so they don't break up in the soup.

INGREDIENTS | SERVES 6

24 meatballs, ½
8 cups chicken broth
1 tablespoon minced fresh basil
2 carrots, thinly sliced
1 cup acini de pepe pasta
2 cups chopped fresh escarole or spinach
Salt and pepper to taste
Freshly grated Parmesan

Meatball Mix

Wedding soup meatballs should be a fine-textured mix of beef or veal, plus either ground pork or ground turkey. To get the right texture, place ground meat with fresh herbs in a food processor and pulse to a fine paste. Mix with eggs and soft bread crumbs and refrigerate until well chilled. Roll the mixture into small meatballs and drop them into boiling water to cook. Remove with a slotted spoon and add to the soup.

1. Bring a soup pot full of water to a boil. Drop meatballs in water; immediately reduce heat to medium. Simmer 10 minutes; remove meatballs with a slotted spoon and reserve. Discard boiling water.

2. Place broth in soup pot. Add basil and carrots; bring to a boil. Cook 5 minutes; add pasta. Stir well; reduce heat to medium. Simmer 10 minutes, stirring often. Add meatballs, escarole or spinach, and salt and pepper to taste. Cook 2 minutes; cover and remove from heat. Let stand 10 minutes before serving. Sprinkle grated Parmesan over each bowl to taste.

Creamy Chicken Velouté

This is a classic soup that can be enhanced with chopped mushrooms, spinach, or asparagus tips.

INGREDIENTS | SERVES 4

2 tablespoons butter

1 shallot, minced

2 tablespoons flour

5 cups hot chicken broth

1 cup heavy cream

1 cup cooked chicken, finely chopped

Salt and white pepper to taste

2 tablespoons minced fresh parsley or tarragon

1. In a heavy saucepan, heat butter over medium-low heat. Add shallot; sauté 3 minutes. Sprinkle in flour; stir well to blend. Continue stirring 2–3 minutes. (Flour should not be allowed to brown.)

2. Add 1 cup broth; whisk until flour is dissolved and mixture is smooth. Slowly add remaining broth. Raise heat to medium; cook 15 minutes.

3. Stir in cream. Add chicken, salt, pepper, and herbs. Remove from heat and serve.

Cock-a-Leekie Soup

Versions of this soup have been made in Scotland for centuries. Some cooks like to add rice or diced potatoes for a heartier soup.

INGREDIENTS | SERVES 6

1 tablespoon butter or chicken fat

6 leeks, well-trimmed and thinly sliced

1 carrot, thinly sliced

1 rib celery, thinly sliced

8 cups chicken broth

2 cups cooked chicken, shredded

Pinch thyme

¼ cup minced fresh parsley

Salt and pepper to taste

1. In a soup pot, melt butter or fat over medium-high heat. Add leeks; sauté 3 minutes. Add carrot and celery; continue to sauté 2 minutes longer.

2. Add broth to pot; bring mixture to a boil. Reduce heat to medium; simmer 10 minutes.

3. Add chicken and thyme; continue to simmer 20 minutes.

4. Add parsley, salt, and pepper. Remove from heat and serve.

Mulligatawny Soup

This is an early example of fusion cuisine; the soup is an English dish that pays homage to Indian curries.

INGREDIENTS | SERVES 8

2 tablespoons butter

2 leeks, trimmed and sliced

1 carrot, sliced

1 rib celery, sliced

1 banana pepper, minced

2 cloves garlic, minced

1 tablespoon curry powder

1 teaspoon cumin

9 cups chicken broth

½ cup uncooked red lentils

1 large russet potato, diced

1 tart apple, cored and diced

1 tablespoon tamarind concentrate

1 tablespoon lemon juice

Salt and pepper to taste

2 cups cooked chicken, shredded

1 (14-ounce) can coconut milk

⅓ cup minced fresh cilantro

1. In a large soup pot, heat butter over medium-high heat. Add leeks, carrot, celery, banana pepper, and garlic; sauté 5 minutes, then sprinkle curry powder and cumin over vegetables. Stirring, cook another 1 minute; add broth.

2. Bring to a boil. Add lentils, potato, and apple. Reduce heat to medium; simmer 30 minutes, stirring occasionally.

3. Remove from heat and, working in batches, purée soup in a blender.

4. Return soup to pot. Add tamarind juice, lemon juice, salt and pepper, and chicken. Turn heat to medium; bring soup to a simmer. Stir in coconut milk; cook 5 minutes.

5. Remove from heat. Add cilantro and serve.

Spanish Chicken and Ham Soup

This is a great soup to prepare in the summertime, when fresh vegetables are abundant.

INGREDIENTS | SERVES 6

1 tablespoon olive oil
1 shallot, minced
8 cups chicken broth
1 zucchini, halved lengthwise and sliced
4 ounces mushrooms, sliced
2 tomatoes, diced
1 cup ham, finely diced
1½ cups cooked chicken, diced
Pinch thyme
Salt and pepper to taste

1. In a soup pot, heat olive oil over medium-high heat. Add shallot; sauté 3 minutes.

2. Add broth, zucchini, mushrooms, and tomatoes; bring mixture to a boil. Reduce heat to medium; simmer 15 minutes.

3. Stir in ham, chicken, thyme, salt, and pepper; continue to simmer 5 minutes. Remove from heat and let stand briefly before serving.

Florentine Chicken Soup

Make this broth-based chicken Florentine for days when velouté with spinach seems a little too fussy.

INGREDIENTS | SERVES 4

2 tablespoons olive oil
1 medium onion, finely chopped
2 cloves garlic, minced
2 tablespoons flour
6 cups hot chicken broth
2 plum tomatoes, diced
2 bay leaves
½ cup raw orzo pasta
2 cups chopped fresh spinach
1 cup cooked chicken, finely chopped
Salt and pepper to taste
2 tablespoons minced fresh parsley

1. In a heavy saucepan, heat oil over medium-high heat. Add onion and garlic; sauté 3 minutes.

2. Sprinkle in flour; stir well to blend. Continue stirring 2–3 minutes.

3. Add broth; whisk until flour is dissolved and mixture is smooth. Add tomatoes and bay leaves. Bring broth to a boil; add orzo pasta. Reduce heat to medium; cook, stirring often, 20 minutes.

4. Add spinach, chicken, salt, pepper, and parsley; simmer an additional 10 minutes. Remove from heat and serve.

German Chicken and Spaetzle Soup

Some cooks like to boil the spaetzle in a separate pot of water to avoid clouding the chicken broth.

INGREDIENTS | SERVES 6

2 tablespoons olive oil

1 small onion, diced

1 rib celery, diced

1 carrot, diced

8 cups chicken broth

½ teaspoon red wine vinegar

1 teaspoon sugar

4 chicken breast halves, diced

1½ cups flour

½ teaspoon salt

¼ teaspoon black pepper

2 eggs, beaten

½ cup milk

¼ cup minced parsley or chives

Noodles Versus Dumplings

Sometimes it's hard to tell the difference between pasta and dumplings. (In fact, in some corners, spaetzle is known as "noodle dumplings.") The truth is, the ingredients are virtually identical—it's all a matter of how they're treated. If the dough is wet, minimally handled, and dropped in boiling liquid in dollops or pieces, it's a dumpling. Roll it out thin, cut and shape it, and it's a noodle.

1. In a heavy soup pot, heat olive oil over medium-high heat. Add onion, celery, and carrot; sauté 5 minutes.

2. Add broth, vinegar, and sugar. Bring to a boil; reduce heat to medium. Simmer 10 minutes.

3. Add chicken to soup; continue to simmer another 10 minutes.

4. In a mixing bowl, combine flour, salt, and pepper. Add eggs and milk. Beat ingredients with a mixer on medium speed until smooth. Stir in parsley or chives.

5. Bring soup to a boil over high heat. Drop spaetzle dough into soup, using about ½ teaspoon of dough for each dumpling. Reduce heat to medium; stir gently. When spaetzle float to top of soup—about 2 or 3 minutes—soup is ready to serve. Add salt and pepper to taste.

Creamy Chicken and Broccoli Soup

This rich soup makes a satisfying lunch entrée. Serve with a lightly dressed salad and crusty bread.

INGREDIENTS | SERVES 6

6 cups chicken broth
2 tablespoons olive oil
1 shallot, minced
2 cups broccoli, cut in small florets
½ cup butter
3 tablespoons flour
1 cup cream, heated
1 cup half-and-half
1 cup cooked chicken breast, chopped
Salt and pepper to taste
Parmesan cheese

1. In a soup pot, bring broth to a boil over medium-high heat.

2. In a skillet, heat oil over medium-high heat; sauté shallot and broccoli 3 minutes. Add to broth; reduce heat to medium.

3. Melt butter in skillet over medium heat. Add flour; stir until mixture forms a smooth paste. When roux begins to bubble, stir in hot cream. Whisk until smooth.

4. Add cream mixture to broth along with half-and-half and chicken. Simmer, without boiling, 10 minutes.

5. Add salt and pepper to taste. Remove from heat and serve with grated Parmesan cheese.

Chicken Artichoke Soup

If you don't have fresh artichokes, use 6 artichoke bottoms.
Purée 2 in a little chicken broth and chop the rest.

INGREDIENTS | SERVES 4

1 tablespoon butter

2 shallots, minced

6 cups chicken broth

½ cup white wine

4 artichokes, steamed

1 cup shredded cooked chicken

1 cup heavy cream

2 tablespoons minced fresh tarragon

Salt and pepper to taste

1. In a soup pot, heat butter over medium-high heat. Add shallots; sauté 3 minutes.

2. Add broth and white wine; allow mixture to come to a boil.

3. Pull artichokes apart and scrape tender pulp from leaves; add pulp to broth. Remove choke from artichokes and finely chop artichoke bottoms; stir into broth. Reduce heat to medium; simmer 15 minutes.

4. Add shredded chicken; cook 5 minutes longer. Add heavy cream, tarragon, salt, and pepper. Stir well and remove from heat.

Chicken, Wild Rice, and Chanterelle Soup

Wild rice isn't rice at all, but a member of the wheat family.
It's a whole grain that adds texture and a light, earthy flavor to soups.

INGREDIENTS | SERVES 8

1 tablespoon butter or chicken fat

10 ounces chanterelle mushrooms, chopped

2 garlic cloves, minced

8 cups chicken broth

2 tablespoons dry sherry

1 rib celery, sliced

1 carrot, sliced

2 cups cooked wild rice

2 cups diced chicken

1 cup heavy cream

¼ cup minced parsley

Salt and pepper to taste

1. In a large soup pot, heat butter over medium-high heat. Add mushrooms and garlic; sauté 3 minutes.

2. Pour in broth and sherry. Add celery and carrot; bring to a boil.

3. Reduce heat to medium. Cover pot; simmer 20 minutes, stirring occasionally.

4. Stir in wild rice, chicken, cream, parsley, salt, and pepper; simmer 10 minutes longer. Remove from heat. Let stand for a few minutes before serving.

Cheesy Chicken Corn Chowder

For a milder-tasting soup, use shredded Colby cheese instead of sharp Cheddar.

INGREDIENTS | SERVES 6

4 slices bacon

1 large onion, diced

2 cloves garlic, minced

6 cups chicken broth

2 russet potatoes, peeled and diced

3 cups corn kernels

1½ cups shredded chicken

2 cups half-and-half

1 cup shredded sharp Cheddar cheese

Pinch cayenne

Salt and pepper to taste

¼ cup minced fresh parsley

1. In a large soup pot, fry bacon over medium-high heat until crisp. Remove bacon strips to a paper towel, leaving bacon fat in pot. Add onion and garlic to bacon fat; sauté 3 minutes.

2. Add broth, diced potatoes, and corn. Bring to a boil; reduce heat to medium.

3. Simmer 20 minutes, stirring often. Return bacon to pot. Stir in chicken and half-and-half. Continue to simmer soup 5 minutes; do not boil.

4. Stir in cheese, cayenne, salt, and pepper. Stir until cheese has melted. Remove from heat and stir in parsley.

CHAPTER 3

Turkey, Duck, and Goose Soups

Turkey Broth

Fresh turkey wings aren't essential to this recipe, but they do give the broth more flavor and body.

INGREDIENTS | SERVES 6

1 turkey carcass
4 turkey wings
2 onions, quartered
3 ribs celery, halved
2 carrots, halved
1 teaspoon salt
6 peppercorns
1 sprig fresh parsley
1 green onion
10 cups water

Easy Does It

Simmering a broth for a few hours coaxes all the flavors and some nutrients from the bones and vegetables piled into the kettle. Don't try to speed up the process by keeping everything at a rolling boil. Boiling for long periods tends to make bone broths turn bitter and cloudy.

1. Combine all ingredients in a large stock pot or Dutch oven; water should cover ingredients. Break up carcass if necessary to fit in pot.

2. Bring water to a boil over high heat. Continue boiling 3 minutes; reduce heat to medium low. Cover pot; simmer 6 hours.

3. Remove from heat; let stand 30 minutes.

4. Ladle broth through a fine sieve into a bowl; discard solids. Cover and refrigerate overnight. Skim off any fat on surface. Use within 3 days, or place in freezer.

Goose or Duck Broth

*Use roasted goose or duck bones for this recipe, or use raw birds
from which the breast meat has been cut and reserved for another recipe.*

INGREDIENTS | SERVES 6

2 duck or 1 goose carcass

2 bay leaves

3 celery ribs, halved

2 onions, quartered

2 carrots, halved

2 sprigs fresh thyme

10 peppercorns

1 teaspoon salt

10 cups water

1. Combine all ingredients in a large soup pot or Dutch oven; water should cover ingredients. Break up carcasses if necessary. Bring mixture to a boil over high heat. Boil 3 minutes, skimming off any foam that rises to top of water.

2. Reduce heat to medium low. Cover pot; simmer 6 hours.

3. Remove from heat; let stand 30 minutes. Ladle broth through a fine sieve into a bowl; discard solids. Cover and refrigerate overnight.

4. In the morning, scrape off congealed fat on surface. Store fat in refrigerator to use in recipes. Use broth within 3 days, or store in freezer.

Thanksgiving Turkey Noodle Soup

For a soupier soup, reduce noodle quantity to 1–1½ cups.
Or substitute 1 cup of orzo pasta or elbow macaroni for the noodles.

INGREDIENTS | SERVES 6–8

8 cups turkey broth

1 rib celery, diced

1 small onion, diced

1 carrot, diced

1 cup peas (optional)

1 teaspoon dried Italian herb seasoning

2 cups medium-width noodles, uncooked

1–2 cups chopped or shredded turkey meat

Salt and pepper to taste

¼ cup minced fresh parsley

1. Combine broth, celery, onion, carrot, and peas, if desired, in a large soup pot. Sprinkle in herbs; bring to a boil over medium-high heat. Reduce heat to medium; simmer 20 minutes, or until carrots are tender.

2. Bring to a boil over high heat; add noodles. Cook 7–10 minutes, or until noodles are tender.

3. Stir in turkey meat, salt, pepper, and fresh parsley. Remove from heat and let stand 5 minutes before serving.

Using Your Noodles

If you really want to go old school, try making your own noodles. Combine 1 cup of flour, an egg, a pinch of salt, and a few tablespoons of milk in a bowl. Stir together to make a soft dough. Sprinkle on extra flour, roll the dough out to ⅛ thickness, then cut the noodles into your favorite width. Boil noodles 7–9 minutes in the soup.

Turkey Soup with Dumplings

*This variation on chicken and dumplings offers a lighter alternative
to the traditional gravy-laden dish.*

INGREDIENTS | SERVES 8

8 cups turkey broth

1 (14-ounce) can diced tomatoes with onion

1½ cups chopped turkey meat

2 cups mixed vegetables

1½ cups flour

2 teaspoons baking powder

1 teaspoon salt

2 tablespoons butter

¾ cup milk

3 tablespoons minced fresh parsley

Salt and pepper to taste

1. In a large soup pot, bring broth and tomatoes to a boil over high heat. Stir in turkey and mixed vegetables.

2. In a bowl, combine flour, baking powder, and salt. Whisk together to blend and remove any lumps. Cut in butter with 2 knives or a pastry blender until mixture resembles coarse meal. Stir in milk to form a moist dough. Add parsley; stir until evenly distributed through dough.

3. Drop dumplings by tablespoons into boiling stock. Reduce heat to medium and cover; simmer 15 minutes. Remove from heat and add salt and pepper.

Quicky Dumplings

Feathery-light homemade dumplings are a thing of beauty. But if you're pressed for time, refrigerated biscuit dough can be pressed into service. Buy nonflakey canned biscuits, cut them into quarters, and drop them into boiling broth. After 8–10 minutes, the dumplings should be cooked through.

Turkey, White Bean, and Escarole Soup

For a heartier soup, sauté a bit of sliced Italian sausage with the onion mixture.

INGREDIENTS | SERVES 6

2 tablespoons olive oil

1 small onion, diced

1 rib celery, diced

1 carrot, diced

½ red bell pepper, diced

8 cups turkey broth

1 cup diced turkey

1 (16-ounce) can cannellini beans

2 cups trimmed and chopped fresh escarole

Salt and pepper to taste

1. In a large soup pot, combine olive oil, onion, celery, carrot, and bell pepper. Sauté over medium-high heat 3 minutes.

2. Add broth; bring to a boil. Reduce heat to medium; cover and simmer 10 minutes.

3. Add turkey, beans, and escarole; simmer uncovered 10–15 minutes. Remove from heat and add salt and pepper.

The Role of Escarole

Escarole is a variety of endive characterized by broad, ruffled green leaves. The slightly bitter flavor of the leaves—particularly the dark-green outer leaves—make this Mediterranean vegetable a favorite accent for soups and salads. Creamy white beans make a particularly nice backdrop for sautéed escarole spiked with garlic.

Turkey Barley Soup

Tomatoes and green chilies give this otherwise unassuming soup a spicy kick.
If you prefer a milder broth, omit the tomatoes and chilies.

INGREDIENTS | SERVES 6

1 tablespoon olive oil
1 rib celery, diced
1 small onion, diced
2 carrots, diced
8 cups turkey broth
1 (10-ounce) can tomatoes and green chilies
½ cup pearl barley
1½ cups diced cooked turkey
⅓ cup fresh parsley, minced
½ teaspoon dried thyme
Salt and pepper to taste

1. In a heavy soup pot, combine oil, celery, onion, and carrots. Sauté 3 minutes over high heat.

2. Add broth and tomatoes and green chilies; bring to a boil. Stir in barley; reduce heat to medium and simmer 30 minutes.

3. Add turkey, parsley, and thyme. Continue cooking 30 minutes longer, or until barley is tender; season with salt and pepper. Remove from heat and serve.

Smoked Turkey, Tomato, and Cabbage Soup

A smoked turkey carcass will make this broth more flavorful.
You can also use ham broth in place of the turkey broth.

INGREDIENTS | SERVES 6

6 cups turkey broth
1 (15-ounce) can diced tomatoes
1 (15-ounce) can tomato sauce
2 bay leaves
1 large onion, diced
3 garlic cloves, minced
3 cups chopped cabbage
2 cups diced smoked turkey
¼ cup chopped fresh basil
Salt and pepper to taste

1. Combine broth, tomatoes, tomato sauce, bay leaves, onion, and minced garlic in a large soup pot; bring to a boil over high heat. Reduce heat to medium; simmer 10 minutes.

2. Add cabbage and turkey; continue to cook 30 minutes.

3. Stir in basil, salt, and pepper. Remove from heat and let stand 10 minutes before serving.

Duck, Fennel, and Orzo Soup

Fresh fennel has a fresh, sweet anise-like flavor that pairs very well with the rich duck.

INGREDIENTS | SERVES 4

1 tablespoon duck fat or butter
1 small onion, diced
½ red bell pepper, cored and diced
2 cloves garlic, minced
1½ cups thinly sliced fennel
7 cups duck broth
1 cup uncooked orzo pasta
1 cup shredded duck meat
¼ cup minced green onion
Salt and pepper to taste

1. In a large soup pot, heat fat over medium-high heat until hot. Add onion, bell pepper, and garlic; sauté 3 minutes.

2. Add fennel; cook 2 minutes longer, then add broth.

3. Bring to a boil; cook 5 minutes.

4. Stir in orzo; reduce heat to medium. Add meat; simmer 15 minutes, stirring often.

5. Add onion, salt, and pepper. Remove from heat. Let stand briefly before serving.

Duck and Wild Rice Soup

For a lighter soup, the heavy cream can be omitted or replaced with evaporated milk.

INGREDIENTS | SERVES 4

1 tablespoon duck fat
1 tablespoon vegetable oil
2 leeks, sliced
1 rib celery, sliced
1 cup sliced mushrooms
2 garlic cloves, minced
6 cups duck broth
½ cup wild rice
1 cup finely chopped duck
1 cup heavy cream
Salt and pepper to taste
¼ cup minced parsley

1. In a large soup pot, combine fat, oil, leeks, celery, mushrooms, and garlic; sauté over medium-high heat 3–5 minutes, or until mushrooms become tender.

2. Add broth; bring to a boil. Stir in wild rice; reduce heat to medium and simmer 45 minutes, stirring often.

3. Stir in duck; continue cooking 15–20 minutes, or until rice is completely tender.

4. Remove from heat; add cream, salt, and pepper. Serve garnished with parsley.

Smoked Duck and Squash Soup

Pie pumpkin or acorn squash can be substituted for butternut squash in this recipe.

INGREDIENTS | **SERVES 6**

1 tablespoon duck fat or vegetable oil

3 green onions, diced

1 jalapeño pepper, minced

6 cups duck broth

2 cups butternut squash, peeled and diced

1 cup shredded smoked duck

1 teaspoon fresh thyme leaves

1 tablespoon minced fresh cilantro

½ teaspoon cumin

Pinch cinnamon

Salt and pepper to taste

1. In a large soup pot, combine fat, onions, and jalapeño pepper; sauté over high heat 3 minutes.

2. Add broth; bring to a boil. Reduce heat to medium; add diced squash. Simmer 10 minutes.

3. Add duck, thyme, cilantro, cumin, and cinnamon; cook 5 minutes more.

4. Add salt and pepper. Remove from heat and let stand briefly before serving.

Pick Your Squash

Hard-skinned winter squash—such as acorn, butternut, and pie pumpkins—can be used interchangeably in most recipes. The easiest way to cook squash is to cut it in half, scoop out the seeds, then bake the halves face down in a 350°F oven until tender. Try not to overcook cut squash in soups and stews or the pieces will begin to break up.

Duck Confit and Lentil Soup

Duck confit is made from salt-cured duck leg meat that's been poached and preserved in duck fat. It's available at specialty markets.

INGREDIENTS | SERVES 6

1 tablespoon duck fat
1 onion, diced
1 rib celery, diced
2 cloves garlic, minced
2 carrots, peeled and diced
1 pound brown lentils, rinsed
8 cups duck or chicken broth
½ cup minced sundried tomatoes
¼ teaspoon dried thyme leaves
¼ teaspoon cayenne pepper
1 cup shredded duck confit
Salt and pepper to taste

1. In a large soup pot over medium-high heat, combine fat, onion, celery, garlic, and carrots; sauté 3–5 minutes.

2. Add lentils, broth, and sundried tomatoes; bring to a boil. Reduce heat to medium; cook 1 hour, stirring occasionally.

3. Add thyme, cayenne, and confit; continue cooking 20 minutes.

4. Season with salt and pepper. Remove from heat and let stand 10 minutes before serving.

Confit Confidential

Duck confit originated as a method of preserving duck meat for future meals. Poaching and encasing the meat in duck fat protects it from spoilage-inducing oxygen. Making confit isn't difficult, but it does require either rendering fat from ducks or buying expensive duck fat. If you're not inclined to make or buy confit, try using a combination of unpreserved duck and bacon in recipes.

Duck Sausage and Three-Bean Soup

Look for smoked duck sausage at large supermarkets, meat markets, and gourmet shops.

INGREDIENTS | **SERVES 8–10**

1 tablespoon duck fat or vegetable oil

½ pound duck sausage, sliced

1 medium onion, diced

3 cloves garlic, minced

1 green bell pepper, cored and diced

8 cups duck or chicken broth

1 (16-ounce) can cannellini beans

1 (16-ounce) can garbanzo beans

1 (16-ounce) can red kidney beans

1 teaspoon Tabasco sauce

⅓ cup fresh parsley, minced

⅓ cup green onions, minced

Salt and pepper to taste

1. In a large soup pot, combine fat or oil, sausage, onion, garlic, and bell pepper; sauté 5 minutes over high heat.

2. Add broth; bring to a boil. Reduce heat to medium; stir in beans and Tabasco. Simmer 20 minutes.

3. Add parsley and green onion; simmer 5 minutes.

4. Add salt and pepper. Remove from heat and let stand a few minutes before serving.

Gingered Duck Soup

This light but flavorful soup is perfect for a first course.
Add ramen noodles to the broth for a heartier dish.

INGREDIENTS | SERVES 4

6 cups duck broth

2 tablespoons soy sauce

1 tablespoon minced fresh ginger

½ cup julienned carrots

½ cup julienned daikon radish

½ cup shredded duck

1 green onion, minced

2 tablespoons minced cilantro

Salt and pepper to taste

1. Combine broth, soy sauce, and ginger in a soup pot; bring to a boil over high heat, then reduce heat to medium.

2. Add carrots, radish, and duck; simmer 10 minutes.

3. Stir in onion, cilantro, salt, and pepper. Remove from heat and serve.

Flavorful Roots

Fresh ginger brings a clean, pungent aroma to soups and sauces. To use fresh ginger root, peel the tough outer skin of the root and grate the juicy flesh. Slices of ginger can be used to flavor sauces, but should be removed before serving the dish. Cut fresh ginger will keep 2–3 weeks in the refrigerator if carefully wrapped.

Duck and Andouille Gumbo

*Filé powder is made from the dried, ground leaves of the sassafras tree.
It's used for both flavoring and thickening gumbos. Find it in the spice aisle.*

INGREDIENTS | SERVES 8

2 ducklings, quartered

¾ cup vegetable oil

1 cup granulated flour

2 medium onions, diced

10 cups hot duck stock or water

2 ribs celery, sliced

1 large green bell pepper, cored and diced

3 cloves garlic, minced

1 pound andouille sausage, sliced

1 teaspoon cayenne pepper

½ teaspoon dried thyme leaves

1 teaspoon rubbed sage

2 green onions, sliced

⅓ cup minced parsley

1 tablespoon filé powder

Salt and pepper to taste

All-American Andouille

Andouille sausage is a specialty of Cajun cuisine. While it shares the name of a traditional French tripe sausage, the recipe for Louisiana andouille is quite different. Cajun cooks prepare the thick sausage with coarsely ground pork, pork fat, and a generous amount of pepper and other seasonings. The sausage is then smoked for many hours, resulting in the characteristic firm texture and smoky, spicy flavor.

1. Place quartered duckling pieces in a roasting pan. Prick skin with a fork; place in 350°F oven 1 hour. Remove from oven and let stand until cool enough to handle; remove skin.

2. In a large, heavy soup pot, combine oil and flour to make a roux. (Melted duck fat can be used to make up some of the oil.) Cook over medium-high heat, stirring constantly, until mixture turns a dark, reddish-brown.

3. Turn off heat; carefully add half of diced onion. Continue stirring until onion begins to turn translucent.

4. Slowly add hot broth; stir until roux dissolves in liquid and broth begins to thicken. Turn heat to medium high; bring to a boil. Reduce heat to medium; place duck pieces in broth; simmer 1 hour.

5. Remove duck and set aside to cool. Add remaining onion, celery, bell pepper, garlic, and andouille; continue cooking over medium heat 1½ hours.

6. Stir in cayenne, thyme, and sage; remove from heat and let stand 15 minutes. Skim off any fat that rises to top. Remove duck meat from bones and cut into bite-sized pieces; add with onion and parsley.

7. Reheat gumbo over medium heat. When very hot, turn off heat and stir in filé powder. Add salt and pepper and serve over steamed rice.

Polish Duck Soup

This unusual, sweet-and-sour soup is also known as Czarina Soup. Some cooks prefer to strain the solids from the soup before returning the duck meat to the pot.

INGREDIENTS | SERVES 6

1 duckling
10 cups water
1 medium onion, diced
1 rib celery, diced
1 carrot, diced
4 dried apricots, quartered
8 prunes, halved
½ cup golden raisins
1 pint sour cream
4 tablespoons flour
1 tablespoon apple cider vinegar
2 tablespoons sugar
Salt and pepper to taste

1. Cut duckling into pieces, reserving blood.

2. Place duck, water, onion, celery, and carrot in large soup pot; bring to a boil over high heat, then reduce heat to medium. Add apricots, prunes, and raisins; simmer 2 hours, skimming any foam or fat that rises to surface.

3. Remove duck from broth. When cool enough to handle, debone meat and cut into pieces. In a medium bowl, whisk together duck blood, sour cream, and flour. Slowly ladle in some hot stock, whisking constantly, to temper the mixture. Quickly stir sour cream mixture into soup.

4. Continue cooking soup over medium heat until soup thickens, about 5 minutes; add duck. Stir in vinegar and sugar. Add salt and pepper and serve.

Goose and Wild Rice Soup

Use leftover roast goose to make this easy, hearty soup.

INGREDIENTS | SERVES 6–8

½ cup diced pancetta

1 medium onion, diced

1 rib celery, diced

1 large carrot, diced

2 bay leaves

8 cups goose broth

1½ cups chopped cabbage

1½ cups cooked wild rice

1–2 cups shredded cooked goose

Pinch dried thyme

Salt and pepper to taste

1. In a large soup pot, fry pancetta over medium-high heat 2 minutes, stirring constantly.

2. Add onion, celery, and carrot; continue sautéing 3 minutes.

3. Add bay leaves and broth; bring to a boil. Reduce heat to medium; simmer 30 minutes.

4. Stir in cabbage, wild rice, and goose meat. Add thyme; simmer an additional 20 minutes, or until cabbage is tender. Add salt and pepper and serve.

Goose Giblet Soup

Some cooks like to add a bit of beef broth or a beef bouillon cube to this soup to make a heartier broth.

INGREDIENTS | SERVES 4

2 tablespoons oil or butter

1 medium onion, diced

1 rib celery, diced

Giblets from 1 goose, minced

1 (14-ounce) can diced tomatoes

6 cups goose broth

1 teaspoon mixed Italian herb seasoning

½ cup pearl barley

Salt and pepper to taste

1. In a large soup pot, combine oil or butter, onion, and celery; sauté over medium-high heat 3 minutes.

2. Add giblets; sauté an additional 3 minutes.

3. Add tomatoes, broth, and Italian seasoning. Bring soup to a boil; reduce heat to medium. Simmer 45 minutes.

4. Raise heat and bring to a boil again; stir in barley. Reduce heat to medium; simmer 1 hour.

5. Season with salt and pepper. Remove from heat and serve.

Goose and Beet Soup

Goose broth gives this Norwegian borscht cousin a rich, meaty flavor.
Some cooks use goose broth but omit goose meat from the recipe.

INGREDIENTS | SERVES 4–6

2 tablespoons butter

2 shallots, minced

2 cloves garlic, minced

2 cups diced raw beets

1 carrot, diced

6 cups goose broth

2 bay leaves

½ teaspoon cayenne

1 tablespoon lemon juice

Salt and pepper to taste

1 cup finely chopped goose meat

Chopped fresh dill

Sour cream

1. In a large soup pot, combine butter, shallots, and garlic; sauté over medium-high heat 3 minutes.

2. Add beets and carrots; continue to sauté, stirring constantly, 3 minutes longer.

3. Add broth, bay leaves, and cayenne; bring to a boil. Reduce heat to medium; simmer 40 minutes, or until beets are tender.

4. Working in batches, purée soup in a blender or food processor.

5. Return to pot; stir in lemon juice and salt and pepper. Add meat and reheat. Serve in bowls garnished with fresh dill and sour cream.

Red or Gold?

Nutrient-rich beets are oft maligned. Diners —many of whom have been subjected to strongly flavored pickled beets—complain about the veggie "bleeding" all over their plates and dying other foods red. If you're not a fan of red soup, try using young gold or white beets in this recipe. You'll get mild beet flavor and won't have to worry about permanent stains in your kitchen.

Autumn Goose and Cabbage Soup

Make this hearty soup for a comforting between-the-holidays supper.

INGREDIENTS | SERVES 6–8

1 tablespoon oil or goose fat
1 medium onion, diced
1 rib celery, diced
1 red bell pepper, diced
2 cloves garlic, minced
8 cups goose stock
1 large white potato, peeled and diced
1 turnip, peeled and diced
1 carrot, diced
2 cups shredded cabbage
1½ cups shredded goose
½ teaspoon dried thyme leaves
Salt and pepper to taste

1. In a large soup pot, heat oil or fat over medium-high heat. Add onion, celery, bell pepper, and garlic; sauté 5 minutes.

2. Add stock, potato, turnip, and carrot; bring to a boil. Reduce heat to medium; simmer 30 minutes.

3. Add cabbage, goose meat, and thyme; simmer another 30 minutes.

4. Remove from heat. Add salt and pepper.

CHAPTER 4

Meaty Soups

Basic Meat Broth

This broth has a meaty flavor, but not much color.
Add it to dishes that don't require a caramel-colored broth.

INGREDIENTS | SERVES 6

1 pound beef, pork, lamb, or venison, diced

2 pounds meaty bones, reserved from diced meat or purchased separately

2 onions, quartered

2 cloves garlic

2 carrots, cut in pieces

2 ribs celery, cut in pieces

2 bay leaves

6 black peppercorns

10 cups water

Salt to taste

1. Combine all ingredients in a large soup pot. Bring to a boil over high heat; reduce heat to medium. Simmer 3–4 hours, skimming foam that rises to top.

2. Remove broth from heat; let stand 20 minutes.

3. Strain through a fine sieve; refrigerate several hours or overnight.

4. Skim off fat and discard. Use broth as needed in recipes or freeze for later use.

Roasted Beef or Lamb Broth

This recipe produces the dark, rich meat broth preferred for most beef- or lamb-based soups.

INGREDIENTS | SERVES 6

3 pounds meaty beef or lamb bones (shanks, necks, ribs)

2 tablespoons olive oil

10 cups water

2 onions, quartered

2 cloves garlic

2 carrots, cut in pieces

2 ribs celery, cut in pieces

2 bay leaves

6 black peppercorns

Salt and pepper to taste

Beautiful Bones

Although beef broth can be made from ingredients bought just for that purpose, it doesn't have to be. Some of the richest broths are a byproduct of dinner entrees. Prime rib roasts and even bone-in chuck roasts have meaty trimmings that produce excellent, rich-tasting beef broths. Lamb shanks and breast of veal bones can be pressed into service as well. Don't forget to add leftover au jus to the stock pot as well.

1. Preheat oven to 350°F. Place beef bones in a shallow roasting pan; coat well with olive oil. Roast uncovered 2 hours, turning occasionally to allow all sides to brown.

2. Remove from oven and place in a large soup pot. Pour 1 cup of water in roasting pan; scrape pan to loosen browned bits. Pour water from roasting pan into soup pot. Add remaining water and other ingredients to pot.

3. Bring to a boil over medium-high heat. Boil 2 minutes; reduce heat to medium. Simmer uncovered 4 hours or longer, replenishing liquid as needed.

4. Remove from heat; allow to cool. Strain through a fine sieve; discard solids.

5. Refrigerate until chilled. Remove fat and discard. Use broth as directed in recipes, or freeze.

Old-Fashioned Vegetable Beef Soup

Leftover pot roast can be substituted for the raw beef in this recipe. Just reduce the cooking time.

INGREDIENTS | SERVES 8

2 tablespoons olive oil
2 cups diced lean round or chuck roast
1 large onion, diced
1 rib celery, sliced
8 cups beef broth
2 cups diced tomatoes, fresh or canned
1 cup tomato sauce
2 bay leaves
1 large russet potato, peeled and diced
2 cloves garlic, pressed
3 cups frozen mixed vegetables
3 ounces dried vermicelli, broken up
Salt and pepper to taste
¼ cup minced fresh herbs (parsley, basil, oregano, thyme)

1. In a large, heavy soup pot, heat olive oil over medium-high heat. Working in batches, brown beef cubes on all sides. Remove beef to a bowl; add onion and celery to remaining oil. Sauté 3 minutes; return beef cubes to pot.

2. Add broth, tomatoes, tomato sauce, and bay leaves; bring to a boil, then reduce heat to medium. Cook 2 hours, or until beef is very tender.

3. Add diced potato, garlic, and vegetables; simmer 1 hour longer.

4. Bring to a boil over high heat; stir in vermicelli. Cook just until pasta is tender, about 10 minutes.

5. Season with salt and pepper and stir in fresh herbs. Remove from heat and let stand a few minutes before serving.

Alphabet Soup, Anyone?

Vegetable beef soup is often made from leftovers and things the cook has on hand. Spaghetti or vermicelli can be found in most pantries, and therefore show up in many soup pots. Elbow macaroni and various-width noodles are the other favorites. But there are some 350 different pasta shapes in the world—including alphabets, stars, and trees. Feel free to add your favorites to your soup.

Beef Barley Soup

Cooked ground beef can be used in place of shredded beef in this recipe.

INGREDIENTS | SERVES 4–6

½ pound cooked shredded beef

1 medium onion, diced

1 rib celery, diced

½ small green bell pepper, cored and diced

1 carrot, diced

1 (16-ounce) can diced tomatoes

2 bay leaves

6 cups beef broth

½ cup pearl barley

Salt and pepper to taste

1. In a large soup pot, combine beef, onion, celery, green pepper, carrot, and tomatoes; cook over high heat, stirring constantly, 3 minutes.

2. Add bay leaves and broth; bring to a boil. Stir in barley; continue boiling 5 minutes.

3. Reduce heat to medium; cover and cook 1 hour. Stir and check liquid level frequently. Season with salt and pepper to taste.

Good Carbs, Good Soups

Barley is a whole-grain, high-fiber, low-fat carbohydrate that actually tastes good. It has the texture of small, al dente pasta when cooked, making it an excellent addition to soups, stews, and casseroles. As a bonus, barley contains disease-fighting antioxidants and phytochemicals. In the United States, half the barley harvest goes to animal feed and more than 40 percent is used in beer production.

Beef Ramen

Substitute your own aromatic beef broth for the powdered bouillon in the ramen packet for a real treat.

INGREDIENTS | SERVES 4

⅓ cup julienned carrots
1 clove garlic, pressed
6 cups beef broth
1 teaspoon soy sauce
2 packs instant ramen noodles
1 green onion, minced

1. In medium soup pot, combine carrots, garlic, and broth. Bring to a boil over high heat; cook 5 minutes.

2. Add soy sauce and ramen noodles; stir noodles to separate. Reduce heat to medium.

3. Simmer 5 minutes, or until noodles are tender. Serve garnished with green onion.

Root Vegetables in Beef Broth

Experiment with other root vegetables in this soup, including rutabagas, beets, and yuca.

INGREDIENTS | SERVES 8

2 tablespoons butter
1 medium onion, diced
1 rib celery, diced
1 carrot, diced
1 turnip, diced
1 russet potato, peeled and diced
1 parsnip, diced
1 small sweet potato, peeled and diced
8 cups beef broth
2 bay leaves
½ teaspoon dried thyme leaves
1 teaspoon grated orange zest
Salt and pepper to taste

1. In a large soup pot over medium-high heat, melt butter. Add onion; sauté 3 minutes.

2. Add celery and carrot; sauté 3 minutes more.

3. Add turnip, potato, parsnip, and sweet potato, then broth and bay leaves; bring to a boil. Reduce heat to medium; simmer 25 minutes.

4. Stir in thyme, orange zest, salt, and pepper; cover. Let stand 10 minutes before serving.

Taco Soup

This is a very forgiving recipe. Use more or less taco seasoning, corn, or beans as you like.

INGREDIENTS | SERVES 8

2 pounds ground beef

2 packets taco seasoning

1 (10-ounce) can Mexican-style tomatoes and green chilies

1 (16-ounce) can tomato sauce

3 cups frozen corn

2 (16-ounce) cans chili-seasoned beans

2 cups water

½ teaspoon cumin

¼ cup minced fresh cilantro

Shredded Cheddar and Monterey jack cheese

Sour cream

1. In a large soup pot over high heat, brown ground beef. Remove from heat; drain off fat.

2. Sprinkle taco seasoning over top; stir to blend. Add tomatoes and chilies, tomato sauce, corn, beans, and water.

3. Bring to a boil over high heat; stir in cumin. Reduce heat to medium; simmer 30 minutes.

4. Remove from heat; stir in cilantro. Serve garnished with cheese and sour cream.

Turn Up the Heat—Quick!

Always keep a can of tomatoes and green chilies in your pantry. This magical product can add an instant flavor kick to any soup. The chilies give heat and the tomatoes add both taste and texture. In addition, tomatoes and chilies now come in varying levels of heat as well as added seasonings.

Thai Beef Soup

This soup is a sinus-clearing take on beef noodle soup.
Cook the round steak slices just until done for tender results.

INGREDIENTS | SERVES 4

½ pound round steak
2 tablespoons peanut oil
½ teaspoon sesame oil
1 tablespoon red curry paste
1 sweet onion, cut in eighths
1 rib celery, sliced diagonally
1 hot red pepper, minced
3 green onions, sliced
3 cloves garlic, minced
6 cups beef broth
1 tablespoon fish sauce
8 ounces rice noodles
1 teaspoon sugar
1 teaspoon rice vinegar
¼ cup minced cilantro

1. Cut round steak into thin strips. In a large wok or soup pot, heat peanut and sesame oils over high heat until a drop of water sizzles. Quickly stir-fry beef; remove to a platter.

2. Add curry paste; stir constantly 1 minute. Add onion, celery, hot pepper, green onions, and garlic; cook 3 minutes.

3. Reduce heat to medium; add broth and fish sauce. Simmer 15 minutes. Meanwhile, soften noodles in cold water 10 minutes.

4. Bring soup to a boil over high heat; drain noodles and add to soup. Separate noodles with a fork or chopsticks; cook just until tender, 1–2 minutes.

5. Remove from heat; stir in sugar, vinegar, and cilantro. Return beef to pot; let stand briefly before serving.

Oxtail Soup

To serve "boneless" oxtail soup, just remove the oxtails from the finished soup with a slotted spoon, remove the morsels of meat, and return them to the pot.

INGREDIENTS | SERVES 6

2 pounds oxtails

1 medium onion, diced

2 carrots, diced

2 leeks, sliced

1 celery rib, diced

3 garlic cloves, minced

8 ounces mushrooms, sliced

1 large russet potato, peeled and diced

8 cups beef broth

2 bay leaves

¼ cup red wine

¼ cup minced fresh parsley

Salt and pepper to taste

Oxtail Tales

Oxtail dishes first appeared on peasant tables, in an attempt to use all parts of a slaughtered animal. Today, oxtail soups and stews are found on gourmet menus as well as in homey kitchens. Most oxtails are actually harvested from beef cattle of both sexes. These boney, muscled cuts of meat are extremely gelatinous and make a rich broth. Long, slow cooking is needed to tenderize the meat. Oxtails are a favorite Caribbean treat and oxtail broth is a U.K. staple.

1. Place oxtails in a single layer in a roasting pan; roast in 400°F oven 40 minutes, turning occasionally.

2. Remove from oven; place on a platter. Drain fat from roasting pan; set aside. Pour 1 cup of water in pan; stir to deglaze.

3. In a heavy soup pot, combine 2 tablespoons of fat from roasted oxtails, onion, carrots, leeks, celery, garlic, and mushrooms. Sauté 5 minutes over high heat.

4. Add potato, broth, and water from roasting pan; bring to a boil.

5. Add bay leaves and wine; reduce heat to medium. Add oxtails; simmer 2 hours.

6. Add parsley, salt, and pepper; remove from heat. Let stand a few minutes before serving.

Beefy Cabbage Borscht

For an extra flourish, some cooks like to add a cup of heavy cream to the soup before serving.

INGREDIENTS | SERVES 8

2 tablespoons olive oil
1 pound lean round or chuck, diced
1 large onion, diced
1 rib celery, sliced
1 green bell pepper, cored and diced
1 beet, peeled and diced
1 large potato, peeled and diced
2 (16-ounce) cans diced tomatoes
8 cups beef broth
1 teaspoon caraway seed
1 small cabbage, cored and diced
1 tablespoon lemon juice
Salt and pepper to taste

1. In a large, heavy soup pan, heat oil over medium-high heat. Brown beef cubes; remove to a plate. Add onion, celery, and green pepper; sauté over medium-high heat 3 minutes.

2. Add beet, potato, tomatoes, and broth. Return beef to pot; bring to a boil.

3. Reduce heat to medium; add caraway; simmer 30 minutes.

4. Add cabbage; continue cooking 1½ hours.

5. Stir in lemon juice, salt, and pepper. Remove from heat; let stand briefly before serving.

French Onion Soup

If you have authentic onion soup crocks, you can melt the cheese quickly under a broiler. Otherwise, a few minutes in the oven works fine.

INGREDIENTS | SERVES 4

4 tablespoons butter

3 sweet onions, halved vertically and thinly sliced

1 tablespoon flour

6 cups roasted beef broth

½ cup red wine

2 bay leaves

½ teaspoon fresh thyme leaves

1 clove garlic, minced

1 tablespoon fresh parsley, minced

Salt and pepper to taste

1 baguette, sliced

4 thick slices Gruyere cheese

1. In a large soup pot, melt butter over medium heat. Add onions; cook, stirring, until onions are a rich brown color. Sprinkle flour over onions; stir until blended. Add broth and wine; simmer 5 minutes.

2. Reduce heat to low; add bay leaves, thyme, garlic, and parsley. Cover pot; continue to simmer 20 minutes.

3. Remove from heat; remove bay leaves and add salt and pepper.

4. Cut 4 slices from baguette, 1 thick. Toast bread in 350°F oven 10 minutes, turning once.

5. Ladle into 4 oven-safe bowls. Place one toasted bread slice over each bowl; top with cheese. Place bowls on baking sheet; bake at 400°F just until cheese is melted. Serve with extra bread.

Ginger Beef Soup with Dumplings

Frozen, ready-made Chinese dumplings are available in most supermarkets.
Or, you can substitute cooked, meat-filled tortellini.

INGREDIENTS | SERVES 4

6 cups beef broth
1 tablespoon grated fresh ginger
1 tablespoon soy sauce
1 tablespoon sherry
1 clove garlic, pressed
½ teaspoon sugar
8 steamed meat dumplings
¼ cup minced green onion

1. In a large soup pot, combine broth, ginger, soy sauce, sherry, garlic, and sugar; bring to a boil over medium-high heat. Reduce heat to medium; cover and simmer 15 minutes.

2. Remove from heat; place 2 steamed dumplings in each soup bowl. Ladle broth over dumplings; garnish with green onions.

Roast Pork and Garlic Soup

Garlic takes on a mild, sweet flavor when baked, making this soup rich but not too pungent.

INGREDIENTS | SERVES 4

1 large head of garlic
2 tablespoons olive oil
1 small onion, finely chopped
8 ounces mushrooms, sliced
5 cups pork or chicken broth
½ cup white wine
1 cup heavy cream
1 cup roasted pork, cut in thin strips
Salt and pepper to taste
¼ cup minced fresh parsley

1. Coat garlic head with 1 teaspoon olive oil. Wrap securely in foil; bake at 350°F for 1 hour. Set aside to cool.

2. In a soup pot, heat remaining oil over medium-high heat. Add onion and mushrooms; sauté 5 minutes.

3. Add broth and wine; bring to a boil. Reduce heat to medium; simmer 15 minutes.

4. Press roasted garlic from each clove into a blender container. Add heavy cream; pulse to blend. Whisk cream into soup; add pork strips. Simmer to heat through.

5. Season with salt and pepper; remove from heat. Garnish with parsley.

Pho (Vietnamese Beef Noodle Soup)

The Vietnamese eat Pho in big, steaming bowls filled with rice noodles.
If your Pho is an appetizer, you may opt for smaller portions.

INGREDIENTS | SERVES 4

6 cups beef broth

1 small onion, quartered

1 slice fresh ginger

1 star anise

2 whole cloves

¼ teaspoon coriander seeds

1 teaspoon sugar

4 ounces rice noodles

½ pound boneless sirloin steak, trimmed

1 tablespoon fish sauce

1 cup bean sprouts

⅓ cup whole fresh basil leaves

Salt and pepper to taste

¼ cup minced green onion

¼ cup minced fresh cilantro

1 small hot pepper, sliced

Lime wedges

Fabulous Pho

Some food historians believe pho, pronounced "fuh," got its name from *feu*, the French word for fire. This ubiquitous Vietnamese dish originated during the French occupation of the country. Although the Vietnamese traditionally don't eat much beef, this soup has become the quintessential Vietnamese comfort food. It combines French-style boiled beef in broth, Chinese noodles, and Southeast Asian spices and herbs.

1. In a large soup pot, combine broth, onion, ginger, anise, cloves, coriander, and sugar. Bring to a boil over high heat; stir well, then reduce heat to medium. Cover and simmer 15 minutes.

2. Soften noodles in hot water 10 minutes.

3. Bring a pot of water to a boil; add noodles. Cook 1 minute, or until noodles are soft; drain. With a sharp knife, cut steak into very thin slices.

4. Strain broth into a heat-safe bowl; discard solids. Return broth to soup pot; add fish sauce, sprouts, and basil. Cook 1 minute over medium heat; add sliced steak. Continue cooking just until beef is no longer pink, about 1 minute. Season with salt and pepper; remove from heat.

5. Divide noodles into 4 large soup bowls. Ladle broth over noodles; sprinkle with green onions, cilantro, and sliced pepper. Serve with lime wedges.

Pancetta and Potato Soup

Pancetta is Italian bacon. It's salt cured and spiced, but not smoked. It may be sold in chunks or rolls.

INGREDIENTS | SERVES 6

4 ounces pancetta

2 shallots, minced

3 white potatoes, peeled and diced

6 cups ham or chicken broth

Salt and pepper to taste

¼ cup fresh parsley, minced

2 cups shredded Cheddar cheese

1. Cut pancetta into very small dice. In a heavy soup pot over medium-high heat, fry until bits are slightly crisp. Remove to a plate; leaving fat in pot. Add shallots; sauté 3 minutes.

2. Add potatoes and broth; bring to a boil, then reduce heat to medium. Simmer 20 minutes, checking liquid occasionally.

3. When potatoes are completely tender, ladle half of soup into blender container; pulse to purée. Return puréed soup to pot; mix well.

4. Stir in pancetta; heat on medium until bubbly. Add salt and pepper. Ladle into bowls; garnish with parsley and shredded cheese.

Hot and Sour Soup

Buy tiger lily buds and dried wood ear mushrooms at Asian specialty stores
or in the Asian food section of some supermarkets.

INGREDIENTS | SERVES 4

6 tiger lily buds

¼ cup dried wood ear mushrooms, chopped

3 ounces boneless pork chops

¼ cup soy sauce, divided use

1 tablespoon sesame oil, divided use

1 tablespoon cornstarch, divided use

2 ounces firm tofu

⅓ cup sliced mushrooms

½ cup julienne-sliced bamboo shoots

⅓ cup julienne-sliced carrots

6 cups chicken or pork broth

2 tablespoons rice wine vinegar

1 egg

1 teaspoon freshly ground black pepper

1 green onion, minced

Hot chili oil to taste

Salt to taste

The Chinese Soup Pot

Chinese cuisine varies dramatically from one end of the vast country to the other. However, one commonality is soup. Whether you're dining on Mandarin, Cantonese, Szechwan, or Hunan fare, you'll find steaming bowls of soup on the table. Critical to serving authentic Chinese soups is to use high-quality ingredients and to pay close attention to preparation details.

1. Place tiger lily buds in a small heat-safe bowl; place dried mushrooms in another bowl. Pour boiling water into each bowl; let ingredients soften 30 minutes.

2. Slice pork into very thin strips; place in a third bowl. Combine a tablespoon of soy sauce and a teaspoon of sesame oil; pour over pork and mix well. Sprinkle 1 teaspoon of cornstarch over pork; toss to coat. Let stand 15 minutes.

3. Cut tofu into thin strips. In a soup pot, combine tofu, fresh mushrooms, bamboo shoots, carrots, and broth; bring to a boil over high heat.

4. Drain lily buds and dried mushrooms; add to pot with pork, remaining soy sauce, and sesame oil. Stir well; reduce heat to medium. Simmer 5 minutes.

5. Stir in vinegar. Dissolve remaining cornstarch in 2 tablespoons cold water. Bring soup to a boil again; stir in cornstarch. Cook, stirring, 1 minute, or until soup thickens. Beat egg; slowly pour into soup while stirring.

6. Remove from heat. Add pepper, green onion, hot oil, and salt; serve.

Lamb Kibbe Soup

The kibbe can be made a day or two in advance and refrigerated.
Just heat the kibbe in the soup broth when you're ready to serve it.

INGREDIENTS | SERVES 4–6

¼ pound medium-grain bulgur wheat

1 pound finely ground lamb

Salt and pepper to taste

1 large onion, finely chopped

¼ cup minced fresh parsley

½ teaspoon allspice

Pinch ground cloves

1 teaspoon cumin

Vegetable oil

6 cups beef or lamb broth

1 (16-ounce) can diced tomatoes

1 teaspoon sugar

1 teaspoon lemon juice

2 green onions, minced

Plain yogurt

Toasted pine nuts

A National Treasure

Kibbe is considered the national dish of Lebanon; however, versions are made in Syria, Armenia, and throughout the eastern Mediterranean. The stuffed, fried ovals served with this soup usually show up on buffet and banquet tables. Other forms include a baked kibbe casserole that layers the bulgur-meat crust mixture over spiced ground lamb. There's even a raw kibbe dish that resembles steak tartar, but made with lamb.

1. Place bulgur wheat in a bowl; fill with cold water to cover. Soak 30 minutes.

2. Drain bulgur; press excess moisture out with paper towels. Place bulgur and ½ of ground lamb in a food processor; add salt and pepper and ½ of onion. Process until a fine paste forms. Refrigerate until ready to use.

3. In a skillet, combine rest of ground lamb, remaining onion, parsley, allspice, cloves, cumin, salt, and pepper (if desired). Sauté over high heat 3–5 minutes, until lamb is no longer pink. Drain off fat; allow to cool.

4. With wet hands, shape chilled bulgur mixture into golf ball–sized balls. Make an indentation in each ball; stuff with cooked ground lamb. Press bulgur mixture around ground lamb; shape into ovals. Continue until all ingredients have been used, making 12–15 kibbe.

5. In a large Dutch oven, pour enough oil to reach a depth of 2. Fry kibbe for 10 minutes, turning gently, until nicely browned. Drain on paper towels.

6. In a soup pot, combine broth, tomatoes, sugar, and lemon juice; bring to a boil over high heat. Reduce heat to medium; simmer 10 minutes.

7. Stir in green onions; add salt and pepper. To serve, place kibbe in bowls and ladle broth over. Garnish with yogurt and pine nuts.

Spiced Lamb and Chickpea Soup

Some cooks make this soup with braised lamb shanks instead of diced lamb.
Just debone the meat after cooking and return it to the pot.

INGREDIENTS | SERVES 8

1 pound boneless lamb, diced
2 tablespoons olive oil
1 large onion, diced
1 rib celery, diced
2 cloves garlic, minced
1 cup dry red lentils, rinsed
1 (16-ounce) can diced tomatoes
1 tablespoon tomato paste
8 cups lamb broth
2 cups cooked chickpeas
½ teaspoon turmeric
½ teaspoon cinnamon
½ teaspoon cumin
½ teaspoon ground ginger
1 teaspoon grated orange zest
Salt and pepper to taste
⅓ cup minced fresh cilantro
Lemon wedges

1. In a heavy soup pot over medium-high heat, brown lamb cubes in olive oil; remove to a plate. Sauté onion and celery in oil 3 minutes.

2. Return lamb to pot; add garlic, lentils, tomatoes, tomato paste, and broth. Bring to a boil; reduce heat to medium. Simmer uncovered 30 minutes.

3. Add chickpeas, turmeric, cinnamon, cumin, ginger, and orange zest; cover and cook 1 hour more.

4. Remove from heat; stir in salt, pepper, and cilantro. Serve with lemon wedges.

Sweet and Spicy

North African and Middle Eastern dishes intrigue palates with aromatic, unusual spice blends. Curry powders offer shortcuts to these melded flavors, but it's worth the effort to experiment with your own blends. Try for a balance of sweet, hot, and fragrant spices and don't be afraid to toast spices in a dry skillet for a richer, deeper flavor.

Veal Florentine Soup

This elegant but easy soup is a great way to use leftover veal roast or chops.

INGREDIENTS	SERVES 4

2 tablespoons butter

1 shallot, minced

4 ounces mushrooms, chopped

1 cup cooked veal, shredded

4 cups veal stock

2 cups stemmed fresh spinach, chopped

1 cup heavy cream

Pinch nutmeg

Salt and pepper to taste

1. In a heavy soup pot, melt butter over medium-high heat. Add shallots and mushrooms; sauté 5 minutes.

2. Add cooked veal and veal stock; bring to a boil. Reduce heat to medium; simmer 10 minutes.

3. Add spinach; cook 5 minutes.

4. Stir in heavy cream, nutmeg, salt, and pepper. Remove from heat and serve immediately.

Veal Variables

Veal factory farming practices have raised eyebrows among some consumers. Although there are efforts being made to raise veal cattle more humanely, some cooks still prefer to avoid this meat. Fortunately, there are alternatives; virtually any recipe calling for veal can be prepared using lean pork or chicken.

Venison Soup

Small venison meatballs star in this easy-to-make soup.
The meatballs can be made in advance and frozen for up to six months.

INGREDIENTS | SERVES 6

1 pound ground venison

1 egg

½ cup bread crumbs

1 tablespoon minced parsley

1 teaspoon Worcestershire sauce

Salt and pepper to taste

6 cups venison or beef broth

1 (16-ounce) can diced tomatoes

1 teaspoon mixed Italian herb seasoning

1 teaspoon Tabasco

2 green onions, sliced

1 rib celery, sliced

1 carrot, sliced

1 cup green peas

1 cup chopped mushrooms

⅔ cup dried orzo pasta

1. In a large bowl, combine ground venison, egg, bread crumbs, parsley, and Worcestershire sauce. Add salt and pepper; mix until well blended. Roll into 18–24 small, tightly packed meatballs. Place meatballs on low-sided baking sheet lined with nonstick foil; bake at 350°F until browned, about 20 minutes.

2. In a large soup pot, combine broth, tomatoes, herb seasoning, Tabasco, green onions, celery, carrot, peas, and mushrooms. Bring mixture to a boil over high heat; cook 5 minutes. Reduce heat to medium; simmer 30 minutes.

3. Over high heat, bring soup to a boil again; stir in orzo. Cook until orzo is tender, about 10 minutes.

4. Reduce heat to medium; add meatballs. Season with salt and pepper; simmer 5 minutes. Remove from heat and let stand briefly before serving.

Moose Soup

If you don't have easy access to moose meat, you can substitute venison, bison, or beef.

INGREDIENTS | SERVES 6

3 tablespoons vegetable oil

2 pounds moose meat, diced

1 large onion, finely diced

1 jalapeño pepper, minced

1 rib celery, diced

2 cloves garlic, minced

10 cups water or beef broth

2 carrots, trimmed and sliced

2 parsnips, trimmed and sliced

1 (16-ounce) can diced tomatoes

2 cups cooked wild rice

Salt and pepper to taste

1. In a deep skillet or Dutch oven, heat oil over medium-high heat. Working in batches, brown moose cubes; remove to a plate. Add onion, jalapeño, celery, and garlic; sauté 3 minutes.

2. Add water or broth and reserved meat; bring to a boil, then reduce heat to medium. Add carrots, parsnips, and tomatoes; cook, stirring occasionally, 2 hours.

3. Stir in rice; add salt and pepper. Remove from heat; let stand 5 minutes before serving.

Mighty Moose

North-country denizens love moose soups, stews, and even burgers. Like most game meats, moose can be relatively mild or gamey, depending on the age of the animal and where it has been grazing. Unlike deer and bison, which are farmed and packaged for supermarkets, moose is still primarily the bounty of hunters. Nonhunters can satisfy their curiosity through online vendors.

CHAPTER 5

Vegetable Soups

Basic Vegetable Broth

Adding tomatoes will give this broth both color and flavor.
If you would prefer a pale broth, omit the ripe tomatoes.

INGREDIENTS | **SERVES 8**

2 large onions, chopped

6 ribs celery, leaves removed, chopped

3 large carrots, chopped

2 parsnips, chopped

6 white mushrooms, chopped

1 ear corn on the cob, husked

½ cup sliced fennel

4 green onions, including tops, chopped

3 ripe tomatoes, chopped (optional)

4 whole garlic cloves

½ cup chopped fresh parsley

2 sprigs fresh thyme

8 black peppercorns

6 quarts water

1 teaspoon kosher salt

1. Add prepared vegetables and herbs to a large soup kettle, including tomatoes, if desired. Sprinkle peppercorns over top; add cold water. Bring to a boil over high heat; reduce heat to medium. Simmer 90 minutes.

2. Remove corn on the cob; continue cooking remaining ingredients 90 minutes longer, adding more water if needed.

3. Stir in salt; remove from heat. Let stand 10 minutes.

4. Ladle through fine-mesh strainer into a clean bowl or pan. Press as much liquid from vegetables as possible; discard solids. Broth can be used immediately, refrigerated for up to 3 days, or frozen for later use.

Broth Options

To make roasted vegetable broth, place ingredients listed in a large roasting pan or Dutch oven and drizzle with ⅓ cup olive oil. Stir to mix, then place in a 400°F oven for an hour, stirring every 15 minutes or so. When vegetables are browned, carefully spoon them into a soup kettle, cover with cold water, and bring to a boil. Simmer for 2 hours, strain, and use as desired.

Vichyssoise

If you prefer your potato-leek soup warm, by all means enjoy.
Just return it to the saucepan after puréeing, add cream, and heat—do not boil.

INGREDIENTS | SERVES 6

4 tablespoons butter

4 leeks, white and light green parts, sliced

1 medium onion, diced

3 pounds russet potatoes, peeled and thinly sliced

5 cups chicken broth

Salt and pepper to taste

1 cup heavy cream

Chopped fresh parsley or chives

Freedom Soup?

There's no question that potato-leek soup is a French farmhouse favorite. But despite the name—Vichyssoise is named for the town of Vichy, France—the cold, creamy version of this soup is an American creation. Louis Diat, the French-born chef of the Ritz-Carlton Hotel in New York, invented the dish in 1917. Oh, and the correct pronunciation does have a "z" sound at the end.

1. In a large soup pot, melt butter over medium-high heat. Add leeks and onion; cook, stirring often, just until vegetables soften—do not brown. Add potatoes and broth; bring to a boil. Reduce heat to medium; simmer 1 hour, or until potatoes are very soft.

2. Remove from heat. Either purée soup in a food processor or press through a fine mesh strainer into a bowl. Season with salt and pepper.

3. Chill until ready to serve. Before serving, whisk in heavy cream. Check seasoning. Ladle into bowls; garnish with parsley or chives.

Gazpacho

Garnish this refreshing salad in a cup with diced avocado or a dollop of sour cream.
Or, add a tablespoon of fresh mango or black bean salsa.

INGREDIENTS | SERVES 6

4 large ripe tomatoes, chopped

1 small red onion, chopped

1 small cucumber, peeled and chopped

1 small green bell pepper, cored and chopped

2 cloves garlic, peeled and chopped

1 rib celery, chopped

¼ cup fresh parsley

¼ cup red wine vinegar

¼ cup extra-virgin olive oil

1 teaspoon Worcestershire sauce

1 teaspoon Tabasco sauce

1 teaspoon sugar

Pinch dried oregano

Salt and pepper to taste

2 cups tomato juice

1. Combine all ingredients except tomato juice in a blender or food processor; pulse until puréed. Add tomato juice. Chill.

2. Ladle into bowls or soup cups; garnish as desired.

White Gazpacho

There are many versions of white gazpacho, including one that mimics cucumber-yogurt soup. This recipe is based on the Spanish aji blanco.

INGREDIENTS | SERVES 4

1 cup slivered almonds
4 slices white bread, crust removed
⅓ cup water
2 cloves garlic
1 green onion, chopped
⅓ cup olive oil
2 cups buttermilk
1 cup heavy cream
Salt and pepper to taste
1 cup halved green grapes
½ cup sliced almonds

1. Place slivered almonds in a food processor; pulse to grind. Soak bread in water 10 minutes; add to food processor with garlic and green onion. With motor running, add olive oil in a steady stream until mixture is thick and creamy.

2. Pour almond-bread mixture into a bowl; whisk in buttermilk. Whip cream until slightly thickened; gently stir into soup. Season with salt and pepper.

3. Ladle soup into bowls; garnish with grapes and sliced almonds.

Spring Snow Pea and Mushroom Soup

This is a light first-course soup. To make it heartier, add a package of ramen noodles during the last two minutes of cooking.

INGREDIENTS | SERVES 6

1 teaspoon sesame oil
1 tablespoon peanut oil
1 clove garlic, minced
1 cup thinly sliced white mushrooms
6 cups chicken broth
1 teaspoon grated fresh ginger
1½ cups trimmed and halved snow pea pods
½ cup shredded carrots
Salt and pepper to taste
¼ cup minced green onion

1. In a large saucepan, combine sesame oil and peanut oil. Add garlic and mushrooms; sauté over high heat 2 minutes.

2. Add broth; bring to a boil. Reduce heat to medium; add ginger, pea pods, and shredded carrots. Simmer just until pea pods become tender, about 3 minutes.

3. Season soup with salt and pepper. Ladle into bowls and garnish with green onion.

Creamy Asparagus Soup

To make this a vegetarian soup, buy extra asparagus and simmer in water for one hour.
Strain the broth and use in place of chicken broth.

INGREDIENTS | **SERVES 4–6**

1 pound fresh asparagus
3 shallots, chopped
1 clove garlic, chopped
2 tablespoons butter
4 cups chicken broth
Pinch nutmeg
Salt and white pepper to taste
1 cup heavy cream

Creamy Comfort

A little cream goes a long way in creamed soups. Mostly, the creamy texture of most creamed soups comes from puréed ingredients. A little heavy cream gives soups a rich but delicate flavor. For a little more oomph and fewer calories, consider a splash of buttermilk or yogurt instead of cream. For a low-fat creamed soup, stir in evaporated skimmed milk instead of cream.

1. Wash asparagus; trim 1 from bottom of stalks and discard. Cut tips (about 1) from half of stalks and reserve. Cut remaining stalks into 1 pieces; place in a large, heavy saucepan with shallots, garlic, and butter. Sauté over medium-high heat 3 minutes.

2. Add broth; bring to a boil. Reduce heat to medium; simmer 30 minutes, or until asparagus is very soft.

3. Remove from heat. Working in batches, purée asparagus and broth in a food processor or blender. (You can also press it through a fine-mesh sieve.)

4. Return mixture to pot; bring to a simmer over medium heat. Add reserved asparagus tips; cook just until tips are crisp-tender, about 2 minutes. Season with nutmeg, salt, and pepper. Stir in cream.

Smokey Sweet Potato Soup

This soup can also be made with leftover baked sweet potatoes.
Simply scrape the cooked sweet potato pulp from the peeling.

INGREDIENTS | SERVES 4

2 large sweet potatoes, peeled and diced

3 slices bacon

1 onion, diced

2 cups water

Pinch cinnamon

Salt and pepper to taste

Sour cream

1. Place diced sweet potatoes in a large, heavy saucepan over medium-high heat. Fill pan with water to cover potatoes; bring to a boil. Reduce heat to medium; cook until potatoes are tender, about 20–30 minutes. Drain potatoes.

2. In a clean soup pot over medium-high heat, fry bacon until crisp. Remove; set aside. Add onion to bacon grease; sauté until onion is lightly browned, about 5 minutes.

3. Add water and sweet potatoes; bring to a boil. Cook 5 minutes, adding more water if necessary.

4. Remove from heat; purée in food processor. Return to pan; thin with more water, if desired. Season with cinnamon, salt, and pepper. Crumble reserved bacon into soup and serve with a dollop of sour cream.

Minestrone

*Use leftover chuck roast or round roast for the beef in this recipe.
If you don't have leftovers, quickly sear a small chuck or round steak.*

INGREDIENTS | SERVES 10

⅓ cup olive oil

1 large onion, diced

2 ribs celery, sliced

1 green bell pepper, cored and diced

2 carrots, sliced

3 garlic cloves, minced

6 cups beef broth

2 (15-ounce) cans tomato sauce

1 (15-ounce) can diced tomatoes

2 cups water

2 bay leaves

1 teaspoon dried oregano

½ teaspoon dried basil

2 cups diced or shredded cooked beef

1 (15-ounce) can kidney beans

1 (15-ounce) can cannellini beans

1 cup fresh or frozen Italian green beans

1 large baking potato, peeled and diced

⅔ cup dried elbow macaroni or ditalini

1 large zucchini, halved lengthwise and sliced

2 cups fresh spinach, washed and chopped

⅓ cup minced fresh parsley

Salt and pepper to taste

Grated Parmesan cheese

Red pepper flakes

1. In a large, heavy soup pot, heat olive oil over medium-high heat. Add onion, celery, bell pepper, carrots, and garlic; sauté until vegetables are crisp-tender, about 5 minutes.

2. Add broth, tomato sauce, tomatoes, water, and bay leaves; stir in oregano and basil. Bring to a boil; reduce heat to medium and simmer 30 minutes, allowing liquid to reduce in volume.

3. Add beef; continue cooking 1 hour.

4. Add kidney and cannellini beans, green beans, and potato. Turn heat to high; bring to a boil. Add pasta; boil 3 minutes, stirring frequently to keep pasta from sticking to bottom of pot.

5. Reduce heat to medium; cook until pasta and potatoes are tender, about 15–20 minutes.

6. Stir in zucchini, spinach, and parsley; cook just until zucchini is tender, about 5 minutes. Season with salt and pepper; serve with grated Parmesan cheese and red pepper flakes. Remove bay leaves if desired.

Cook's Choice

As with most vegetable soup recipes, minestrone can contain a variety of different ingredients. Some cooks prefer to include only cannellini beans, while others always add lima beans or garbanzos. Potatoes can be omitted. Savoy cabbage can be added in place of spinach. For a starchier broth, dry beans can replace canned; just add more liquid and plan on a longer cooking time.

Sorrel Soup

Sorrel is a perennial green, leafy vegetable. Young leaves have a fruity flavor while older leaves are acidic and taste more like mature spinach.

INGREDIENTS | SERVES 4

4 cups chicken or vegetable broth
1 small onion, finely chopped
1 baking potato, peeled and diced
2 cups chopped fresh sorrel
2 cups light cream
3 egg yolks, beaten
Salt and pepper to taste
2 hardboiled eggs, sliced
Sour cream

1. In a heavy soup pot, combine broth, onion, and potato; bring to a boil over high heat. Reduce heat to medium; cover. Simmer 10–15 minutes, until potatoes are tender.

2. Add sorrel and cream; raise heat to medium high. When soup begins to bubble, add egg yolks in a steady stream, whisking constantly until eggs have been incorporated. Remove soup from heat.

3. Season with salt and pepper. Ladle into bowls and garnish with sliced boiled eggs and sour cream.

Cucumber and Yogurt Soup

Cold cucumber and yogurt soup is a refreshing lunchtime treat that's as easy to make as a smoothie. Throw in a slice of jalapeño for kick.

INGREDIENTS | SERVES 4

3 cups seedless cucumber, peeled and diced
2 cups plain yogurt
2 cloves garlic
1 tablespoon olive oil
1 teaspoon honey
2 tablespoons chopped fresh mint leaves
1 tablespoon chopped fresh dill leaves
Pinch cumin
Salt and pepper to taste
Whole mint leaves

1. Combine all ingredients except salt and pepper and mint in blender or food processor; purée. Add salt and pepper.

2. Chill soup until ready to serve. Ladle into bowls and garnish with mint leaves.

Mediterranean Magic

Yogurt and cucumber combinations turn up in the cuisines of Greece, Turkey, Israel, Lebanon, and a few other countries. Often, the combination isn't a soup, but a sauce or salad dressing. The yogurt may be drained to thicken it or combined with a bit of sour cream. Sometimes parsley replaces the dill, and often diced onions and tomatoes are tossed in as well as feta cheese.

Olive Soup with Sherry

This extraordinary soup is for olive lovers only.
Feel free to experiment with different varieties of olives.

INGREDIENTS | SERVES 4–6

2 cups pitted green Greek olives
1 medium onion, chopped
3 cloves garlic, chopped
½ cup olive oil
4 cups chicken or vegetable broth
⅓ cup flour
1 cup heavy cream
Pinch cayenne
Pinch oregano
Salt and pepper to taste
¼ cup sherry
¼ cup minced parsley

1. Rinse olives in cold water. Place 1½ cups olives, onion, and garlic in a heavy soup pot with 2 tablespoons of olive oil; sauté over medium-high heat 3 minutes, or until onions begin to wilt.

2. Place contents of pot into a blender or food processor with 1 cup of broth; pulse until puréed.

3. Pour remaining olive oil into soup pot; whisk in flour. Cook over medium-high heat, stirring constantly, until roux turns pale brown. Carefully whisk in remaining broth; stir until completely smooth. Bring to a boil; cook 10 minutes.

4. Reduce heat to medium; stir in olive mixture from blender. Continue to simmer 20 minutes. While soup simmers, chop remaining olives.

5. Add cream, cayenne, and oregano. Simmer 5 minutes.

6. Add chopped olives, salt, and pepper; stir in sherry. Cook 2 minutes; ladle into bowls and garnish with parsley.

Southwestern Corn Soup

Crisp-fried corn tortilla strips make a nice garnish for this summertime favorite.

INGREDIENTS | SERVES 6–8

4 cups freshly cut corn kernels

1 medium onion, diced

1 red bell pepper, cored and diced

2 jalapeño peppers, seeded and minced

¼ cup olive oil

1 teaspoon chili powder

½ teaspoon cumin

6 cups vegetable or chicken broth

1 cup heavy cream

Salt and pepper to taste

1 teaspoon lime zest

⅓ cup minced fresh cilantro

Shredded Cheddar or Monterey jack cheese

1. In a large, heavy soup pot, combine fresh corn, onion, bell pepper, jalapeño peppers, and olive oil. Sauté 5 minutes over medium-high heat, stirring constantly.

2. Add chili powder and cumin; slowly stir in broth. Bring to a boil; reduce heat to medium and simmer 45 minutes.

3. Add cream, salt, and pepper; cook 5 minutes.

4. Remove from heat; stir in lime zest and cilantro. Serve garnished with grated cheese.

Corny Business

Fresh corn on the cob adds just-picked flavor to any soup or vegetable dish. To prepare, remove the husk and any trace of corn silk. Rinse well, then place the corn cob, one end down, in a heavy bowl. With a sharp paring knife, carefully cut the kernels from the cob in even, downward strokes. Then scrape the cob to get corn "milk" from the kernels. Kernels and corn milk should fall into the bowl, ready to use.

Parmesan Spinach Soup

To make this a meatless soup, substitute 2 tablespoons olive oil for the pancetta and use vegetable broth in place of the chicken broth.

INGREDIENTS | SERVES 4

⅓ cup diced pancetta
1 small onion, minced
3 cloves garlic
1 rib celery, finely diced
1 carrot, finely diced
3 cups chicken broth
1 cup white wine
4 cups chopped fresh spinach leaves
1 cup light cream
Salt and pepper to taste
½ cup shredded Parmesan cheese
4 toasted baguette slices

1. In a heavy soup pot over medium-high heat, cook pancetta until it begins to release fat. Add onion, garlic, celery, and carrot; sauté, stirring frequently, 5 minutes.

2. Pour in broth and wine; bring to a boil. Reduce heat to medium; simmer 10 minutes.

3. Add spinach to the broth and wine; simmer 5 minutes.

4. Add cream, salt, and pepper; simmer 5 minutes.

5. Remove from heat; ladle into bowls. Divide Parmesan over each bowl; top with a toasted baguette round.

Curried Acorn Squash Soup

Pour this soup into insulated jars to serve at autumn tailgate parties. Or, serve it in small cups with Thanksgiving hors d'oeuvres.

INGREDIENTS | SERVES 6

4 cups baked acorn squash pulp
2 cups cooked apples
4 cups vegetable broth
2 teaspoons curry powder
1 teaspoon cinnamon
¼ teaspoon ginger
1 cup heavy cream
Salt and pepper to taste
Sour cream
Chopped walnuts

1. Working in batches, place squash, apples, and broth into a blender; process until puréed. Pour into a large sauce pan; stir in curry powder, cinnamon, and ginger. Place over medium heat; simmer 15 minutes. Add more water or broth if necessary.

2. Stir in heavy cream and add salt and pepper; simmer 5 minutes.

3. Remove from heat. Ladle soup into bowls; garnish with sour cream and chopped walnuts.

Summer Squash Soup

This simple, quick-fix soup brings the flavors of a summer vegetable garden into the kitchen.

INGREDIENTS | SERVES 8–10

3 tablespoons olive oil

2 zucchini, diced

4 yellow squash, diced

8 ounces white mushrooms, sliced

2 shallots, minced

6 ripe, fresh tomatoes, peeled, seeded, and diced

1 teaspoon sugar

8 cups chicken broth

⅓ cup chopped fresh basil

Salt and pepper to taste

1. In a large soup pot, combine olive oil, zucchini, yellow squash, mushrooms, and shallots. Sauté over high heat, stirring constantly, 5 minutes.

2. Add tomatoes; continue cooking and stirring an additional 3 minutes.

3. Sprinkle in sugar. Reduce heat to medium; add broth. Simmer 20 minutes.

4. Stir in basil, salt, and pepper. Serve with crusty bread.

Beet Borscht

*Beet borscht, not to be confused with meaty cabbage borscht,
is a cold summer soup for beet lovers only.*

INGREDIENTS | SERVES 6–8

4 cups fresh beets, peeled and shredded

1 whole onion, peeled and stuck with 4 cloves

2 quarts water

¼ cup lemon juice

2 tablespoons sugar

3 eggs

Salt and pepper to taste

Sour cream

1. In a soup pot, combine beets, onion, and water; bring to a boil over high heat. Reduce heat to medium; simmer 1 hour, or until shredded beets are tender.

2. Remove onion and cloves; discard. Stir in lemon juice and sugar; continue cooking 30 minutes.

3. Place eggs in food processor; pulse to whip. Ladle 2 cups soup into large heat-safe measuring cup. With processor running, slowly pour soup into eggs. Immediately stir egg mixture back into soup pot; stir well. Add salt and pepper to taste.

4. Allow soup to cool; refrigerate until chilled. Serve cold with a dollop of sour cream on top.

Roasted Tomato Bisque with Crème Fraîche

*Roasting gives tomatoes a deeper, richer flavor. For added smokiness,
you can also roast tomatoes in a grill basket over hot coals.*

INGREDIENTS | **SERVES 8**

10 ripe plum tomatoes

⅓ cup olive oil

3 garlic cloves, minced

1 teaspoon mixed Italian herb seasoning

1 tablespoon butter

1 green onion, chopped

¼ cup parsley chopped

4 cups chicken or vegetable broth

2 cups heavy cream

Kosher salt and freshly ground black pepper to taste

⅔ cup crème fraîche

Fresh basil leaves

Homemade Crème Fraîche

To make your own crème fraîche, simply whisk together 1¼ cups heavy cream with ¼ cup buttermilk. Pour in a glass jar or narrow ceramic bowl and cover well. Let stand at room temperature for 12 hours, or until mixture begins to thicken. Stir and refrigerate. Use within one week.

1. Cut tomatoes in half lengthwise; place in roasting pan lined with nonstick foil. Combine olive oil, garlic, and Italian herbs; drizzle oil mixture over tomatoes and toss to coat. Place tomatoes cut side down in 350°F oven; roast 40 minutes. When tomatoes are cool enough to handle, remove skin. Coarsely chop tomatoes.

2. In a soup pot, heat butter over medium-high heat; sauté green onion and parsley 3 minutes.

3. Add chopped tomatoes and broth; bring mixture to a boil. Simmer 5 minutes.

4. Remove from heat. Working in batches, purée in a blender or food processor. Strain mixture back into soup pot; bring to a simmer over medium-high heat. Whisk in heavy cream and season with salt and pepper.

5. Remove from heat. Ladle into shallow bowls; garnish with dollops of crème fraîche and basil leaves.

Wild Mushroom Soup

Buy dried porcini mushrooms at gourmet food stores or markets that specialize in imported Italian ingredients.

INGREDIENTS | SERVES 4–6

½ cup dried porcini mushrooms

1½ cups boiling water

2 tablespoons butter

1 pound mixed wild mushrooms, trimmed and chopped

2 shallots, minced

2 tomatoes, peeled, seeded, and chopped

¼ teaspoon dried thyme leaves

2½ cups beef or vegetable broth

1 cup heavy cream

Salt and pepper to taste

Chopped parsley

1. In a heat-safe bowl, pour boiling water over porcini mushrooms; let stand 30 minutes.

2. Drain mushrooms, reserving 1 cup of soaking liquid. Place in a food processor; pulse to chop finely.

3. In a heavy soup pot, melt butter over medium-high heat. Add fresh mushrooms and shallots; sauté 5 minutes, or until mushrooms are soft.

4. Add tomatoes; cook 3 minutes longer.

5. Sprinkle thyme over mushrooms and tomatoes. Add broth, reserved cup of mushroom-soaking water, and soaked chopped porcini mushrooms. Bring to a boil; reduce heat to medium. Simmer 10 minutes.

6. Stir in heavy cream; season with salt and pepper. Serve garnished with chopped parsley.

Creamy Mushroom Bisque

Truffle oil can be found at some supermarkets and many gourmet food shops, as well as by mail order. It's expensive, but a little goes a very long way.

INGREDIENTS | SERVES 4

3 tablespoons butter

2 garlic cloves

1 pound white mushrooms, trimmed and chopped

1 shallot or small onion, chopped

2 tablespoons granulated flour

3 cups vegetable or mushroom broth

1 tablespoon fresh thyme leaves

1½ cups half-and-half

Salt and pepper to taste

Splash white truffle oil

Minced chives

1. In a soup pot, combine butter, garlic, mushrooms, and shallot over medium-high heat. Sauté 5 minutes, until mushrooms are tender.

2. Sprinkle with granulated flour; mix well.

3. Slowly add broth; whisk to remove any lumps of flour. Bring to a boil; reduce heat to medium. Simmer 10 minutes.

4. Add thyme leaves. Remove from heat; purée in food processor until smooth.

5. Return to pot; stir in half-and-half. Season with salt and pepper; cook until just heated. Before serving, drizzle in a little truffle oil; garnish with chives.

Miso Soup

Dashi is a Japanese soup stock made from boiling dried seaweed and bonita fish flakes in water. Instant dashi powder is available in some supermarkets.

INGREDIENTS | SERVES 4

5 cups dashi stock or vegetable broth

1 cup thinly sliced mushrooms

1 thinly sliced green onion, divided

6 ounces silken tofu, diced

3 tablespoons miso paste

Drizzle dark sesame oil, optional

1. In a soup pot, bring broth to a boil. Add mushrooms and half of green onion. Reduce heat to medium low; simmer 3 minutes.

2. Add tofu; simmer 2 minutes.

3. In a small bowl, combine miso paste and 1 cup of hot stock; stir until smooth. Slowly return to pot; mix well and remove from heat.

4. Add remaining green onions and, if desired, sesame oil. Serve immediately.

Pimiento Cheese Soup

This soup can be thinned with extra milk or turned into a cheese sauce by omitting the broth and cutting the milk in half.

INGREDIENTS | SERVES 6

2 tablespoons butter

2 tablespoons flour

2 cups chicken broth or water

4 cups milk

3 ounces cream cheese

2 cups shredded mild Cheddar cheese

Dash Worcestershire sauce

½ teaspoon cayenne pepper

½ cup chopped pimientos

Salt and pepper to taste

Cheesy Choices

Cheese soup can be enhanced by adding a splash of beer, crumbled bacon, or chopped broccoli, or by changing the types of cheese used. Pimiento Cheese Soup pays homage to a favorite Southern sandwich spread, often found in tea sandwiches and on hors d'oeuvres trays.

1. In a large saucepan, combine butter and flour. Cook over medium-high heat, stirring constantly, until mixture forms a bubbly paste.

2. Slowly add broth or water; whisk until completely smooth. Bring to a boil; reduce heat to medium. Simmer 10 minutes.

3. Add milk, cream cheese, and shredded cheese. Cook, stirring constantly, until soup is thick and cheese is completely melted. Add Worcestershire, cayenne, and pimientos; simmer 3 minutes.

4. Season with salt and pepper; remove from heat.

Beer Cheese Soup

This super-rich soup is a gift from America's Midwest dairy and beer belt. Serve it at fall football parties.

INGREDIENTS | SERVES 6

2 tablespoons butter or vegetable oil

1 large onion, diced

2 ribs celery, diced

2 carrots, diced

3 cloves garlic, minced

1 teaspoon Worcestershire sauce

1 teaspoon Tabasco

2 cups water or chicken broth

2 cups beer

¼ cup flour

¼ cup butter

2 cups half-and-half

4 cups shredded Cheddar cheese

1 teaspoon Dijon mustard

Salt and pepper to taste

2 cups popped popcorn or croutons

1. In a soup pot over medium-high heat, combine butter or oil, onion, celery, carrots, and garlic; sauté 5 minutes.

2. Add Worcestershire, Tabasco, broth, and beer; bring to a boil, then reduce heat to medium. Simmer 15 minutes.

3. In a saucepan over medium-high heat, combine flour and butter; cook, stirring constantly, until roux is smooth and bubbly. Reduce heat to medium; slowly whisk in half-and-half. Keep stirring until mixture thickens and half-and-half is hot. Remove from heat; add cheese, stirring until melted.

4. Whisk cheese mixture into beer broth mixture; add mustard, salt, and pepper. Simmer without boiling 10 minutes, stirring often.

5. Ladle into soup mugs; garnish with popcorn or croutons.

Stuffed Baked Potato Soup

Anything you might put on a baked potato you can stir into this soup.
To keep it vegetarian, add imitation bacon bits or croutons in place of bacon.

INGREDIENTS | SERVES 6

3 tablespoons butter

1 medium onion, minced

4 cups vegetable or chicken broth

3 white potatoes, peeled and diced

2 cups half-and-half

2 cups shredded Cheddar cheese

3 tablespoons sour cream

1 large russet potato, baked until tender and diced

Salt and pepper to taste

⅓ cup cooked bacon crumbles

¼ cup green onion, minced

1. In a heavy soup pot over medium-high heat, combine butter and onion; sauté 5 minutes.

2. Add broth and diced white potatoes; bring to a boil. Reduce heat to medium; simmer 20 minutes, or until potatoes are very tender.

3. Remove soup from heat. Working in batches, ladle into blender; pulse to purée. Return pureed to pot; add half-and-half. Heat on medium just until hot and bubbly. Whisk in cheese; stir until melted.

4. Remove from heat; whisk in sour cream. Add diced baked potato, salt, and pepper. Ladle into bowls; garnish with bacon crumbles and green onion.

Callaloo Soup

Callaloo soup is a Caribbean staple, where cooks sometimes add bits of crab or spiny lobster tail to the mix.

INGREDIENTS | SERVES 6

1 tablespoon oil or butter

1 large onion, diced

1 rib celery, diced

1 green bell pepper, cored and diced

2 cloves garlic, minced

1 pound callaloo leaves, trimmed and chopped

4 cups vegetable or chicken broth

2 cups okra, sliced

1 (14-ounce) can coconut milk

¼ teaspoon dried thyme leaves

¼ teaspoon cloves

¼ teaspoon cayenne

Salt and pepper to taste

Croutons or chopped herbs

1. In a large soup pot, combine oil or butter, onion, celery, green pepper, and garlic; sauté over medium-high heat 3 minutes.

2. Add callaloo leaves and broth; stir in okra. Bring to a boil; reduce heat to medium. Simmer 20 minutes.

3. Add coconut milk, thyme, cloves, cayenne, salt, and pepper; simmer 10–15 minutes, or until vegetables are very tender.

4. Working in batches, purée soup. Return to soup pot; cook just until hot. Serve garnished with croutons or fresh herbs.

CHAPTER 6

Fish and Seafood Soups

Basic Fish Broth

Snapper, sole, cod, halibut, flounder, sea bass, and haddock
are some of the nonoily fish suitable for stock making.

INGREDIENTS | SERVES 6

1 tablespoon butter

1 tablespoon olive oil

2 onions, diced

2 ribs celery, chopped

1 carrot, chopped

3 pounds nonoily fish heads and meaty carcasses

2 sprigs thyme

2 bay leaves

3 sprigs parsley

8 cups water

1 cup white wine

3 peppercorns

1 tablespoon vinegar

1. Combine butter and oil in a heavy stock pot. Add onions, celery, and carrot; sauté over medium-high heat 5 minutes.

2. Add fish and remaining ingredients. Bring to a boil; reduce heat to medium. Cover pot; simmer 4–6 hours, occasionally skimming foam off top.

3. Remove from heat; let stand 30 minutes.

4. Remove bones and vegetables with slotted spoon; discard. Strain broth through fine sieve into a bowl. Cover; refrigerate until chilled. Skim off any fat that rises to top. Use broth within a few days, or freeze for later.

Shellfish Broth

Shellfish broth can be a mix of shells or shells from only one type of shellfish. For bisques, cook strained broth until reduced by half to concentrate flavors.

INGREDIENTS | SERVES 6

8 cups broken shells from shrimp, crabs, or lobsters

8 cups water

1 onion, sliced

2 ribs celery, chopped

1 carrot, chopped

1 cup white wine

1 tablespoon tomato paste

2 sprigs thyme

3 sprigs parsley

10 peppercorns

1 bay leaf

1. In a large stock pot, combine shells and water. Cook over medium heat 1 hour without allowing mixture to boil; skim foam as it rises to top.

2. Add remaining ingredients; cover and simmer 2 hours.

3. Remove from heat; let stand 30 minutes.

4. Strain broth through fine sieve into a bowl; discard solids. Cover; refrigerate, or freeze until needed.

Cooking Liquid as Broth

The cooking liquid from steamed clams, mussels, lobster, and shrimp is very flavorful and should never be discarded. Strain the liquid to remove any shell bits, then add to soup or freeze for later use. In a pinch, these cooking broths can be combined with clam juice to make an acceptable base for soups.

Oyster and Artichoke Soup

Purists insist this soup tastes best after being refrigerated for several hours and gently reheated.

INGREDIENTS | **SERVES 4**

3 tablespoons butter
4 green onions, finely chopped
1 rib celery, finely chopped
3 cloves garlic, minced
2 cups fresh or frozen artichoke hearts, chopped
2 tablespoons flour
4 cups chicken or seafood broth
1 teaspoon Tabasco
¼ teaspoon dried thyme
1 teaspoon Worcestershire sauce
1 pint oysters
¼ cup sherry
1 cup heavy cream
¼ cup minced fresh parsley
Salt and pepper to taste

1. In a large, heavy soup pot, melt butter over medium-high heat. Add green onions, celery, and garlic; sauté 1 minute. Add chopped artichoke hearts; continue to cook, stirring constantly, 3 minutes.

2. Sprinkle flour over vegetables; stir to coat. Slowly add broth to vegetables; stir until flour has dissolved. Add Tabasco, thyme, and Worcestershire sauce. Bring to a boil; reduce heat to medium. Cover pot; cook 1 hour and 15 minutes, adding more liquid if needed.

3. Drain oysters; reserve liquid. Chop oysters; add to soup. Stir in oyster liquid and sherry; simmer uncovered 10 minutes, never allowing mixture to boil.

4. Stir in heavy cream, parsley, salt, and pepper; remove from heat. Serve immediately, or cool and refrigerate for later.

Heaven on the Half Shell

Oysters are filter feeders, and their flavor and wholesomeness reflects the quality of the waters where they spend their lives. Many cooks insist on North American-produced oysters—particularly when serving raw oysters—because the industry is strictly regulated in the United States and Canada. Even so, *vibrio vulnificus* bacteria can live in the raw tissues, which is why unprocessed, raw oysters are ill advised for children, the elderly, and those with compromised immune systems.

Oysters Rockefeller Soup

This soup pays homage to Oysters Rockefeller, the fabulous broiled oyster appetizer that originated in Antoine's Restaurant in New Orleans.

INGREDIENTS | SERVES 4

4 tablespoons butter
1 small onion, finely chopped
1 green onion, finely chopped
1 rib celery, finely chopped
3 cloves garlic, minced
4 cups water or seafood broth
1 teaspoon Tabasco
1 tablespoon Herbsaint liqueur
1 pint oysters
2 cups fresh spinach, chopped
2 tablespoons minced fresh parsley
1 cup heavy cream
¼ cup grated Parmesan cheese
Salt and pepper to taste

1. In a heavy soup pot, melt butter over medium-high heat. Add onion, green onion, celery, and garlic; sauté 3 minutes.

2. Sprinkle flour over mixture; stir to blend. Slowly add broth; stir until flour has dissolved. Bring mixture to a boil; add Tabasco and reduce heat to medium. Simmer, covered, 30 minutes.

3. Add Herbsaint; drain oysters and reserve liquid. Chop oysters; add with oyster liquid to soup pot. Simmer 2 minutes.

4. Stir in spinach and parsley; simmer 5 minutes.

5. Remove from heat; stir in cream and Parmesan, season with salt and pepper. Serve immediately.

Marmitako (Basque Fish Soup)

This main-dish fisherman's soup comes from the Basque coast of Spain.
The name means "from the pot."

INGREDIENTS | **SERVES 4–6**

3 tablespoons olive oil

1 medium onion, diced

1 green bell pepper, cored and cut into strips

2 cloves garlic, minced

1 small hot pepper, minced

2 cups seeded, diced plum tomatoes

½ cup dry white wine

6 cups water or chicken broth

3 large white potatoes, peeled and cut into ½ slices

1 pound tuna fillet

Salt and pepper to taste

Lemon quarters

1. In a heavy Dutch oven, heat olive oil over medium-high heat. Add onion, green pepper, garlic, and hot pepper; sauté 3 minutes.

2. Add tomatoes; continue to cook, stirring, 5 minutes.

3. Reduce heat to medium; add wine and 1 cup broth. Cover; simmer 10 minutes, stirring occasionally.

4. Add remaining broth and potatoes; cover and cook 30 minutes.

5. Rinse tuna fillet, pat dry, and dice. Sprinkle a little salt over fish; add to soup. Stir in salt and pepper; cover and simmer 5 minutes.

6. Serve immediately with lemon wedges and crusty bread.

New England Clam Chowder

If you prefer a thinner chowder, just omit the flour.
Some cooks like to add corn or diced carrots to the soup for color.

INGREDIENTS | SERVES 4–6

4 slices bacon

1 large onion, diced

2 cloves garlic, minced

3 russet potatoes, peeled and diced

1 tablespoon flour

½ cup white wine

1½ cups clam juice

1 cup water or fish stock

18 large clams, steamed and chopped

½ teaspoon thyme

1½ cups milk

1 cup heavy cream

Salt and pepper to taste

¼ cup minced fresh parsley

1. In a large soup pot, fry bacon over medium-high heat until crisp; remove to a paper towel, leaving fat in pot. Add onion and garlic to fat; sauté 3 minutes.

2. Add diced potatoes; cook, stirring, 5 minutes.

3. Sprinkle flour over potatoes and onion; carefully stir in wine, clam juice, and water or fish stock. Bring to a boil; reduce heat to medium. Add chopped clams and thyme; cover and simmer 20 minutes, stirring occasionally.

4. Add milk and cream; crumble in reserved bacon. Simmer, uncovered, 10 minutes.

5. Add salt and pepper. Remove from heat; add parsley.

Chowder Chops

Heavy cream usually contains 36 percent fat. It is the only milk product that can be boiled and reduced to a smooth, thick texture. Milk and light creams separate into curds and whey when boiled, which results in soup with an unpleasant texture and appearance.

Manhattan Clam Chowder

This dairy-free chowder closely resembles vegetable soup, but using clams instead of beef.

INGREDIENTS | SERVES 6

3 strips bacon

1 large onion, diced

1 green bell pepper, cored and diced

1 rib celery, diced

3 cloves garlic, minced

2 (16-ounce) cans diced tomatoes

4 cups clam juice

1 cup water

4 white potatoes, diced

1 large carrot, diced

24 Cherrystone clams, steamed and chopped

½ teaspoon dried oregano

½ teaspoon red pepper flakes

Salt and pepper to taste

¼ cup minced fresh parsley

1. In a heavy soup pot over medium-high heat, fry bacon until crisp; remove to paper towels to drain. Add onion, green pepper, celery, and garlic to fat; sauté 3 minutes.

2. Stir in tomatoes, clam juice and water; bring to a boil. Reduce heat to medium; add potatoes and carrot. Simmer, uncovered, 30 minutes, stirring occasionally.

3. Add clams, oregano, and red pepper flakes; simmer 15 minutes.

4. Remove from heat. Season with salt and pepper; add parsley.

Red Versus White Chowder

Manhattan clam chowder isn't from Manhattan at all. One story suggests it originated in Rhode Island in the late 1800s, when Portuguese cooks opted to add tomatoes to the clam-and-potato soup instead of milk. Old-line New England chowder lovers considered this a travesty, and dubbed the creation Manhattan Clam Chowder as a snub. Over the years, the dish has been adopted by New Yorkers and given a decidedly Italian twist.

Mussels in Saffron Soup

Small, farm-raised mussels are sweet tasting and often grit free. They're perfect for this rich soup.

INGREDIENTS | SERVES 4

4 dozen mussels, scrubbed and debearded
2 cups white wine
2 cups clam juice
2 bay leaves
1 sprig thyme
¼ teaspoon crushed saffron threads
1 tablespoon butter
2 shallots, minced
2 garlic cloves
2 cups half-and-half
Salt and pepper to taste
2 tablespoons minced fresh parsley
2 tablespoons minced fresh chervil

1. Place cleaned mussels in a heavy soup pot or Dutch oven; pour in wine and clam juice. Add bay leaves, thyme sprig, and saffron threads; bring to a boil and cover well. Cook 5 minutes; mussels should be done and shells open. Discard any unopened mussels.

2. With a slotted spoon, remove mussels in shells to a bowl. Strain cooking liquid through a fine sieve into another bowl. Melt butter over medium-high heat in soup pot. Add shallots and garlic; sauté 3 minutes.

3. Pour reserved cooking liquid from mussels into pot. Bring to a boil; reduce heat to medium.

4. Reserve 8 mussels in shells; remove meat from remaining mussels. Coarsely chop meat; add to simmering liquid. Cook 5 minutes.

5. Add half-and-half; continue cooking 1 minute.

6. Remove from heat; season with salt and pepper. Ladle soup into bowls; garnish with reserved mussels in shells. Sprinkle parsley and chervil over each bowl. Serve immediately.

Corn and Crab Soup

Freshly cut corn gives this soup extra flavor. In a pinch, frozen corn kernels or frozen creamed corn can be used.

INGREDIENTS | SERVES 6

3 tablespoons butter

1 medium onion, diced

3 tablespoons flour

4 cups chicken broth

2 cups corn kernels, scraped from cob

2 cloves garlic, pressed

½ teaspoon cayenne pepper

Pinch cumin

1 green onion, minced

2 cups cream

1 pound lump crabmeat

Salt and pepper to taste

2 tablespoons minced parsley

Feeling Crabby

Ever wonder why crabmeat is so expensive? Well, it takes 18–20 whole blue crabs to equal 1 pound of crabmeat. Crabs are steamed before being shelled, and the crabmeat separated into prized backfin lump crabmeat, white body crabmeat, and less expensive (but flavorful) claw crabmeat. Packaged fresh crabmeat is heat processed to kill bacteria. Just-picked crabmeat can also be frozen or canned.

1. In a heavy soup pot, melt butter over medium-high heat. Add onion; sauté 3 minutes.

2. Sprinkle with flour; stir to coat. Add broth; stir until flour has dissolved. Bring mixture to a boil; add corn. Reduce heat to medium; simmer 15 minutes.

3. Add garlic, cayenne, cumin, and green onion; cook 5 minutes, stirring often.

4. Ladle 2 cups of broth and corn into a blender. Pour in 1 cup of cream; blend to purée. Pour purée back into pot; stir in remaining cup of cream.

5. Reduce heat to low; carefully stir in crabmeat. Cook 1–2 minutes; remove from heat.

6. Season with salt and pepper; stir in parsley. Serve immediately.

She-Crab Soup

Authentic Charleston She-Crab Soup features the fatty meat of female blue crabs and crab roe. If you can't find crab roe, substitute crumbled egg yolks.

INGREDIENTS | SERVES 4

3 tablespoons butter

2 tablespoons granulated flour

3 cups half-and-half

½ small onion, very finely chopped

1 teaspoon Worcestershire sauce

¼ teaspoon cayenne

¼ teaspoon mace

1 pound lump crabmeat

3 tablespoons crab roe or 2 crumbled boiled egg yolks

Salt and pepper to taste

¼ cup sherry

¼ cup minced fresh parsley

1 teaspoon grated lemon zest

1. In a heavy soup pot over medium low heat, melt 2 tablespoons butter; stir in flour and stir until blended into a smooth paste. Add half-and-half; whisk constantly until mixture begins to thicken. Add onion, Worcestershire, cayenne, and mace. Allow cream to begin to bubble around the edges of the pot; reduce heat to low.

2. Continue to simmer, not allowing it to boil, 5 minutes. Stir in crabmeat and crab roe or crumbled egg yolks. Season with salt and pepper; cook an additional minute.

3. Add sherry; remove from heat. Let stand briefly before serving. Ladle into bowls; garnish with parsley and lemon zest.

Minorcan Conch Chowder

Datil peppers are small, very hot peppers native to St. Augustine, Florida.
If you can't find them, substitute any hot peppers.

INGREDIENTS | SERVES 6

3 ounces slab bacon, diced

1 medium onion, diced

1 green bell pepper, cored and diced

1 rib celery, diced

2 cloves garlic, minced

2 datil peppers, minced

1 (28-ounce) can plum tomatoes, crushed

1 cup tomato sauce

5 cups clam juice

2 bay leaves

½ teaspoon dried thyme leaves

2 russet potatoes, peeled and diced

1 cup minced conch meat

Salt and pepper to taste

1. In a heavy soup pot, fry diced bacon over medium-high heat. When bacon bits have browned, remove from pot; reserve. Add onion, green pepper, celery, garlic, and datil peppers; sauté 5 minutes.

2. Add tomatoes, tomato sauce, clam juice, and bay leaves. Bring to a boil; reduce heat to medium. Simmer 30 minutes, adding more clam juice or water if needed.

3. Add thyme, potatoes, and conch meat; simmer 45 minutes.

4. Season with salt and pepper; remove from heat. Let stand a few minutes before serving.

Conch Cuisine

Conch is a large mollusk with a beautiful curved and fluted shell. It's native to the Caribbean and South Atlantic waters, and it turns up in fritters, stews, soups, and occasionally in salads. Conch meat can be rubbery, so it's usually either marinated or finely chopped before cooking. Fresh conch can be found in some markets, while frozen conch is more widely available. Clams are a good substitute in recipes.

Spicy Cod Soup

This light soup can be turned into a hearty main dish with the addition of diced potatoes or pasta.

INGREDIENTS | **SERVES 4–6**

1 tablespoon olive oil
1 medium onion, diced
1 green bell pepper, cored and diced
3 cloves garlic
1 jalapeño pepper, minced
2 (16-ounce) cans diced tomatoes
4 cups fish broth
½ cup orange juice
½ cup white wine
½ teaspoon cumin
¼ teaspoon cayenne
½ cup sliced black olives
1 pound cod fish fillet, diced
Salt and pepper to taste
¼ cup fresh basil ribbons

1. In a large soup pot, heat olive oil over medium-high heat. Add onion, green pepper, garlic, and jalapeño pepper; sauté 3 minutes.

2. Add tomatoes, broth, orange juice, wine, cumin, and cayenne. Bring to a boil; reduce heat to medium. Simmer 1 hour.

3. Add olives and diced cod; simmer 10 minutes, or until fish is opaque.

4. Season with salt and pepper; remove from heat. Stir in fresh basil.

Hot and Sour Seafood Soup

Crab leg meat can be added to this soup, but avoid surimi or artificial crab.

INGREDIENTS | SERVES 4

6 tiger lily buds

¼ cup dried wood ear mushrooms, chopped

8 large shrimp, peeled and halved vertically

8 sea scallops, quartered

¼ cup soy sauce, divided use

1 tablespoon sesame oil, divided use

1 tablespoon cornstarch, divided use

2 ounces firm tofu

⅓ cup sliced mushrooms

½ cup julienne-sliced bamboo shoots

⅓ cup julienne-sliced carrots

6 cups fish broth

2 tablespoons rice wine vinegar

2 tablespoons cold water

1 egg

1 teaspoon freshly ground black pepper

1 green onion, minced

Hot chili oil to taste

Salt to taste

1. Place tiger lily buds in a small heat-safe bowl; place dried mushrooms in another bowl. Pour boiling water into each bowl; let ingredients soften 30 minutes.

2. Place shrimp and scallops in third bowl. Combine 1 tablespoon soy sauce and 1 teaspoon sesame oil; pour over seafood and mix well. Sprinkle 1 teaspoon cornstarch over shrimp and scallops; toss to coat. Let stand 15 minutes.

3. Cut tofu into thin strips. In a soup pot, combine tofu, fresh mushrooms, bamboo shoots, carrots, and broth; bring to a boil over high heat. Drain lily buds and dried mushrooms; add to pot with seafood, remaining soy sauce, and sesame oil. Stir well; reduce heat to medium. Simmer 8 minutes.

4. Stir in vinegar. Dissolve remaining cornstarch in 2 tablespoons cold water. Bring to a boil again; stir in cornstarch. Stirring, cook 1 minute, or until soup thickens.

5. Beat egg; slowly pour into soup while stirring. Remove from heat. Add pepper, green onion, hot oil, and salt; serve.

Bouillabaisse

Serve this classic Provençal fish soup with lots of crusty bread and a crisp white wine.

INGREDIENTS | **SERVES 6**

6 cups fish broth

½ cup white wine

2 large tomatoes, peeled, seeded, and diced

2 leeks, trimmed and julienned

1 cup sliced fennel

3 garlic cloves, minced

1 sprig fresh thyme

⅓ cup orange juice

⅛ teaspoon saffron threads

Salt and pepper to taste

1 dozen mussels, scrubbed

1 dozen small clams, scrubbed

1 pound assorted fish fillets, diced

2 dozen large shrimp, peeled and deveined

3 steamed lobster tails, cut in half lengthwise

¼ cup minced fresh parsley

1. In a large Dutch oven, combine broth, wine, tomatoes, leeks, fennel, garlic, thyme, orange juice, and saffron threads. Bring to a boil over medium-high heat. Reduce heat to medium; simmer 15 minutes.

2. Add salt and pepper. Raise heat to medium high; bring to a boil. Add mussels and clams. Cover; cook 5 minutes, or until shells are open.

3. Reduce heat to medium. Add fish, shrimp, and lobster; cook, uncovered, until fish and shrimp turn opaque, about 5 minutes.

4. Remove from heat; cover. Let stand a few minutes before serving in large, shallow bowls. Garnish with parsley.

Cioppino

Cioppino is a favorite San Francisco dish, with strong Italian roots.

INGREDIENTS | SERVES 4

2 tablespoons olive oil

1 medium onion, diced

1 green bell pepper, cored and diced

4 cloves garlic, minced

1 (28-ounce) can plum tomatoes, crushed

1 cup tomato juice

3 cups fish broth or clam juice

1 cup dry red wine

1 teaspoon Italian herb seasoning

1 tablespoon Pernod

1 teaspoon Tabasco

1 dozen steamed clams or mussels in shells

4 steamed crab halves, outer shells and gills removed

1 dozen large shrimp, peeled and deveined

½ pound diced sea bass, red snapper, or halibut

¼ cup minced fresh parsley or basil

1. In a large soup pot, heat olive oil over medium-high heat. Add onion, green pepper, and garlic; sauté 3 minutes.

2. Add tomatoes, tomato juice, broth, wine, and Italian seasoning. Bring to a boil; reduce heat to medium. Simmer 15 minutes.

3. Stir in Pernod and Tabasco; add mussels or clams, crabs, shrimp, and fish. Cook until fish and shrimp are opaque, about 5 minutes.

4. Serve in large bowls. Sprinkle with parsley or basil.

Cioppino Versus Bouillabaisse Versus Zuppa de Pesce

There are no hard-and-fast rules about what combinations of fish and shellfish go into a mixed seafood soup. That means Italian-American Cioppino, French Bouilla-baisse, and Southern Italian Zuppa de Pesce may all boast the same oceanic array of seafood. Herbs, spices, and broth thickness may vary, and—in the case of Zuppa de Pesce—there may be a dense tangle of spaghetti at the bottom of the bowl. But the wonderful concept is all the same.

Catfish Courtbouillon

*French courtbouillon is a delicate fish broth. This is a Louisiana dish that bears
very little resemblance to the mother-country versions.*

INGREDIENTS | SERVES 6

2 pounds catfish fillet, cut into 2 wide pieces

2 teaspoons kosher salt

1 teaspoon cayenne pepper

½ teaspoon garlic powder

¼ teaspoon onion powder

½ teaspoon black pepper

3 tablespoons melted bacon fat or vegetable oil

1 medium onion, diced

1 green bell pepper, cored and diced

1 rib celery, diced

3 garlic cloves, minced

2 tablespoons granulated flour

1 cup fish broth

1 (28-ounce) can plum tomatoes, crushed

1 tablespoon Tabasco

2 bay leaves

1 (16-ounce) can tomato sauce

2 green onions, white and green parts, finely chopped

¼ cup minced parsley

1. Rinse catfish pieces; pat dry. Combine kosher salt, cayenne, garlic powder, onion powder, and pepper; sprinkle liberally on fish and set aside.

2. In a heavy Dutch oven, heat fat or oil over medium-high heat. Add onion, green pepper, celery, and garlic; sauté 5 minutes.

3. Sprinkle flour over mixture; stir well to combine. Add broth; stir until flour dissolves and mixture is thickened. Add tomatoes, Tabasco, bay leaves, and tomato sauce. Bring mixture to a boil; reduce heat to medium low. Simmer 10 minutes.

4. Add catfish carefully, trying to avoid overlapping pieces. Add additional broth or water if mixture seems too thick. Sprinkle top with green onions and parsley. Cover; simmer 45 minutes. Add water if needed, but do not stir.

5. Remove from heat; check seasoning—sprinkle more of spice mixture into sauce if needed. Carefully ladle soup into bowls over steamed rice.

About Catfish

Cajun courtbouillon purists insist that the soup must be made with wild-caught catfish, not farmed, and that whole fish or fish steaks must be cooked in the sauce to give it authentic flavor. If you're willing to engage yourself in removing bones and skin from your plate, by all means try the whole-fish version. Wild-caught catfish has a much stronger flavor than farm-raised catfish. You'll either find it to be a revelation or an acquired taste.

Mexican Vigil Soup

This soup is often served on Good Friday.
If you can't find Mexican dried fish, substitute 1 cup of flaked dried cod.

INGREDIENTS | SERVES 6

1 pound dried fish

1 cup milk

2 tablespoons vegetable oil

1 medium onion, diced

1 Anaheim pepper, diced

2 cloves garlic, minced

1 (16-ounce) can diced tomatoes

6 cups water or fish broth

2 russet potatoes, peeled and diced

1 cup green beans

1 cup peas

1 cup blanched nopalitos (cactus pads), diced

2 eggs, beaten

Salt and pepper to taste

1. Clean dried fish, removing scales and bones; flake remaining fish. (You should have about 1 cup of boneless fish flakes.) Place fish and milk in a bowl; set aside.

2. In a heavy soup pot over medium-high heat, combine oil, onion, pepper, and garlic; sauté 5 minutes.

3. Add tomatoes and water or broth. Bring to a boil; reduce heat to medium. Add potatoes, green beans, and peas.

4. Strain fish; discard milk. Add flaked fish to pot. Simmer 40 minutes.

5. Add blanched nopalitos; cook 5 minutes.

6. Slowly pour beaten eggs into soup, stirring. Remove heat; add salt and pepper.

Lobster Bisque

Give this bisque extra flavor by roasting lobster shells in butter for 45 minutes before making broth from the shells and water.

INGREDIENTS | SERVES 4

½ cup butter

½ cup flour

1 minced shallot

2 tablespoons tomato purée

6 cups lobster broth

2 cups heavy cream

¼ cup sherry

1 tablespoon brandy

2 lobster tails, finely chopped

1 tablespoon chopped fresh tarragon

Salt and pepper to taste

Lobster Lumps

Many older recipes for lobster bisque call for puréed lobster meat to make a perfectly smooth soup. If you prefer that option, just reserve a few bits of lobster for garnish, then purée the lobster meat with the cream before adding it to the soup. The important thing is to strain the lobster-cream mixture through a fine sieve to keep the soup from tasting grainy.

1. In a soup pot over medium-high heat, melt butter. Add flour; stir until mixture forms a paste. Cook until bubbly, but not browned.

2. Add shallot and cook 1 minute; carefully add broth. Whisk until flour is dissolved and mixture is slightly thickened. Stir in tomato purée. Bring to a boil; reduce heat to medium.

3. Simmer until broth is reduced by one third, about 20–30 minutes.

4. Stir in cream, sherry, and brandy; simmer, without boiling, 20 minutes.

5. Add chopped lobster meat and tarragon. Remove from heat; add salt and pepper. Serve in creamed soup bowls with baguette slices.

Creole Seafood Gumbo

This recipe makes Creole gumbo, the type often found in New Orleans homes and bistros. Cajun gumbo rarely contains both roux and okra.

INGREDIENTS | SERVES 8

⅔ cup vegetable oil
⅔ cup granulated flour
2 onions, diced
2 cups sliced okra
10 cups hot shellfish or fish broth
1 green bell pepper, cored and diced
1 rib celery, diced
3 cloves garlic, minced
2 tomatoes, diced (optional)
2 bay leaves
½ teaspoon cayenne pepper
½ teaspoon garlic powder
½ teaspoon onion powder
½ teaspoon dried thyme leaves
1 pound medium shrimp, peeled and deveined
1 pound peeled crawfish tails
1 dozen oysters
1 pound crabmeat
Salt and pepper to taste
¼ cup minced fresh parsley
¼ cup minced green onion

1. In a heavy soup pot over medium heat, combine oil and flour; stir until mixture forms a smooth paste. Continue to cook, stirring constantly, until roux turns a toasty brown. Add 1 onion to roux; stir until onion turns translucent. Add okra; stirring, continue to cook 3 minutes.

2. Slowly add hot broth; stir until flour mixture is dissolved. Bring mixture to a boil. Cook 10 minutes.

3. Reduce heat to medium; add remaining onion, green pepper, celery, and garlic. Stir in tomatoes, bay leaves, cayenne, garlic powder, onion powder, and thyme. Simmer 1½ hours, adding more stock if needed.

4. Add shrimp, crawfish, oysters, and crabmeat; continue to simmer, stirring occasionally, 20 minutes.

5. Add salt and pepper; stir in parsley and green onion. Serve over steamed rice.

Czech Christmas Fish Soup

Families with roots in the Czech Republic enjoy a seafood supper on Christmas Eve, and this soup stars.

INGREDIENTS | **SERVES 6–8**

4 tablespoons butter

1 medium onion, diced

2 tablespoons flour

8 cups fish broth

2 ribs celery, sliced

½ bulb celery root, trimmed and chopped

5 whole allspice berries

½ teaspoon mace

1 cup half-and-half

1 pound mild white fish, diced

1 dozen oysters, with liquid

Salt and pepper to taste

¼ cup minced fresh parsley

1. In a heavy soup pot, melt butter over medium-high heat. Add onion; sauté 3 minutes.

2. Sprinkle flour over mixture; stir until well blended. Slowly add broth; stir until flour dissolves. Bring to a boil; reduce heat to medium. Add celery, celery root, allspice, and mace. Simmer 40 minutes.

3. Stir in half-and-half. Add fish and oysters; continue to cook 20 minutes. Do not allow soup to boil.

4. Season with salt and pepper. Remove from heat; stir in parsley. Serve in shallow bowls.

Thai Lobster Soup

This soup can be enriched by adding coconut milk or by stirring in softened rice noodles.

INGREDIENTS | SERVES 4

1 stalk fresh lemongrass

6 cups shellfish broth or chicken broth

1 clove garlic, pressed

Juice of 1 lime

Zest of 1 lime, grated

1 tablespoon fish sauce

1 hot chili pepper, chopped

4 ounces mushrooms, sliced

2 green onions, sliced

1 cup lobster meat, chopped

¼ cup minced fresh cilantro

Salt and pepper to taste

1. Trim lemongrass; cut a few diagonal slices to use as garnish. Set aside. Cut remaining stalk into strips.

2. In a soup pot, combine lemongrass and broth. Bring broth to a boil; reduce heat to medium. Simmer 10 minutes.

3. Remove lemongrass; discard. Add garlic, lime juice and zest, fish sauce, hot pepper, and mushrooms; Simmer 10 minutes.

4. Stir in green onions, lobster, and cilantro; cook 10 minutes.

5. Add salt and pepper. Ladle into bowls; garnish with reserved lemongrass slices.

Salmon Chowder

This chowder is a great way to use leftover salmon.
A tablespoon of tomato juice can be added to give the soup a nice pink color.

INGREDIENTS | SERVES 4–6

4 slices bacon

1 large onion, diced

2 cloves garlic, minced

2 russet potatoes, peeled and diced

1 tablespoon flour

½ cup white wine

3 cups fish broth

1 cup corn kernels

1 pound fresh salmon, poached and flaked

1½ cups heavy cream

Salt and pepper to taste

2 tablespoons minced fresh dill

1. In a large soup pot, fry bacon over medium-high heat until crisp. Remove to a paper towel; leave fat in pot. Add onion and garlic to fat; sauté 3 minutes.

2. Add diced potatoes; stirring, cook 5 minutes.

3. Sprinkle flour over potatoes and onion; carefully stir in wine and broth. Bring mixture to a boil; reduce heat to medium. Add corn; cover and simmer 20 minutes, stirring occasionally.

4. Add salmon and cream. Crumble in reserved bacon; simmer, uncovered, 10 minutes.

5. Add salt and pepper. Remove from heat; add dill.

Crawfish and Wild Rice Soup

If you don't have access to crawfish, you can substitute peeled and deveined shrimp.

INGREDIENTS | SERVES 4

2 tablespoons butter

1 small onion, minced

1 rib celery, minced

6 ounces mushrooms, sliced

2 tablespoons flour

6 cups fish or shellfish broth

1 pound crawfish tails

1 cup cooked wild rice

1 cup heavy cream

Salt and pepper to taste

1. In a heavy soup pot, melt butter over medium-high heat. Add onion, celery, and mushrooms; sauté 3 minutes.

2. Sprinkle with flour; stir until well blended. Slowly add broth. Bring to a boil; reduce heat to medium. Simmer 15 minutes.

3. Add crawfish and wild rice; simmer 15 minutes.

4. Stir in cream, salt, and pepper; cook 5 minutes longer. Remove from heat and serve.

Scallop Soup

This fresh-tasting soup offers a nice diversion from chowders and creamy bisques.

INGREDIENTS | SERVES 4–6

2 tablespoons olive oil

1 leek, white part only, trimmed and sliced

⅓ cup diced fennel bulb

1 carrot, trimmed and sliced

2 large tomatoes, peeled, seeded, and diced

6 cups fish broth

2 tablespoons vermouth

1 pound sea scallops, quartered

⅓ cup fresh basil leaves

Zest of 1 lemon

1 garlic clove

Salt and pepper to taste

Freshly grated Parmesan

1. In a heavy soup pot, heat oil over medium-high heat. Add leek; sauté 2 minutes.

2. Stir in fennel and carrot; sauté 3 minutes.

3. Add tomatoes and broth. Bring mixture to a boil; reduce heat to medium and add vermouth. Simmer 15 minutes.

4. Add scallops; simmer 3–5 minutes, or just until scallops turn opaque.

5. Combine basil, lemon zest, and garlic in a blender; pulse until finely ground. Stir into soup; add salt and pepper.

6. Remove from heat; serve. Pass the Parmesan at the table.

CHAPTER 7

Legumes in a Bowl

Black Bean Soup with Salsa

*This vegetarian soup offers a nice contrast between the smooth,
mellow flavor of the beans and the spicy-tart salsa.*

INGREDIENTS | SERVES 8

2 pounds dry black beans

3 quarts water or vegetable broth

2 bay leaves

1 tablespoon unsweetened cocoa powder

1 large onion, diced

1 green bell pepper, cored and diced

2 cloves garlic, minced

2 tablespoons olive oil

1 tablespoon red wine vinegar

1 teaspoon cumin

½ teaspoon black pepper

1 teaspoon kosher salt

Salsa Ingredients:

2 large tomatoes, diced small

1 small red onion, minced

2 jalapeño peppers, minced

1 firm ripe avocado, diced

Juice of 2 limes

¼ cup minced cilantro

Sour cream

1. Rinse black beans thoroughly; pick out any specks of dirt or discolored beans. Soak beans in enough cold water to cover for 8 hours, or overnight. Discard soaking water.

2. Place beans in a large soup pot; add water or broth. Add bay leaves and cocoa. Bring to a boil over high heat; reduce to medium. Simmer, uncovered, 2 hours.

3. In a skillet, sauté onion, green pepper, and garlic in oil until crisp-tender, about 3–5 minutes.

4. Add contents of skillet to soup, along with vinegar, cumin, pepper, and salt; continue cooking 1 hour.

5. Adjust salt and pepper; remove from heat.

6. In a bowl, combine tomatoes, onion, jalapeño peppers, avocado, lime juice, and cilantro. Ladle soup into bowls; top each bowl with a spoonful of sour cream and a spoonful of salsa. Serve immediately.

Chocolate in Soup?

Cocoa powder or unsweetened chocolate adds depth of flavor and richness to soups and sauces. Although most consumers associate chocolate with sweet confections, it isn't unusual to find it as an ingredient in savory dishes from Mexico and Central and South America. In fact, the national dish of Mexico, Turkey Mole, is built on a thick, chocolate-laced sauce. Chocolate or cocoa powder is especially good in vegetarian black bean dishes.

Lentil and Spinach Soup

Dried lentils don't have to be soaked, and they cook more quickly than other dried beans, making these legumes perfect for a hearty, last-minute soup.

INGREDIENTS | SERVES 4

1 tablespoon olive oil

1 onion, diced

1 rib celery, diced

2 cloves garlic, minced

2 carrots, peeled and diced

1 pound brown lentils, rinsed

1 (14-ounce) can diced tomatoes with oregano

2 quarts water or vegetable broth

1 teaspoon Tabasco

1 cup fresh spinach, cleaned and chopped

Salt and pepper to taste

1. In a large soup pot over medium-high heat, combine oil, onion, celery, garlic, and carrots; sauté 3–5 minutes.

2. Add lentils and tomatoes; bring to a boil. Pour in water or broth and Tabasco; reduce heat to medium. Cook 1 hour and 15 minutes, stirring occasionally.

3. Add spinach; continue cooking until spinach wilts, about 1 minute. Season with salt and pepper. Serve immediately.

Edamame Soup

Buy cooked, ready-to-shell edamame beans in your produce section or use frozen edamame beans.

INGREDIENTS | SERVES 4

6 cups chicken or vegetable broth

2 cups fresh-cooked shelled edamame beans

1 cup finely sliced white mushrooms

1 teaspoon grated fresh ginger

1 tablespoon soy sauce

Dash dark sesame oil

2 tablespoons minced fresh cilantro

Salt and pepper to taste

1. Combine all ingredients in a large saucepan over high heat; stir well.

2. Bring to a boil; reduce heat to medium. Simmer 15 minutes.

3. Serve in shallow bowls.

Senate White Bean Soup

This super-simple soup has been on the menu of the U.S. Senate restaurant every day for more than 100 years.

INGREDIENTS | SERVES 8

2 pounds dried navy beans

4 quarts water

1½ pounds smoked ham hocks

1 onion, chopped

2 tablespoons butter

Salt and pepper to taste

History in a Bowl

There are several stories about how the famous bean soup got onto the Senate restaurant menu. Most suggest that Senator Fred Thomas Dubois of Idaho, who served from 1901 to 1907 and chaired the committee supervising the Senate restaurant, put through a resolution demanding the soup be served each day. Another story has Senator Knute Nelson of Minnesota declaring his love for the soup in 1903, prompting the restaurant cooks to satisfy his cravings.

1. Wash navy beans in a colander; pick out any dark beans or specks of dirt. Place beans in a heavy soup pot with 4 quarts of hot water. Add ham hocks; bring mixture to a boil over high heat. Reduce heat to medium; cover and cook, stirring occasionally, 3 hours.

2. Remove ham hocks; set aside to cool. Cut meat from ham hocks; dice and return to soup.

3. In a skillet over high heat, sauté onion in butter until lightly browned. Pour contents of skillet into soup. Season with salt and pepper just before serving.

Ribollita

This Tuscan peasant dish gets added heartiness from crusty Italian bread, usually added the second day to stretch a pot of soup. The word ribollita means "reboiled."

INGREDIENTS | SERVES 6

4 ounces pancetta, diced small

1 red onion, finely chopped

1 leek, cleaned and chopped

2 carrots, diced

3 cloves garlic, minced

1 tablespoon tomato paste

1 (14-ounce) can diced tomatoes

1 bay leaf

6 cups chicken broth or water

3 cups chopped black cabbage or Savoy cabbage

3 cups cooked cannellini beans

2 tablespoons minced fresh basil

⅓ cup extra virgin olive oil

8 thick slices Italian bread

2 tablespoons chopped fresh basil

Freshly grated Parmesan (optional)

Of Cabbages and Cabbages

Cavalo nero or black cabbage is a leafy, dark-green winter vegetable grown in Tuscany. Although widely available in Europe, it is less so in the United States. Savoy cabbage, kale, or a combination of Savoy cabbage and Swiss chard make good substitutes.

1. In a large soup pot over medium-high heat, brown pancetta. Add onion, leek, carrots, and garlic; sauté 3 minutes.

2. Add tomato paste; cook, stirring constantly, 1 minute. Stir in tomatoes, bay leaf, and broth or water. Bring to a boil; reduce heat to medium. Simmer 10 minutes.

3. Add chopped cabbage. Purée 1 cup of beans in a food processor; add to the broth along with remaining beans. Continue to cook 30 minutes, stirring occasionally.

4. When soup is almost ready, brush a little olive oil on tops of bread slices; toast bread in oven until browned. Place a slice of toast in each serving bowl. Remove soup from heat; stir in remaining olive oil and the basil. Ladle ribollita over bread in bowls and serve immediately. Pass freshly grated Parmesan.

Split Pea Soup with Turkey Tasso

The longer split pea soup cooks the creamier it gets. For a soup that's more like a purée, add an extra half-hour cooking time to this recipe.

INGREDIENTS | SERVES 6

1 pound green split peas, rinsed

1 cup diced turkey tasso

2 green onions, minced

1 small onion, diced

1 rib celery, sliced

1 small red bell pepper, cored and diced

2 carrots, peeled and sliced

¼ cup minced fresh parsley

1 clove garlic, minced

8 cups water

6 small red potatoes, peeled and quartered

Salt and pepper to taste

1. Rinse peas in strainer; pick out any bits of dirt or discolored peas.

2. In a large, heavy soup pot, combine tasso, peas, green onions, onion, celery, red bell pepper, carrots, parsley, and garlic. Stir in water; bring to a boil over medium-high heat. Reduce heat to medium; simmer 2 hours, stirring often.

3. Add potatoes; cook 20–30 minutes, or until potatoes are tender. Let stand 5 minutes before serving. Add salt and pepper as desired.

Lasso Some Tasso

Tasso is a smoked meat product made throughout Southwest Louisiana. Lean strips of pork, beef, or turkey are marinated in a spicy brine, then smoked. The resulting meat has a more pronounced smoky flavor than most sausage, and keeps very well. Locals eat thin slices of tasso as a snack, but mostly people use it to flavor beans, soups, and pasta dishes. Some specialty meat markets outside of Louisiana carry tasso, but it's also available through online venues.

Hoppin' John Soup

Hoppin' John—a dish of black-eyed peas with rice—is traditionally eaten on New Year's for good luck; collard greens are eaten to bring money. This dish combines the two!

INGREDIENTS | SERVES 4

1 pound dried black-eyed peas

1 large smoked ham hock

1 onion, chopped

1 green bell pepper, cored and chopped

1 rib celery, sliced

1 (14-ounce) can diced tomatoes with roasted garlic

2 quarts water

1 teaspoon Tabasco

1 cup diced, lean ham

2 cups cleaned, chopped collard greens

1 cup cooked and refrigerated rice (optional)

Salt and pepper to taste

¼ cup minced fresh parsley

1. Wash peas in colander; pick out any discolored ones or specks of dirt. Place in a heavy soup pot with ham hock, onion, green pepper, celery, tomatoes, and 2 quarts of water. Bring mixture to a boil over high heat. Reduce heat to medium and cover; stirring occasionally, cook 2 hours.

2. Remove ham hock; set aside to cool. Stir in Tabasco, ham cubes, and collard greens. Add additional water or broth if needed; simmer, uncovered, 25 minutes.

3. Remove meat from ham hock; shred and add to soup. Sprinkle rice over soup, if desired; cook an additional 5 minutes.

4. Season with salt and pepper; garnish with parsley. Serve immediately.

Sticky Business

Raw rice cooks best when added to thin, broth-based soups. When adding rice to thick soups, it's best to precook the rice and chill it before stirring it into the pot. Refrigeration dehydrates the rice slightly and makes it easier to disperse the rice throughout the soup. The hot soup heats and rehydrates the rice.

Red Beans and Rice Soup

The only difference between this dish and the classic red beans and rice is the amount of liquid in the beans and the relatively minor role of the rice.

INGREDIENTS | SERVES 10

2 pounds dried red kidney beans

1 pound andouille sausage, sliced

1 large onion, diced

1 green bell pepper, cored and diced

2 ribs celery, sliced

3 garlic cloves, minced

2 bay leaves

¼ teaspoon thyme leaves

1 teaspoon Tabasco

½ teaspoon cayenne

3 quarts broth or water

1 tablespoon lemon juice

2 green onions, sliced

⅓ cup chopped parsley

Salt and pepper to taste

5 cups cooked white rice

Tabasco (optional)

1. Place beans in colander; rinse well, picking out any bits of dirt and damaged beans. Put in a large bowl; add enough cold water to cover by several inches. Let soak 8 hours. or overnight, adding more water if needed.

2. In a large, heavy soup pot over medium-high heat, cook sausage 3 minutes, stirring.

3. Add onion, bell pepper, celery and garlic; sauté 5 minutes.

4. Add bay leaves, thyme, Tabasco, and cayenne. Drain beans; add to pot, along with 3 quarts broth or water. Bring to a boil; reduce heat to medium. Simmer 2½ hours, stirring often and adding more water or broth as needed.

5. Stir in lemon juice, green onions, and parsley; add salt and pepper. To serve, place a large spoonful of cooked rice in each bowl; ladle bean soup over top. Pass the Tabasco at the table.

Cranberry Bean Soup with Mixed Herbs

Some cooks like to add a little cooked spaghetti or macaroni to this soup,
making it a more substantial dish.

INGREDIENTS | SERVES 4–6

1 pound dried cranberry beans

6 slices bacon, cut into pieces

1 large onion, diced

1 green bell pepper, cored and diced

2 ribs celery, sliced

3 garlic cloves, minced

2 large tomatoes, diced

2 bay leaves

2 quarts chicken broth or water

¼ cup chopped basil leaves

2 green onions, sliced

¼ cup chopped parsley

2 tablespoons fresh tarragon leaves

2 teaspoons fresh thyme leaves

Salt and pepper to taste

1. Place cranberry beans in a colander; rinse well, picking out any bits of dirt and damaged beans. Put in a large bowl; add enough cold water to cover by several inches. Let soak 8 hours, or overnight, adding more water if needed.

2. In a large, heavy soup pot over medium-high heat, cook bacon 3 minutes, stirring.

3. Add onion, bell pepper, celery, and garlic; sauté 5 minutes.

4. Add tomatoes and bay leaves; cook until tomatoes begin to release liquid. Drain beans; add to pot with broth or water. Bring mixture to a boil; reduce heat to medium. Simmer 2 hours, stirring often and adding more water or broth as needed.

5. Stir in basil, green onions, parsley, tarragon, and thyme. Add salt and pepper. Remove from heat; let stand 5 minutes before serving.

Fifteen-Bean Soup with Smoked Turkey

This recipe offers a flavorful, robust alternative to seasoning soup with pork or sausage.

INGREDIENTS | **SERVES 6–8**

1 pound fifteen bean soup mix
2 tablespoons olive oil
1 large onion, diced
1 green bell pepper, cored and diced
2 ribs celery, sliced
3 garlic cloves, minced
1 (14-ounce) can diced tomatoes
2 quarts water or chicken broth
2 smoked turkey wings
1 teaspoon Tabasco
1 teaspoon cumin
1 cup diced smoked turkey breast
Salt and pepper to taste
1 green onion, minced

1. Place bean mix in large strainer; rinse thoroughly, picking out any specks of dirt and discolored beans. In a large soup pot over medium-high heat, combine oil, onion, green pepper, celery, and garlic; sauté 3 minutes.

2. Add tomatoes, water or broth, and turkey wings. Add beans; bring to a boil. Reduce heat to medium; simmer 2½ hours, adding more liquid if needed.

3. Remove turkey wings; stir in Tabasco, cumin, and diced turkey. Simmer 30 minutes.

4. Add salt and pepper; remove from heat. Stir in green onion; serve.

Curried Lentil Soup with Caramelized Onions

Sweet and pungent caramelized onions add unexpected flavor and texture to this soup.

INGREDIENTS | SERVES 6

1 pound dried lentils

2 tablespoons oil

2 green onions, sliced

1 large green bell pepper, cored and diced

1 rib celery, sliced

4 cloves garlic, minced

1 jalapeño pepper, minced

6 fresh tomatoes, chopped

2 teaspoons curry powder

1 teaspoon cumin

4 cups water or chicken broth

4 tablespoons butter

2 sweet onions, thinly sliced

1 teaspoon sugar

Salt and pepper to taste

1. Rinse lentils in strainer; pick out any discolored lentils and bits of soil. In a large soup pot, combine oil, green onions, bell pepper, celery, garlic, and jalapeño pepper; sauté over medium-high heat 3 minutes.

2. Stir in fresh tomatoes, curry powder, and cumin; simmer 5 minutes, stirring often.

3. Add lentils and water or broth. Bring to a boil; reduce heat to medium. Cook 1 hour and 15 minutes, stirring occasionally.

4. In a large skillet, melt butter over medium-high heat. Add onions; cook, stirring often, 10 minutes.

5. Sprinkle sugar over onions; cook until sugar dissolves and onions are golden.

6. Add salt and pepper. Ladle into bowls; top each bowl with a portion of caramelized onion rings.

African Groundnut Soup

*This traditional dish from Ghana is often eaten from a communal dish,
with each diner dipping bread or other starch into the bowl.*

INGREDIENTS | SERVES 4–6

2 boneless chicken breasts

2 boneless chicken thighs

2 tablespoons oil

2 onions, diced

2 hot red peppers, chopped

4 tomatoes, diced

1½ cups creamy peanut butter

8 cups hot water

Salt and pepper to taste

1 cup chopped peanuts

Peanut Power

When adding peanut butter to savory dishes, look for natural or homemade-style butters that have no added sugars or emulsifiers. Peanut butter made from fresh-roasted peanuts—which are actually legumes, not nuts—contains protein, vitamins E and B3, folate, magnesium, and antioxidants. To make your own small-batch peanut butter, simply pour roasted peanuts in a food processor with a very small amount of oil. Pulse until puréed. Add salt if needed.

1. In a large soup pot, brown chicken pieces in oil over medium-high heat; set aside to cool slightly. Add onions and hot peppers to pot; sauté 3 minutes.

2. Add tomatoes; cook until tomatoes begin to release juices. Remove pot from heat; carefully ladle contents of pot into blender. Pulse to purée; return to pot.

3. Dice chicken; return to pot over medium heat. Combine peanut butter and 2 cups hot water in blender; pulse to blend peanut butter in water. Add to pot along with remaining water. Simmer 1 hour, stirring often.

4. Add salt and pepper. To serve, ladle into bowls and garnish with peanuts.

Three-Bean Soup with Sausage

Here's proof that a delicious bean soup can be prepared without hours of cooking. The sausage can be cooked the day before and refrigerated.

INGREDIENTS | SERVES 6

½ pound hot Italian sausage, cooked
1 tablespoon olive oil
1 onion, diced
1 green bell pepper, diced
1 (16-ounce) can red kidney beans
1 (16-ounce) can black beans
1 (16-ounce) can cannellini beans
6 cups water or chicken broth
1 (14-ounce) can diced tomatoes
Salt and pepper to taste

1. Remove casing from cooked sausage; coarsely chop meat. In a large soup pot, combine oil, onion, and bell pepper; sauté 3 minutes.

2. Add chopped sausage to pot; cook an additional 2 minutes.

3. Add beans, water or broth, and tomatoes; stir well. Bring to a boil; reduce heat to medium. Cook 20 minutes.

4. Add salt and pepper; remove from heat. Serve with crusty bread.

Homestyle Split Pea Soup

Big, meaty ham bones are troves of rich flavor. Before adding a ham bone to a soup pot, trim off areas of tough skin and any loose fat.

INGREDIENTS | SERVES 8

1 meaty ham bone
2 pounds split peas
1 bay leaf
1 large onion, diced
1 small red bell pepper, cored and diced
1 rib celery, sliced
2 garlic cloves, pressed
2 carrots, peeled and diced
4 white potatoes, peeled and diced
Salt and pepper to taste

1. In a large, heavy soup pot, place ham bone with enough cold water to cover. In strainer, rinse and sort split peas. Add peas to pot with bay leaf; bring to a boil over high heat. Reduce heat to medium; simmer 2 hours, skimming off any foam that rises to the surface. Stir regularly so peas don't scorch.

2. Remove ham bone; set aside to cool. Add remaining ingredients, plus additional water if needed. Simmer 1 hour, stirring frequently.

3. Remove bits of ham from bone; chop or shred. Stir back into soup. Remove from heat; let stand 5 minutes before serving.

Pasta Fagioli

*Some cooks like to add small meatballs, bits of cooked Italian sausage,
or chopped spinach to this hearty bean and pasta soup.*

INGREDIENTS | SERVES 4–6

2 tablespoons olive oil

3 cloves garlic, minced

1 (28-ounce) can tomatoes

1 (8-ounce) can tomato sauce

4 cups chicken broth

½ teaspoon dried Italian seasoning

Splash white wine (optional)

1 (16-ounce) can cannellini beans

1 cup ditalini pasta

Salt and pepper to taste

2 cups freshly grated Parmesan

1. In a heavy saucepan, heat oil over medium-high heat; sauté garlic briefly. Add tomatoes, tomato sauce, broth, seasoning, and wine. Bring to a boil; reduce heat and simmer 30 minutes.

2. Add beans; raise heat to medium high. Add pasta; stirring, cook 15 minutes, or until pasta is tender. Add more liquid if soup becomes too thick.

3. Season with salt and pepper. Serve in bowls topped with generous amounts of grated cheese. Crusty bread is a must with pasta fagioli.

Pasta Primer

Should you cook dried pasta in your soup or in a separate pot of boiling water? That really depends on your desired result. Cooking pasta in a pot of soup allows the noodles to absorb the flavors—and some of the liquid—in the pot. It also releases some of the starch in the pasta back into the broth. The result is a thicker, denser soup. That's probably fine for bean and heavy vegetable soups, but when making a light, broth-based soup, you may want to cook the pasta separately and add the cooked product to the soup.

Garbanzo Bean and Pork Soup

This traditional Cuban soup is both delicious and easy to make. Use 2 jalapeños for a spicy dish.

INGREDIENTS | SERVES 4

1 pound pork tenderloin

1 tablespoon olive oil

1 medium onion, diced

1 cup dry red wine

1 green bell pepper, cored and diced

1 rib celery, diced

1–2 jalapeño peppers, minced

4 cloves garlic, minced

4 cups chicken broth

1 (16-ounce) can garbanzo beans

Salt to taste

1. Trim any fat from pork; dice into ½ cubes. Heat a large, heavy saucepan over medium-high heat; add oil. Brown pork, tossing to keep lean meat from sticking to pan. Add onion; sauté 3 minutes.

2. Pour in wine; bring mixture to a simmer. Add remaining ingredients. Reduce heat to medium; cover pot. Simmer 30 minutes, stirring occasionally.

3. Remove from heat; serve immediately.

Garbanzo Bonanza

Cultivated garbanzo beans—also known as chick peas, Indian peas, and Bengal gram—have been around for some 5,000 years. In the Middle East, remains of wild garbanzo beans have been dated back 7,500 years. Ancient Greeks and Romans ate these buttery, nutty legumes roasted, mixed with rice or sweetened for dessert. The Spanish and Portuguese brought them to the Americas, where they became a popular ingredient in Mexican and Caribbean dishes. Aside from their agreeable flavor, garbanzo beans are high in protein and can be dried or ground into flour for use in breads, fritters, and fillers.

Portuguese Bean Soup

Savoy cabbage, Swiss chard, or spinach can be substituted for the kale in this recipe.
You can also use frozen kale.

INGREDIENTS | SERVES 4–6

½ pound linguica sausage, sliced
2 tablespoons olive oil
1 onion, diced
2 (16-ounce) cans cannellini beans
6 cups chicken broth
2 white potatoes, peeled and diced
4 garlic cloves, pressed
2 cups stemmed and chopped fresh kale
¼ teaspoon paprika
Salt and pepper to taste

1. In a large soup pot, combine sausage, oil, and onion; sauté 3 minutes over medium-high heat.

2. Stir in beans, broth, potatoes, garlic, kale, and paprika.

3. Bring mixture to a boil, then reduce heat to medium. Cook 30 minutes.

4. Add salt and pepper; remove from heat. Serve with crusty bread.

Black Bean Bisque

This rich, decadent soup can be made from ingredients you probably have in your pantry.

INGREDIENTS | SERVES 6

2 tablespoons olive oil
1 onion, chopped
2 garlic cloves, minced
2 jalapeño peppers
1 teaspoon cumin
2 teaspoons chili powder
1 teaspoon Tabasco sauce
3 cups chicken broth
1 (14-ounce) can diced tomatoes
2 (16-ounce) cans black beans
1 cup heavy cream
Salt and pepper to taste
Sour cream and diced red bell pepper for garnish

1. In a large, heavy saucepan, combine oil, onion, garlic, and jalapeño peppers. Cook over medium-high heat, stirring constantly, 3 minutes.

2. Add cumin, chili powder, Tabasco, broth, tomatoes, and beans; bring to a boil. Reduce heat to medium; simmer, stirring often, 30 minutes.

3. Remove from heat. Ladle into blender; purée, working in batches. Return to pot.

4. Reheat soup until simmering. Remove from heat; stir in heavy cream. Adjust salt and pepper to taste. Serve in cream soup bowls garnished with sour cream and diced red pepper.

Barley Bean Soup

This meatless, dairy-free recipe can be served to your vegan friends.
If you prefer a meaty soup, add diced ham or leftover pot roast to the mix.

INGREDIENTS | SERVES 4

½ pound dried pinto beans
½ pound dried pink beans
2 tablespoons olive oil
2 sweet onions, chopped
1 green bell pepper, cored and chopped
1 rib celery, sliced
2 carrots, chopped
2 quarts water or vegetable broth
2 bay leaves
1 teaspoon Tabasco
⅓ cup pearl barley
Salt and pepper to taste
⅓ cup fresh basil leaves
⅓ cup minced fresh parsley

1. Wash beans in colander; pick out any discolored beans or specks of dirt. Place in a bowl with enough water to cover by several inches; let soak 8 hours, or overnight.

2. Drain beans. Heat oil in a heavy soup pot over high heat. Add onions, bell pepper, celery, and carrots; sauté 5 minutes.

3. Add beans along with water or broth, bay leaves, and Tabasco; bring to a boil. Reduce heat to medium; cover and cook, stirring occasionally, 1½ hours.

4. Check consistency of soup. If more liquid is needed, add it. If a thicker soup is desired, purée 1 cup of the soup in a blender, then return to soup pot.

5. Add barley; cook, uncovered, 30 minutes, or until barley is tender.

6. Remove from heat. Season with salt and pepper; stir in basil and parsley. Serve immediately.

Crock-pot Bean Soup

*This recipe calls for unsoaked dried beans. If you prefer beans with softer skins,
by all means soak the beans overnight before cooking.*

INGREDIENTS | SERVES 6

1 cup dried great northern beans
½ cup dried small red beans
½ cup dried pinto beans
1 ham hock
½ pound chorizo, sliced
1 onion, diced
2 cloves garlic, minced
1 (10-ounce) can tomatoes and green chilies
1 (14-ounce) can fire-roasted diced tomatoes
1 teaspoon chili powder
1 teaspoon cumin
½ cup commercial barbecue sauce
6 cups water
⅓ cup minced green onion
Salt and pepper to taste

1. Pour beans into colander; rinse well and remove any specks of dirt or discolored beans.

2. In the pot of a large slow cooker, combine beans with all ingredients. Cook on medium heat 8–10 hours.

3. Stir well. Keep warm until you're ready to serve.

Fresh Lima Bean Soup

Unlike dried bean soups, this dish has a light, fresh flavor that's perfect for summer patio dining.

INGREDIENTS | SERVES 6

1 pound shelled lima beans
¼ pound pancetta, diced
1 onion, diced
1 red bell pepper, diced
1 cup grape tomatoes, halved
6 cups chicken broth
½ cup chopped fresh basil
Salt and pepper to taste

1. Wash lima beans in colander. In a heavy saucepan over medium-high heat, cook pancetta until browned. Add onion and bell pepper; sauté 3 minutes.

2. Add tomatoes and broth; stir in lima beans. Bring to a boil; reduce heat to medium. Simmer 30 minutes, or until beans are tender.

3. Stir in fresh basil; season with salt and pepper just before serving.

CHAPTER 8

All-American Chilies

Family Favorite Chili

This recipe is only mildly spicy. Real chili heads will want to add ½ teaspoon of cayenne to the spice mix.

INGREDIENTS | SERVES 6

2 pounds bottom round roast

1 pound ground beef

1 medium onion, diced

1 small green bell pepper, cored and diced

1 rib celery, sliced

2 cloves garlic, minced

2 tablespoons olive oil

6 tablespoons chili powder

1 teaspoon kosher salt

1 teaspoon cumin

½ teaspoon garlic powder

1 tablespoon sauce and gravy flour

1 (10-ounce) can Mexican-style tomatoes and green chilies

1 (14-ounce) can tomato sauce

1 (10-ounce) can enchilada sauce

1 (16-ounce) can red beans

4 cups water

Shredded cheese (optional)

1. Trim roast; cut into ½ dice. Combine ground beef, onion, bell pepper, celery, and garlic in a skillet. Cook until meat is no longer pink; drain fat.

2. In a heavy soup pot or Dutch oven, heat olive oil over medium-high heat. Add diced roast; cook, stirring often, until meat is no longer pink.

3. Combine chili powder, salt, cumin, garlic powder, and gravy flour in a small bowl. Mix well; sprinkle over roast. Stir well to coat; cook 1 minute.

4. Add 1 can of tomatoes and green chilies, tomato sauce, enchilada sauce, and beans; stir well.

5. Add cooked ground beef and vegetables. Stir in water; mix well. Reduce heat to medium; cook, stirring often, 4 hours. (If chili becomes too thick too quickly, add small amounts of water while simmering.)

6. Serve with shredded cheese, if desired.

Take It Slow

Most chili recipes take only 30 minutes or so to cook. However, diced meats require longer cooking times to tenderize. In addition, slow cooking allows seasonings and flavors to meld more completely, making a richer, fuller-tasting chili.

Easy Homestyle Chili

This is basic, weeknight supper chili.
Make a double batch and keep some in the freezer.

INGREDIENTS | SERVES 4

1 pound lean ground beef
2 tablespoons chili powder
½ teaspoon cumin
1 small onion, diced
1 garlic clove, minced
1 green bell pepper, cored and diced
1 (14-ounce) can diced tomatoes
1 (8-ounce) can tomato sauce
1 (16-ounce) can chili-seasoned beans
1 cup water
Salt and pepper to taste

1. In a heavy saucepan over medium-high heat, brown ground beef. Remove from heat; drain fat. Sprinkle chili powder and cumin over beef; toss to coat.

2. Add onion, garlic, bell pepper, tomatoes, and tomato sauce; stir in beans and water. Return to medium-high heat; bring to a boil. Reduce heat to medium; simmer 30 minutes, or until chili is thick.

3. Add salt and pepper. Let stand five minutes before serving.

California Green Chili

This recipe can be made with a pound of cooked diced turkey,
ground beef, or pork instead of chicken.

INGREDIENTS | SERVES 4

6 cups fresh tomatillos
1 Anaheim chili pepper, roasted and peeled
1 cup chicken broth
1 teaspoon cumin
½ teaspoon oregano
4 cooked chicken breast halves, diced
1 green onion, minced
¼ cup minced cilantro
Salt and pepper to taste
1 ripe avocado, cut into thin wedges
Sour cream

1. Place washed tomatillos in a large, deep saucepan. Cover with water; cook over medium-high heat 30 minutes.

2. Drain tomatillos. Working in batches, place tomatillos, roasted pepper, and broth in blender or food processor; purée.

3. Pour back into saucepan. Add cumin, oregano, and chicken. Stir well; bring to a boil over medium-high heat. If mixture seems too thick, add additional chicken broth.

4. Remove from heat; stir in green onion and cilantro. Add salt and pepper. Serve with wedges of avocado and sour cream for garnish.

San Antonio's Best Beef Chili

Long before Texas became a U.S. state, the "Chili Queens" of San Antonio would sell their chilies from outdoor kettles in the public square.

INGREDIENTS | SERVES 6–8

⅓ cup flour

2 pounds beef shoulder, cut into ½ cubes

1 pound pork shoulder, cut into ½ cubes

⅓ cup bacon fat

2 large onions, diced

6 cloves garlic, minced

1½ cups chicken or beef broth

4 cups water

4 dried ancho chili peppers

3 dried New Mexico chili peppers

3 dried serrano chili peppers

2 teaspoons cumin

1 teaspoon Mexican oregano

A Bowl of Red

Chili lovers are often surprised to learn that the famous southern Texas Bowl of Red is often made without tomatoes, and beans are always served on the side. Chili champions from the Lone Star State may claim to add any number of secret ingredients to their creations—from coffee grounds to rattlesnake meat—but the rich red sauce color comes from sun-ripened chili peppers.

1. Toss flour with beef and pork until meat is lightly coated. In a large, heavy saucepan or Dutch oven, heat bacon fat over medium-high heat. Brown beef and pork; add onions and garlic. Cook 2–3 minutes, or until onions soften.

2. Add broth; stir well. Lower heat to medium; simmer 20 minutes, stirring often.

3. Add 2 cups water. While meat mixture continues to simmer, remove stems and seeds from dried peppers. Cut peppers into pieces; place in a heat-safe bowl. Bring remaining 2 cups water to a boil; pour over chilies. Let stand 20 minutes.

4. Remove chilies from water with slotted spoon; place in food processor or blender with small amount of soaking water. Pulse to purée; add to simmering meat.

5. Add cumin and oregano; stir well. Simmer uncovered 2 hours. Stir often; add water if chili becomes too dry.

Santa Fe–Style Chili

Fresh New Mexico green chilies, a New Mexico–grown variety of Anaheim peppers, are available in many supermarkets. If you can't find them, substitute Anaheims.

INGREDIENTS | SERVES 6

2 pounds pork loin, cut in ½ cubes
⅓ cup flour
⅓ cup olive oil
1 onion, diced
2 cloves garlic, minced
3 cups chicken broth
6 green New Mexico chilies, roasted
2 jalapeño peppers, minced
½ teaspoon cumin
Salt and pepper to taste
⅓ cup fresh cilantro, minced

Pepper Roasts

Fresh peppers take on a richer flavor when roasted. To roast any large pepper, stick a long fork or skewer in the pepper and hold the pepper over a hot burner, turning to roast evenly. When pepper skin becomes blistered and charred, the pepper is done. Drop hot roasted peppers in a resealable plastic bag and seal. Let stand for a few minutes. The steam will loosen the skin of the peppers, making them easier to peel. Peeled peppers can be chopped or slit open and stuffed.

1. Toss pork with a little flour. Heat oil in a large, heavy saucepan over medium-high heat; cook pork until no longer pink. With a slotted spoon, remove to a plate. Add onion and garlic to oil; sauté 3 minutes.

2. Sprinkle remaining flour over onions and garlic; stir until blended. Slowly add broth, stirring until sauce is smooth. Return pork to pot.

3. Peel New Mexico peppers; remove stems and seeds. Finely chop; add to pot along with jalapeños. Stir in cumin, salt, and pepper. Lower heat to medium; simmer 1½–2 hours. If sauce becomes too thick, add small amounts of water.

4. Remove from heat. Add chopped cilantro; serve.

Chicago-Style Chili

Midwestern chili houses usually serve a tomato-rich, hearty bowl that may or may not be highly peppered. For a spicier chili, change the balance of hot versus mild chili powder.

INGREDIENTS | SERVES 6–8

2 pounds coarsely ground chuck

1 pound finely ground chuck

2 tablespoons hot chili powder

3 tablespoons mild chili powder

1 teaspoon cumin

1 large onion, chopped

3 cloves garlic, minced

1 (14-ounce) can tomato sauce

1 (28-ounce) can crushed tomatoes

2 cups water

1 (16-ounce) can pinto beans

Salt and pepper to taste

Shredded cheese and oyster crackers (optional)

1. In a large, heavy soup pot, cook coarse and finely ground beef together over medium-high heat until no longer pink. Drain fat; sprinkle with chili powders and cumin.

2. Add onion, garlic, tomato sauce, and tomatoes. Stir in water; bring to a boil. Reduce heat to medium; simmer, uncovered, 1 hour. Stir frequently.

3. Add beans; cook 1 hour. Add small amounts of water if sauce appears too thick. Add salt and pepper to taste.

4. Serve chili with shredded cheese and oyster crackers.

Pass the Elbows

Many Midwestern towns lay claim to originating Chili Mac, that ubiquitous school lunchroom dish. We won't pretend to know whether the first folks to mix elbow macaroni with chili were from Illinois, Kansas, or Nebraska. But aficionados insist that the best versions start with really good, beefy, spicy chili. The macaroni can be cooked separately and stirred in, or just cooked in the chili. The resulting dish should never be too dry, and should always be served with shredded cheese on top.

Sirloin and Black Bean Chili

This is a composed dish, well suited to dinner parties and special occasions.
Serve with a side of yellow rice and salad topped with sliced avocados.

INGREDIENTS | SERVES 4

2 pounds sirloin steak

2 tablespoons chili powder

1 teaspoon cumin

1 teaspoon kosher salt

1 tablespoon butter

2 tablespoons olive oil

1 medium sweet onion, diced

2 cloves garlic, minced

1 small green bell pepper, cored and diced

1 jalapeño pepper, minced

6 cups diced fresh tomatoes

½ cup water or broth of your choice

4 cups cooked black beans

¼ cup minced cilantro

Salt to taste

Keep It Tender

There are two ways to ensure tender red meat in your chili: either cook it very lightly or cook it for a very long time. Searing naturally tender cuts of meat then cooking the steaks or cubes until just done seals in the juices. Long, slow cooking breaks down fibers in the muscle, also resulting in a tender dish. But beware of the middle ground: Simply overcooking meat dries out the natural juices and toughens fibers, for unacceptably chewy chili.

1. Trim excess fat from steak. Combine 1 teaspoon of chili powder with ½ of cumin and ½ of salt; rub into steak. In a large, deep skillet, melt butter over high heat. Sear steak 2 minutes on each side; reduce heat to medium. Continue cooking 6 minutes more; remove from skillet.

2. Add olive oil to skillet; turn heat to medium high. Add onion, garlic, and peppers; sauté 3 minutes. Add tomatoes; continue to sauté, stirring, until tomatoes begin to release liquid. Add ½ cup of water or broth bring to a boil.

3. Reduce heat to medium; add remaining chili powder, cumin, and salt. Add beans; stir well. Simmer 20 minutes. In last 3 minutes of cooking time, place whole steak in bean mixture to warm it.

4. Remove steak to a cutting surface. Stir cilantro into bean mixture; adjust salt to taste. Slice steak into thin slices. Ladle chili into shallow bowls; fan steak slices over each serving. Serve immediately.

Hearty Bison Chili

Bison is lower in fat than beef, but still has a rich, red-meat flavor, making it perfect for chili. Most supermarkets carry some cuts of bison in either the fresh meat or freezer sections.

INGREDIENTS | **SERVES 6–8**

2 pounds coarsely ground bison

4 tablespoons hot chili powder

1 teaspoon cumin

½ teaspoon oregano

1 large onion, diced

2 cloves garlic, minced

1 green bell pepper, cored and diced

1 large banana pepper, cored and chopped

1 (14-ounce) can roasted diced tomatoes

1 (14-ounce) can tomato sauce

1 (16-ounce) can pinto beans

2 cups water or beef broth

Salt and pepper to taste

1. In a heavy saucepan over medium-high heat, brown bison. Remove from heat; drain fat. Sprinkle chili powder, cumin, and oregano over bison; toss to coat.

2. Add onion, garlic, bell pepper, banana pepper, tomatoes, and tomato sauce. Stir in beans and water or broth. Return to medium-high heat; bring to a boil.

3. Reduce heat to medium; simmer 30 minutes, or until chili is thick. Let stand 5 minutes before serving. Add salt and pepper as desired.

Slow-Cooked Beef Chili

Start this recipe simmering in the morning and serve a hot, satisfying chili for supper.
Ladle the chili into bowls or over split cornbread wedges.

INGREDIENTS | SERVES 6–8

2 pounds beef round or chuck,
cut in 1 cubes

2 tablespoons vegetable oil

2 tablespoons flour

4 tablespoons hot chili powder

1 teaspoon cumin

1 teaspoon salt

½ teaspoon garlic powder

1 (10-ounce) can tomatoes and
green chilies

1 (14-ounce) can tomato sauce

1 onion, diced

1 green bell pepper, cored and diced

1. In a heavy skillet, brown beef in vegetable oil over high heat. Use a slotted spoon to remove to a slow cooker.

2. Combine flour, chili powder, cumin, salt, and garlic powder; sprinkle over beef and toss to coat. Add remaining ingredients to slow cooker. Cover; cook on medium-high heat 6–8 hours. Stir once or twice during cooking.

3. Reduce heat to low to keep chili warm until ready to serve.

Slow Cooker Basics

Searing beef before adding it to a slow cooker seals in the juices and gives the meat a braised rather than boiled texture. Remember that liquids don't evaporate in a slow cooker, so you won't need added water or stock. In fact, slow cookers allow ingredients to stew in their own juices, so if you prefer a drier, tomato-less chili, just omit the tomato sauce.

Venison Chili

*Mild-tasting farm-raised venison is available at many supermarkets and meat markets.
If you prefer, this dish can be made with diced venison.*

INGREDIENTS | SERVES 6

2 pounds ground venison

1 tablespoon oil

1 large onion, diced

1 large green bell pepper, cored and diced

1–2 jalapeño peppers, minced

4 cloves garlic, minced

6 fresh tomatoes, chopped

3 tablespoons chili powder

1 teaspoon cumin

1 teaspoon sugar

1 (8-ounce) can tomato sauce

3 cups water

1 (16-ounce) can black beans

Salt to taste

¼ cup minced fresh parsley

1. In a large soup pot, brown venison in oil over medium-high heat. Add onion, bell pepper, jalapeño peppers to taste, and garlic; sauté until onion begins to soften, about 3–5 minutes.

2. Stir in fresh tomatoes. Lower heat to medium; simmer 5 minutes, stirring often.

3. Sprinkle chili powder, cumin, and sugar over meat mixture; stir well. Stir in tomato sauce, water, and beans; simmer 2 hours, stirring often. Add additional water if mixture seems too dry.

4. Remove from heat. Add salt and minced parsley. Let stand 5 minutes before serving.

Southern Chopped Pork Chili with Black-Eyed Peas

Buy chopped pork from your favorite barbecue hut or make your own by slow smoking a pork shoulder roast, then deboning and chopping the meat.

INGREDIENTS | SERVES 6

2 pounds chopped barbecue pork

3 tablespoons chili powder

1 medium onion, diced

1 green bell pepper, cored and diced

2 garlic cloves, pressed

1 (10-ounce) can tomatoes and green chilies

½ cup hickory-flavored barbecue sauce

1 (14-ounce) can tomato sauce

1 teaspoon Tabasco sauce

1 cup water

1 (16-ounce) can black-eyed peas

Salt and pepper to taste

⅓ cup minced green onion

1. In a large soup pot, combine pork and chili powder; toss to mix. Let stand 5 minutes.

2. Add onion, bell pepper, garlic, tomatoes and green chilies, barbecue sauce, tomato sauce, Tabasco, and water; mix well. Bring to a boil over high heat. Reduce heat to medium; simmer 15 minutes.

3. Add peas; simmer additional 15 minutes, adding small amounts of water if sauce becomes too dry.

4. Remove from heat. Add salt and pepper to your liking. Stir in green onions; let stand 5 minutes before serving.

A Matter of Convenience

Chili powder requires simmering time to dissolve and achieve full flavor, but that doesn't mean every batch of chili has to be a lengthy ordeal. Substituting cooked and shredded beef pot roast, cooked and cubed poultry, or cooked and chopped pork for raw meats can make chili preparations much easier. Allow 20–30 minutes of simmering time for the chili powder, tomatoes, and vegetables. You can add the meat or poultry at any point during the simmering process.

Meatball Chili

This is a super-easy weeknight supper, especially if the meatballs are purchased or made in advance.

INGREDIENTS | SERVES 4

20 cooked meatballs, homemade or frozen

1 onion, halved and sliced

1 green bell pepper, cored and sliced

1 (16-ounce) can red beans

1 (16-ounce) can white beans

2 (14-ounce) cans chili-seasoned tomato sauce

1 (10-ounce) can mild tomatoes and green chilies

Salt and pepper to taste

1. Combine all ingredients in a large saucepan over high heat. Stir well.

2. Bring to a boil; reduce heat to medium. Simmer 15 minutes, or until meatballs are heated through.

3. Serve in shallow bowls.

White Shredded Turkey Chili

Keep this recipe on hand to make Thanksgiving leftovers more exciting. Shred the turkey with your fingers or using two forks.

INGREDIENTS | SERVES 4

2 cups shredded turkey

2 (16-ounce) cans navy beans

2 green onions, minced

2 garlic cloves, minced

2 Anaheim peppers, roasted, peeled, and chopped

1 teaspoon cumin

½ teaspoon oregano

1 teaspoon Tabasco sauce

6 cups turkey stock

Salt and pepper to taste

1. Combine all ingredients except salt and pepper in a large saucepan. Stir well to combine.

2. Bring mixture to a boil over high heat. Reduce heat to medium; continue to cook, stirring often, 30 minutes.

3. Adjust salt and pepper to taste. Serve in shallow bowls with pita crisps.

Cincinnati Chili

Authentic Cincinnati chili begins with beef that's cooked in the chili broth, not browned. It's important to start with very lean meat to avoid a greasy dish.

INGREDIENTS | SERVES 8

2 pounds very lean ground beef

4 cups cold water

1 onion, finely diced

2 garlic cloves, minced

2 bay leaves

1 tablespoon chili powder

1 tablespoon cinnamon

1 tablespoon cumin

1 tablespoon unsweetened cocoa powder

1 teaspoon allspice

½ teaspoon cloves

2 teaspoons red pepper flakes

2 (14-ounce) cans tomato sauce

2 teaspoons Worcestershire sauce

2 teaspoons vinegar

Salt and pepper to taste

1 pound uncooked spaghetti (not angel hair)

Toppings: Shredded Cheddar cheese, chopped onion, cooked kidney beans, and oyster crackers

1. Combine beef and water in a large, heavy soup pot. Stir with a long fork to disperse beef in water. Cook over medium heat until it begins to simmer. Add onion, garlic, and bay leaves; simmer 30 minutes.

2. Combine chili powder, cinnamon, cumin, cocoa powder, allspice, cloves, and red pepper flakes in a small bowl. Mix well; stir into simmering beef.

3. Combine tomato sauce, Worcestershire sauce, and vinegar; stir into pot. Continue simmering 2 hours, or until sauce reaches desired consistency.

4. Add salt and pepper. In a separate pot, boil water; prepare spaghetti according to package directions. Drain.

5. Serve chili over spaghetti; pass the toppings.

An Immigrant Success Story

Cincinnati chili is an all-American dish, created by two brothers from Macedonia at their Greek restaurant in Cincinnati, Ohio. During the 1920s, the Kiradjieffs began making chili with Middle Eastern–style spices like cinnamon and allspice, plus ground chocolate. They served it over spaghetti with a variety of toppings, including Cheddar cheese, onion, and kidney beans. The toppings in your order determined whether you were getting two-, three-, four-, or five-way chili in Cincinnati-chili parlor parlance.

White Chicken Chili

This light, flavorful chili offers a welcome diversion from heavier red chilies.
If you have leftover chicken, allow about 2 cups diced or shredded chicken.

INGREDIENTS | SERVES 4

1 tablespoon olive oil

1 medium onion, diced

2 banana peppers, diced

2 cloves garlic, minced

1 jalapeño pepper, minced

1 teaspoon cumin

½ teaspoon oregano

4 cups chicken broth

2 (16-ounce) cans cannellini beans

4 chicken breast halves, cooked and diced

Salt to taste

¼ cup cilantro, minced

Shredded Monterey jack cheese

1. In a heavy saucepan, heat oil over medium-high heat. Sauté onion, banana peppers, garlic, and jalapeño pepper 3 minutes, or until onion begins to soften.

2. Add cumin and oregano; stir well. Reduce heat to medium; add broth, beans, and chicken. Simmer 20–30 minutes, stirring often.

3. Add salt and stir in fresh cilantro. Remove from heat. Serve topped with shredded cheese.

A Bowl of White

Some cooks don't consider it white chili unless there's a splash—or even a cup or two—of cream involved in the recipe. To make creamy white chili, use concentrated chicken broth or broth reduced by half to give the dish flavor, then make up the volume of the liquid with cream or evaporated milk.

Ground Turkey Chili

This chili is both full-flavor and low-fat.
Top it with a sprinkle of shredded reduced-fat cheese or a dollop of plain yogurt.

INGREDIENTS | SERVES 4

1 pound ground turkey
1 teaspoon olive oil
2 tablespoons chili powder
½ teaspoon cumin
Pinch oregano
1 small onion, diced
1 garlic clove, minced
1 green bell pepper, cored and diced
1 (14-ounce) can fire-roasted tomatoes
1 (8-ounce) can tomato sauce
1 (16-ounce) can red beans
1 cup water
¼ cup minced cilantro
Salt and pepper to taste

1. In a heavy nonstick saucepan over medium-high heat, cook ground turkey in oil until no longer pink. Sprinkle chili powder, cumin, and oregano over turkey; toss to coat.

2. Add onion, garlic, bell pepper, tomatoes, and tomato sauce; stir in beans and water. Return to medium-high heat; bring to a boil. Reduce heat to medium; simmer 30 minutes, or until chili is thick.

3. Add cilantro, salt, and pepper. Let stand five minutes before serving.

Mixed Bean Vegetarian Chili

Even if you aren't a vegetarian, this dish is both healthful and economical.
Use canned or home-cooked beans.

INGREDIENTS | SERVES 8

2 tablespoons olive oil

1 large onion, diced

1 small green bell pepper, cored and diced

1 jalapeño pepper, minced

2 cloves garlic, minced

2 cups cooked black beans

2 cups cooked small red beans

2 cups cooked navy beans

2 cups cooked pinto beans

1 (28-ounce) can crushed tomatoes

1 (14-ounce) can tomato sauce

1 teaspoon balsamic vinegar

3 tablespoons chili powder

1 teaspoon cumin

2 cups water

Salt and pepper to taste

1. In a heavy soup pot, combine oil, onion, peppers, and garlic over medium-high heat; sauté 5 minutes.

2. Reduce heat to medium; add remaining ingredients to pot. Stir well; simmer 1 hour, adding more water if needed.

3. Adjust salt and pepper to taste. Serve alone or with rice.

Tofu Chili

*Bring this chili to your favorite vegetarian potluck. The tofu absorbs
the flavors of the sauce and mimics the texture of meat.*

INGREDIENTS | SERVES 4

2 tablespoons olive oil

1 pound extra-firm tofu, crumbled

1 medium onion, diced

1 green bell pepper, cored and diced

1 jalapeño pepper, minced

2 cloves garlic, minced

2 tablespoons chili powder

1 teaspoon cumin

1 (14-ounce) can diced tomatoes

1 (14-ounce) can tomato sauce

2 cups frozen corn

1 (16-ounce) can black beans

2 cups water

Salt and pepper to taste

1. In a large, heavy saucepan, combine olive oil and tofu; sauté over medium-high heat 1 minute.

2. Add onion, peppers, and garlic; sauté 3 minutes.

3. Reduce heat to medium; add chili powder, cumin, tomatoes, tomato sauce, corn, black beans, and water. Simmer 1 hour, stirring often.

4. Remove from heat; add salt and pepper. Let stand 5 minutes; serve.

Tofu to You

Tofu is an ancient, protein-rich food from Japan, made by coagulating soy milk and pressing the curds into a cake. The process is similar to cheese making, and like cheese, tofu can be made in many forms and textures. Soft tofu can be whipped into drinks and desserts, while firm tofu can resemble meat in texture. Tofu has a very bland flavor and easily absorbs the taste of other ingredients in a dish.

New England Clam Chili

Heavy cream gives this dish a little more richness and balances the tartness of the tomatoes and chilies.

2 cups minced clams

1 cup clam juice

1 small onion, finely diced

1 green bell pepper, cored and diced

1 tablespoon chili powder

1 (14-ounce) can small-diced tomatoes

1 (10-ounce) can tomatoes and green chilies

1 (16-ounce) can navy beans

1 cup heavy cream

Salt and pepper to taste

1. In a large, heavy saucepan, combine clams, clam juice, onion, pepper, chili powder, tomatoes, and tomatoes and green chilies. Bring to a boil over high heat.

2. Reduce heat to medium; stir in navy beans. Simmer 20 minutes.

3. Remove from heat; stir in heavy cream, salt, and pepper. Serve with oyster crackers.

Clammy Business

There are thousands of varieties of clams in the world, including some giant claims that grow to over 100 pounds. Most of those harvested in North America are considerably smaller, ranging 2–5 inches in width. Small, round cherrystone clams and their Pacific Coast counterparts, butter clams, are most often served raw on the half shell. Littleneck, quahog, and longneck clams are a bit tougher and often wind up steamed and in chowders.

Creamy Cold Crab Chili

This makes an elegant luncheon entrée, particularly when served in chilled, oversized martini glasses.

INGREDIENTS | SERVES 4

1 pound lump crabmeat

1 green onion, minced

¼ cup cilantro, mince

1 jalapeño pepper, minced

1 teaspoon cumin

½ teaspoon chili powder

2 cups heavy cream

1 medium seedless cucumber, diced

1 cup grape tomatoes, halved

1 avocado, sliced

Skip the Surimi

Lump crabmeat is expensive, but worth the splurge. Don't try to substitute surimi, or imitation crab meat, for the real thing—especially in a dish where the crabmeat stars. Surimi is made from inexpensive finfish, usually pollock, that's been cooked, minced, flavored, colored, and reshaped. Aside from the appearance, surimi has a telltale sweet aftertaste that can be unpleasant in large quantities.

1. Check crabmeat for shells; discard. Divide crabmeat in half.

2. Place half of crabmeat in chilled bowl; fold in green onion, cilantro, jalapeño, cumin, and chili powder. Whisk in heavy cream; stir until ingredients are evenly distributed. Stir in cucumber and tomatoes.

3. Divide other half of crabmeat into 4 equal portions; place 1 portion in each of 4 chilled bowls or martini glasses.

4. Ladle chili over crabmeat in each dish; garnish with sliced avocados.

Garden Vegetable Chili

*If you don't have time to roast and peel fresh Anaheim peppers,
feel free to substitute minced jalapeños or canned green chilies.*

INGREDIENTS | SERVES 4

2 tablespoons olive oil

1 sweet onion, diced

1 green bell pepper, cored and diced

1 large zucchini, diced

1 large yellow squash, diced

8 ounces white mushrooms, quartered

4 large tomatoes, diced

2 roasted Anaheim peppers, peeled and chopped

1 teaspoon cumin

½ teaspoon oregano

1 cup tomato juice

Salt and pepper to taste

1. In a large, heavy saucepan, combine olive oil and onion over high heat; stirring, sauté 3 minutes.

2. Add bell pepper, zucchini, squash, and mushrooms; continue cooking 2 minutes.

3. Add tomatoes; cook until tomatoes release juices and mixture begins to bubble. Stir in roasted peppers, cumin, oregano, and tomato juice. Reduce heat to medium; cook 15 minutes.

4. Add salt and pepper; serve.

CHAPTER 9

International Chilies

Rajma (Indian Bean Chili)

Serve this vegetarian chili over rice as an entrée or as a spicy side dish with a simple roast chicken. Use canned kidney beans or cook your own.

INGREDIENTS | SERVES 4–6

2 (16-ounce) cans red kidney beans
¼ cup olive oil
8 cloves garlic, minced
3 jalapeño peppers, minced
1 tablespoon grated fresh ginger
1 large onion, finely chopped
4 large tomatoes, diced
½ teaspoon cumin
2 teaspoons garam masala
1 teaspoon chili powder
¼ teaspoon turmeric
2 cups water
Salt to taste
¼ cup minced cilantro

1. Place beans in a colander; rinse and drain. In a large, heavy saucepan over medium-high heat, combine oil, garlic, jalapeños, ginger, and onion; stirring constantly, sauté until mixture begins to brown.

2. Add tomatoes, cumin, garam masala, chili powder, and turmeric; continue cooking and stirring 5 minutes.

3. Add 2 cups of water. Bring to a boil; cook 5 minutes, or until sauce is thick.

4. Add beans and salt. Remove from heat; stir in cilantro. Serve over rice.

What Is Garam Masala?

Garam masala is a fragrant blend of spices commonly found in northern Indian and Pakistani cuisine. The name literally means "warm spice" and it may include peppercorns, cumin, cinnamon, cardamom, cloves, nutmeg, and caraway as well as bits of star anise, red pepper flakes, turmeric, and fennel. Purists make garam masala at home in small batches, by toasting whole spices in a skillet, then grinding the mixture with a mortar and pestle or spice grinder.

Doro Wot (Ethiopian Spicy Chicken)

This fiery Ethiopian dish is traditionally served from a communal pot, with diners grabbing bits with pieces of soft flatbread called injera.

INGREDIENTS | SERVES 4–6

1 chicken, cut into serving pieces
Juice of 1 lemon
½ teaspoon kosher salt
4 tablespoons butter or nitter kibbeh
1 large onion, diced
4 cloves garlic, minced
1 teaspoon grated fresh ginger
Pinch nutmeg
Pinch cardamom
¼ teaspoon fenugreek seeds
¼ cup Berbere Spice Paste (page 160)
1 tablespoon paprika
½ cup red wine
1 cup water or chicken broth
6 hard-boiled eggs
Salt to taste

1. Rinse chicken pieces; pat dry. Coat with lemon juice; sprinkle with salt. Set aside.

2. In a Dutch oven, heat butter over medium-high heat until melted; sauté onion and garlic 3 minutes.

3. Add ginger, nutmeg, cardamom, fenugreek, Berbere Paste, and paprika; stir to mix and cook 3 minutes.

4. Add wine and water or broth; bring to a boil. Reduce heat to medium; simmer 10 minutes.

5. Add chicken to sauce; turn pieces to coat. Cover; cook 15 minutes, adding water if needed. Uncover; continue cooking 10 minutes.

6. Remove chicken to platter. Peel eggs; pierce whites all over, without breaking through to yolk. Gently roll eggs in sauce to coat; remove eggs to platter.

7. Adjust salt in sauce to taste. Ladle sauce over chicken and eggs; serve with flatbread.

Berbere Spice Paste

This fiery paste is at the heart of Ethiopian cuisine. If you have a spice grinder, by all means use freshly ground whole cardamom seeds, cloves, and allspice berries to make this paste.

INGREDIENTS | MAKES ABOUT 2 CUPS

12 small, dried red chili peppers
1 teaspoon ginger
½ teaspoon cardamom
½ teaspoon coriander
½ teaspoon fenugreek seeds
¼ teaspoon nutmeg
¼ teaspoon cinnamon
⅛ teaspoon cloves
⅛ teaspoon allspice
1 small onion, minced
5 cloves garlic, minced
¼ cup dry red wine
2 tablespoons kosher salt
1 cup sweet paprika
½ cup hot paprika
¼ cup cayenne
¼ cup freshly ground black pepper
1½ cups water
¼ cup vegetable oil

1. Remove stems from the red chilies; in a food processor or spice grinder, process until finely chopped.

2. In a heavy, nonstick skillet, combine peppers, ginger, cardamom, coriander, fenugreek, nutmeg, cinnamon, cloves, and allspice. Cook over low heat, stirring constantly, 1–2 minutes, or until spices begin to get toasty and fragrant.

3. Pour hot spices into food processor along with onion and garlic. Add wine and 1 tablespoon salt; pulse until finely ground. Add remaining salt, paprikas, cayenne, and pepper to skillet; Stirring, toast 1 minute.

4. Remove skillet from heat; add onion and spice paste to paprika mix. Add water a little at a time, stirring to blend smoothly. Return skillet to low heat; cook 15 minutes, stirring constantly. Set aside to cool.

5. Pour Berbere Paste into a small glass bowl or jar. Float vegetable oil over top; cover and refrigerate until needed for recipes.

The Life of Spices

Make it a point to clean out your spice cabinet regularly. Dusty dried herbs and crusty, moisture-logged spices may not make you ill, but they won't do anything good for your cooking. Make it a point to toss any ground spices and herb blends that are more than three years old. (You can always drop herbs into cheesecloth bags to make bath sachets.) Store spices in airtight containers in a cool, dark place.

Siga Wot (Ethiopian Spicy Beef)

This dish can be made more or less spicy by changing the amount of Berbere Spice Paste in the mix.

INGREDIENTS | SERVES 6

2 tablespoons vegetable oil

2 pounds bottom round roast, cut into 1 cubes

4 tablespoons butter or nitter kibbeh

3 large onions, diced

¼ cup Berbere Spice Paste (page 160)

1 (28-ounce) can diced tomatoes

2 tablespoons tomato paste

2 cups water or beef broth

Salt to taste

What Is Nitter Kibbeh?

Nitter kibbeh is a spiced butter that's easy to make and can be used to flavor a range of dishes. To make your own, melt a pound of butter in a heavy saucepan. Add minced onion, minced garlic, grated ginger, and pinches of the following spices: cardamom, turmeric, cinnamon, cloves, and nutmeg. Whisk the mixture to blend, then cook over low heat for 45 minutes, allowing the milk solids to settle on the bottom of the pan. Ladle the clarified butter at the top of the pan through a sieve and into a jar or bowl. Cover tightly and refrigerate until ready to use.

1. In a large Dutch oven, heat oil over high heat. Brown beef in batches; set aside in a bowl. Once beef has been browned, add butter and onions to pan. Cook, stirring often, until onions are caramelized, about 5–10 minutes.

2. Stir in Berbere Paste; cook 2 minutes.

3. Add tomatoes and tomato paste; mix to blend. Slowly add broth. Bring mixture to a boil; reduce heat to medium. Add beef to pot; cover and cook 1 hour, adding liquid as needed.

4. Remove cover; cook 20 minutes longer, or until meat is tender and sauce is thick.

5. Adjust salt to taste; remove from heat. Serve with flatbread.

Australian Chili

Purists insist the beer in this thick, meaty chili has to be an Australian brand.

INGREDIENTS | SERVES 8

1 pound top sirloin roast

⅓ cup flour

¼ pound fatback, diced

1 onion, diced

1 rib celery, diced

1 green bell pepper, cored and diced

2 cloves garlic, minced

2 jalapeño peppers, minced

1 pound ground beef

1 pound ground pork

5 tablespoons chili powder

1 teaspoon cumin

½ teaspoon oregano

1 (12-ounce) can beer

1 (14-ounce) can diced tomatoes

1 tablespoon molasses

Water

Salt to taste

Hopping-Good Chili

Australians enjoy a good kangaroo chili. The marsupial is hunted Down Under and the meat is considered a delicacy, with a taste similar to venison. Kangaroo is extremely low in fat and almost always served braised or stewed, often with a wine or fruit-based sauce. If you live outside Australia, kangaroo meat is available via online vendors.

1. Trim roast; cut into 1 cubes. Coat cubes with flour; set aside. In a heavy soup pot or Dutch oven, add diced fatback. Stirring, cook over medium-high heat until bits are browned and oil is released, about 3 minutes. With a slotted spoon, remove fatback bits; reserve.

2. Brown beef cubes in pork fat; set aside. Add onion, celery, bell pepper, garlic, and jalapeño peppers to pot; sauté, stirring constantly, 3 minutes.

3. Reduce heat to medium; return beef to pot with fried fatback bits.

4. In a separate skillet, cook ground beef and pork until no longer pink; drain fat and add meat to soup pot. Sprinkle meat with chili powder, cumin, and oregano; toss to blend seasonings.

5. Add beer, tomatoes, molasses, and enough water to cover meat by 1. Simmer 3 hours, stirring often. Add small amounts of water if needed to keep chili from sticking to pot.

6. Just before serving, add salt.

Island Pork and Black Bean Chili

Some Caribbean chilies are relatively dry dishes, prepared without tomatoes.
If you'd like to omit the tomatoes, just add a little more liquid.

INGREDIENTS | **SERVES 4–6**

2 pounds boneless pork loin

1 cup orange-pineapple juice

Juice of 2 limes

1 tablespoon jerk seasoning

¼ cup flour

⅓ cup olive oil

2 large onions, diced

1 red bell pepper, cored and diced

1 green bell pepper, cored and diced

5 garlic cloves, minced

2 jalapeño peppers, minced

2 teaspoons cumin

1 teaspoon oregano

¼ teaspoon cloves

¼ teaspoon ginger

2 large tomatoes, diced

1 cup red wine

2 (16-ounce) cans black beans

Salt and pepper to taste

¼ cup cilantro, minced

1. Cut pork loin into 1 cubes; place in resealable plastic bag. Whisk together orange-pineapple juice, lime juice, and jerk seasoning; pour over pork loin. Reseal bag; place in refrigerator overnight.

2. Drain marinade; allow cubes to dry. Dust with flour. In a large skillet or Dutch oven, heat oil over medium-high heat. Brown cubes a few at a time; remove to a platter.

3. In same pan, sauté onions, bell peppers, garlic, and jalapeño peppers 3 minutes.

4. Add cumin, oregano, cloves, ginger, tomatoes, and wine. Bring mixture to a boil; return pork to pot. Reduce heat to medium; simmer 1½ hours.

5. Add beans to pot; continue cooking 30 minutes.

6. Stir in salt and pepper; garnish with cilantro.

Caribbean Goat or Mutton Chili

*Goat meat is tough and fibrous, requiring at least two hours of cooking to get it tender.
If you use mutton, you may not have to cook your chili as long.*

INGREDIENTS | SERVES 6

2 pounds boneless goat or mutton

1 tablespoon Madras curry powder

1 tablespoon jerk seasoning

1 tablespoon chili powder

1 teaspoon brown sugar

2 tablespoons vegetable oil

2 tablespoons butter

1 large sweet onion, diced

2 cloves garlic, pressed

2 (14-ounce) cans diced tomatoes

2 green onions, minced

1 Scotch bonnet pepper, minced

2 cups beef broth

Salt and pepper to taste

Getting Your Goat

Goats are small and easy to keep, making them a popular livestock option for families in the Caribbean. Slow-cooked, highly spiced goat dishes are menu staples. Outside the islands, goat meat is usually available at Caribbean specialty markets and markets that cater to Muslim households. Meat markets either carry goat meat or can order it for you, or you can order it yourself online.

1. Cut goat or mutton into 1 cubes. Place in a bowl; sprinkle with curry powder, jerk seasoning, chili powder, and sugar. Cover; refrigerate 30 minutes.

2. In a heavy Dutch oven, combine oil and butter. Brown meat in batches; remove to a platter. Add onion; stirring, cook over high heat until onion begin to brown. Add garlic, tomatoes, green onions, and Scotch bonnet pepper; sauté 3 minutes.

3. Return meat to pan; add broth. Bring mixture to a boil; reduce heat to medium. Cover and simmer 2–3 hours, until meat is tender. Check liquid level occasionally and add more as needed.

4. Add salt and pepper to taste and remove from heat. Serve over rice.

Brazilian Shrimp Chili

*Coconut milk is a staple of Brazilian cuisine, along with cashews.
This chili cooks fairly quickly—just long enough to meld flavors and turn the shrimp opaque.*

INGREDIENTS | SERVES 6–8

¼ cup vegetable oil

2 onions, diced

2 teaspoons paprika

1 tablespoon tomato paste

5 cloves garlic, minced

½ teaspoon coriander

½ teaspoon thyme

4 dried red chili peppers, chopped

½ cup minced cilantro

½ cup minced parsley

1 tablespoon grated lemon zest

4 diced tomatoes

1 cup water or chicken broth

1 (14-ounce) can coconut milk

3 pounds large shrimp, peeled and deveined

Salt to taste

½ cup chopped cashews

1. In a large, heavy saucepan or Dutch oven, combine oil and onions; cook over high heat until onions begin to soften, about 3 minutes.

2. Add paprika; cook 1 minute. Add tomato paste and garlic; continue cooking and stirring until paste begins to darken.

3. Add coriander, thyme, chili peppers, cilantro, parsley, lemon zest, and tomatoes. Stir to blend; slowly add water or stock. Bring mixture to a boil; reduce heat to medium. Simmer 10 minutes.

4. Add coconut milk. As soon as sauce is hot again, stir in shrimp. Cook just until shrimp turn opaque. Add salt to taste.

5. Remove from heat; garnish with cashews. Serve over rice.

Chinese Chicken in Chili Sauce

Chinese chili sauce can be paired with shrimp, scallops, or finely sliced meats as well as chicken.

INGREDIENTS | **SERVES 6**

6 dried red chili peppers

6 garlic cloves

2 tablespoons brown sugar

1 teaspoon kosher salt

1 teaspoon grated orange zest

⅓ cup fresh-squeezed lime juice

2 tablespoons vegetable oil

2 pounds boneless, skinless chicken, diced

1 large onion, diced

1 red bell pepper, cored and cut in strips

1½ cups chicken broth

1 tablespoon cornstarch dissolved in 2 tablespoons cold water

⅓ cup chopped peanuts

Chili on the Side

Chili-garlic sauce is a favorite Chinese condiment as well as a cooking ingredient. To make your own, just combine dried chilies, garlic cloves, sugar, and salt in a food processor. Lemon or orange zest can be added to the mix for another layer of flavor. Pulse until mixture resembles a coarse paste, then blend with a small amount of vegetable oil and refrigerate in a tightly closed container. Dab on prepared foods as desired.

1. In the bowl of a food processor, combine chilies, garlic, sugar, salt, and orange zest; pulse until mixture forms a paste. Add lime juice; pulse just to blend.

2. In a heavy, deep skillet or wok, heat oil over high heat. Add chicken; stir-fry 1 minute.

3. Add onion and bell pepper; cook until vegetables are crisp-tender, about 2 minutes. Add chili paste; stir until chicken and vegetables are well coated. Sauté 2 minutes.

4. Add broth; bring to a boil. Reduce heat to medium; simmer 10 minutes.

5. Stir in cornstarch dissolved in water; continue cooking 1–2 minutes, until sauce thickens.

6. Remove from heat. Garnish with peanuts; serve with rice.

Chicken in Harissa Sauce

This Tunisian-inspired recipe can be made in stages, refrigerating the harissa sauce and cooked chicken until you're ready to put it all together.

INGREDIENTS | SERVES 6

Harissa:

10 dried red hot peppers, stemmed
3 cloves garlic, peeled
1 teaspoon cumin
½ teaspoon caraway seeds
¼ teaspoon cloves
½ teaspoon kosher salt
½ cup olive oil

Chili:

1 (3-pound) chicken
Water
2 cinnamon sticks
1 orange, quartered
2 tablespoons olive oil
1 large onion, diced
1 green bell pepper, cored and diced
1 tablespoon granulated flour
6 tomatoes, peeled, seeded, and diced
½ cup coarsely chopped black olives
½ cup minced parsley
Salt to taste

1. To make harissa, soak red peppers in hot water 20 minutes; drain. Combine hot peppers, garlic, cumin, caraway seeds, cloves, and salt in food processor; pulse until mixture forms a coarse paste. With processor running, add ⅔ of olive oil in a slow stream. Scrape harissa into a small container; pour remaining olive oil over top.

2. To make chili, wash chicken; place in a soup pot with enough water to cover. Add cinnamon sticks and quartered orange. On high heat, bring to a boil. Reduce heat; simmer, uncovered, 1 hour. Allow chicken to cool in the broth.

3. Remove chicken from broth; reserve broth. Pull chicken from bones; skin and shred meat. Strain reserved broth; add enough liquid, if necessary, to make 2 cups. Pour 1 cup over shredded chicken.

4. In a deep, heavy saucepan or Dutch oven, heat 2 tablespoons olive oil over high heat. Add onion and bell pepper; sauté 3 minutes.

5. Sprinkle with granulated flour; stirring, sauté 2 minutes.

6. Slowly add remaining cup of broth; stir until sauce is smooth. Add tomatoes and 3 tablespoons harissa sauce. Bring mixture to a boil. Reduce heat to medium; cook 10 minutes, stirring frequently.

7. Add reserved shredded chicken, olives, and parsley. Simmer 5 minutes, or until chicken is heated through. Add salt; serve over couscous.

Beef in Piri-Piri Sauce

If you prefer, this dish can be made with cubed rump roast or other cuts of beef.
It's also excellent with venison.

INGREDIENTS | SERVES 4

1½ pounds London broil

1 cup balsamic vinegar

1 cup vegetable oil

1 onion, sliced

2 tablespoons olive oil

1 (14-ounce) can fire-roasted diced tomatoes

1 cup beef broth

½ cup butter, softened

1 roasted red bell pepper, peeled and chopped

4 small hot red peppers

6 cloves garlic

1 teaspoon paprika

1 teaspoon chili powder

Juice of 1 lemon

Salt to taste

Piri Piri Primer

Piri Piri is both the name of a tiny, hot red pepper—also known as bird or birdseye peppers—and a pepper sauce. The pepper grows in both wild and cultivated patches in Africa, and the sauce made from the peppers originates with the Portuguese, who once colonized Mozambique and Angola. Therefore, it's common to find piri-piri sauce (essentially ground peppers, garlic, and a few spices mixed in butter or oil) in recipes from Portugal, Africa, and even Brazil.

1. Rinse London broil; pat dry. Place in a resealable plastic bag. Whisk together vinegar and oil; pour over beef. Add sliced onion; seal, pressing out as much air as possible. Place on a plate; marinate 6 hours, or overnight, turning occasionally.

2. Place a stovetop-safe roasting pan on burner over high heat; pour in olive oil. Drain beef and onions from marinade; sear beef until browned on each side. Add drained onion, tomatoes, and broth; remove from heat. Cover tightly with heavy foil; bake at 325°F for 2 hours.

3. Remove beef from oven; place on platter to cool slightly. Place butter, peppers, garlic, paprika, chili powder, and lemon juice in food processor; pulse to purée.

4. Scrape mixture from food processor into Dutch oven over medium heat; stirring, cook 3 minutes.

5. Add tomato and broth mixture from roasting pan to food processor; pulse to purée. Add tomato mixture to Dutch oven; continue simmering 5 minutes.

6. Cut and shred London broil; add to Dutch oven. When mixture is heated through, check for salt. Serve with boiled potatoes or couscous.

Portuguese Chili with Red Beans

The broth from the cooked red beans adds to the flavor and texture of this chili.
You can use canned beans, but the end result will be different.

INGREDIENTS | SERVES 6–8

1 pound dried red kidney beans

1 tablespoon olive oil

1 onion, diced

1 green bell pepper, cored and diced

3 cloves garlic, minced

2 hot red peppers, minced

½ pound linguica sausage, chopped

1 pound ground beef

1 (14-ounce) can diced tomatoes

1 (8-ounce) can tomato sauce

2 tablespoons chili powder

¼ teaspoon cloves

1 cup beef broth

1 teaspoon Tabasco

Salt and pepper to taste

⅓ cup minced parsley

1. Rinse red beans; pick out any bits of soil or discolored beans. Place in a large bowl; fill with water to cover by several inches. Soak several hours, or overnight. Drain; place in a tall soup pot and cover with fresh water. Bring to a boil over high heat; reduce heat. Simmer until beans are tender, about 3 hours. Add water as needed, but after cooking broth should be thick.

2. In a heavy Dutch oven over high heat, combine oil, onion, bell pepper, garlic, and hot red peppers.; sauté 3 minutes.

3. Add sausage and beef; continue cooking until ground beef is no longer pink. Drain fat; add tomatoes, tomato sauce, chili powder, cloves, and broth. Stir in beans with cooking broth and Tabasco. Reduce heat to medium; simmer 1 hour, stirring often and adding small amounts of liquid if needed.

4. Add salt and pepper. Remove from heat; stir in parsley. Serve with crusty bread and extra hot sauce.

Canadian Chili

Canadian chili isn't a lot different than U.S. chili, although cooks tend to be a little more willing to add a variety of meats and extra veggies to a single batch.

INGREDIENTS | SERVES 6

½ pound bacon

1 onion, diced

1 green bell pepper, cored and diced

1 rib celery, diced

8 ounces sliced mushrooms

2 pounds ground beef

½ pound chopped smoked sausage

5 tablespoons chili powder

1 teaspoon cumin

1 (4-ounce) can tomato paste

1 (28-ounce) can diced tomatoes

1 (16-ounce) can red kidney beans

4 cups water or beef broth

Salt and pepper to taste

1. In a heavy soup pot or Dutch oven, fry bacon over medium-high heat. Set aside; leave fat in pot. Add onion, bell pepper, celery, and mushrooms; sauté 5 minutes.

2. Add ground beef and chopped sausage; continue cooking until beef is no longer pink. Drain fat; sprinkle with chili powder and cumin and stir to toss. Add tomato paste, tomatoes, kidney beans, and water or broth. Stir well; allow mixture to simmer 2 hours, stirring regularly.

3. Remove from heat; add salt and pepper. Serve in bowls, topped with crumbled bacon.

French Lentil Chili

Serve this chili as a vegetarian alternative to meat-based chilies or as a spicy alternative to ordinary lentil soup.

INGREDIENTS | SERVES 4

2 tablespoons olive oil

1 onion, diced

2 garlic cloves, minced

1 pound green lentils

6 cups water or vegetable broth

2 (14-ounce) cans diced tomatoes

1 tablespoon chili powder

1 teaspoon cumin

Pinch thyme

Salt and pepper to taste

¼ cup minced parsley

1. In a heavy soup pot, combine oil, onion, and garlic; sauté over medium-high heat 3 minutes.

2. Place lentils in strainer; rinse well. Pick out any bits of debris or discolored lentils. Add to pot along with 6 cups of water or broth. Reduce heat to medium; cook 30 minutes.

3. Add tomatoes, chili powder, cumin, and a pinch of thyme; continue cooking 30 minutes, or until lentils are tender and chili reaches desired consistency.

4. Season with salt and pepper; remove from heat. Garnish with parsley.

Peruvian Chicken Chili with Potatoes

*Think of this recipe as chicken salad with a major kick. Serve it in bowls
with tortilla chips or over crisp shredded cabbage.*

INGREDIENTS | SERVES 4–6

3 cups diced cooked chicken
breast, chilled

2 cups diced cooked Peruvian
potatoes, chilled

1 cup grape tomatoes

1 cup sliced celery

1 cup chopped cilantro

3 jalapeño peppers

1 clove garlic

½ teaspoon kosher salt

⅓ cup olive oil

Juice of 1 lime

3 tablespoons sour cream

1. Toss chicken and potatoes with tomatoes and celery; place in a shallow serving bowl.

2. In a food processor, combine cilantro, peppers, garlic, and salt; pulse to a paste. With processor running, add olive oil in a steady stream.

3. Spoon chili mixture into a small bowl; whisk in lime juice and sour cream. If sauce is too thick, add 1 tablespoon of water. Drizzle sauce evenly over chicken and potato mixture; toss lightly to coat. Serve immediately.

A Passion for Purple Potatoes

A few years ago, thin, long, purple potatoes became widely available in supermarkets. The striking tubers are among the oldest heirloom varieties, dating back to the earliest potatoes harvested in the Andes foothills. Like all potatoes, the purple gems originated in Peru, some 10,000 years ago. They're known for their creamy flavor and firm texture, making them excellent salad potatoes.

Basque Bean Chili with Ham

Dry-cured Bayonne ham is a specialty of the Basque region, adding a distinctive, sweet, lightly smoked flavor to dishes.

INGREDIENTS | SERVES 4

¼ cup olive oil

1 red bell pepper, cored and diced

1 green bell pepper, cored and diced

1 onion, diced

3 cloves garlic

2 cups diced fresh tomatoes

2 cups chicken broth

2 cups cooked haricot beans

1 cup cooked fava beans

1 cup cooked garbanzo beans

1 tablespoon chili powder

½ teaspoon ground Basque chili powder or cayenne

Pinch oregano

1 cup diced Bayonne ham

Salt and pepper to taste

1. In a heavy soup pot, heat oil over high heat. Add bell peppers, onion, and garlic; sauté 3–5 minutes, or until vegetables are crisp-tender.

2. Add tomatoes and broth; bring to a boil. Reduce heat to medium; add beans, chili powder, Basque chili powder, and oregano. Simmer 30 minutes.

3. Stir in ham and add salt and pepper; remove from heat. Serve immediately.

Uniquely Basque

The Basque region of Europe covers the Pyrenees Mountains and portions of both Spain and France. The Basques have their own language and culture, and a delicious culinary tradition. Fresh, colorful sweet and hot peppers play a significant role in Basque dishes, along with salt cod, baby eels, herbed marinades and broths, lamb, beans, and potatoes. Bayonne ham is a particular delicacy. Basque dishes tend to be more strongly flavored than similar recipes in France and Spain.

Moroccan Chili

To make this a vegetarian dish, skip the ground meat and double the garbanzo beans.
Add water or veggie broth in place of the beef broth.

INGREDIENTS | SERVES 4

1 tablespoon olive oil

1 onion, diced

1 rib celery, diced

1 carrot, diced

1 pound ground lamb or beef

1 (16-ounce) can garbanzo beans

2 teaspoons cumin

½ teaspoon cinnamon

½ teaspoon cayenne

¼ teaspoon cloves

¼ teaspoon ginger

¼ teaspoon turmeric

2 tomatoes, diced

½ cup raisins

2 cups beef broth

Salt to taste

½ cup slivered almonds

1. In a large soup pot, combine oil, onion, celery, and carrot; sauté over high heat 5 minutes, stirring constantly.

2. Add ground lamb or beef; stirring, cook until meat is no longer pink. Drain fat.

3. Add garbanzo beans, cumin, cinnamon, cayenne, cloves, ginger, and turmeric; stir until well blended. Add tomatoes, raisins and broth. Bring mixture to a boil; reduce heat to medium. Simmer 1 hour, adding more liquid as needed.

4. Remove from heat; add salt. Serve over couscous garnished with almonds.

Mango Chicken Chili

Sweet and hot flavors combine to make this simple-to-make dish both unusual and exciting.

INGREDIENTS | SERVES 4

2 tablespoons vegetable oil

2 tablespoons Mussamen curry paste

1 onion, sliced

1 green bell pepper, sliced

1 jalapeño or other hot pepper, minced

1 (14-ounce) can coconut milk

½ cup chicken broth

1 teaspoon lime zest

2 firm-ripe mangoes, diced

4 boneless chicken breast halves, cut in large pieces

½ cup cilantro, minced

Salt to taste

1. In a heavy saucepan or Dutch oven, heat oil over medium-high heat. Add curry paste; sauté 1 minute.

2. Add onion, bell pepper, and jalapeño pepper; sauté 3 minutes longer.

3. Slowly stir in coconut milk and broth; reduce heat to medium. Simmer 10 minutes.

4. Add lime zest, mangoes, and chicken breast; continue simmering until chicken is cooked, about 10–15 minutes.

5. Stir in cilantro and salt; remove from heat. Serve with jasmine rice.

Mango Madness

Mangoes are among the oldest-known cultivated fruits. Although only a few varieties appear in markets, scientists have cataloged more than 1,000 varieties. The tree fruit—which can be used interchangeably with peaches and nectarines in many recipes—originated in India and now grows in semitropical regions throughout the world. To dice a mango, slice the "cheeks" of the fruit from either side of the large center seed. Score the flesh diagonally with a sharp knife, then pull back on the leathery peel. The cubes will pop up and can be sliced off the peel easily.

Argentine Rolled Steak in Chili Sauce

*Argentina is second only to the U.S. in per-capita beef consumption; like the U.S.,
it is also a country of immigrants. This dish has both Italian and South American influences.*

INGREDIENTS | SERVES 4

½ cup red wine vinegar

½ cup beer

½ cup olive oil

2 pounds flank steak

Salt and pepper to taste

2 large Idaho potatoes, peeled and julienned

2 carrots, scraped and julienned

1 red bell pepper, roasted, cored, and cut in strips

4 strips bacon

1 onion, diced

3 cloves garlic, minced

6 New Mexico chili peppers, roasted and peeled

1 (14-ounce) can tomato sauce

1 (14-ounce) can tomatoes

2 teaspoons cumin

1 cup beef broth

1. Whisk together vinegar, beer and ½ cup olive oil. Place steak in resealable bag; pour marinade over. Seal tightly; place in refrigerator several hours, or overnight, turning occasionally.

2. Remove steak from marinade; discard marinade. Place steak on cutting board; place sheet of waxed paper or thick plastic wrap over steak and pound or roll into a thin sheet.

3. Remove wrap; sprinkle salt and pepper over steak. Place strips of potato, carrots, and red bell pepper on top of steak; roll into a tight pinwheel with veggies inside. Tie securely with kitchen twine.

4. In an oblong Dutch oven, cook bacon over high heat until crisp. Remove; add rolled steak to pan. Carefully brown on all sides. Add onions, garlic, and New Mexico peppers; cook 2 minutes.

5. Pour in tomato sauce and tomatoes; bring to a boil. Sprinkle in cumin; slowly add broth. Cover mixture; reduce heat to medium. Simmer 2 hours, turning steak roll occasionally and adding liquid if needed.

6. Remove from heat; let stand 10 minutes. To serve, cut slices of rolled steak and ladle chili sauce over top.

Malaysian Sambal Chicken

In its purest form, sambal sauce is ground chilies and salt.
From that base, other ingredients have been added to make a wide array of dishes.

INGREDIENTS | SERVES 4

4 dried hot chilies
½ teaspoon kosher salt
1 slice fresh ginger
1 piece lemongrass, white part
3 tablespoons olive oil
4 chicken breast halves, sliced crosswise
1 medium onion, diced
2 garlic cloves, minced
3 plum tomatoes, diced
½ teaspoon turmeric
1 cup coconut milk
½ teaspoon cardamom
⅓ cup minced cilantro
Salt to taste

1. Remove stems from chilies; place in small bowl. Add water to cover; soak ½ hour. Drain water; reserve 1 teaspoon. Place soaking water, chilies, salt, ginger, and lemongrass in food processor; pulse to grind.

2. In a heavy skillet, heat 2 tablespoons oil over high heat. Working in batches, sear chicken pieces; remove platter. Add remaining oil and chili mixture; Sauté, stirring constantly, 1–2 minutes.

3. Add onion, garlic, and tomatoes; continue cooking and stirring 3 minutes.

4. Reduce heat to medium; add turmeric and coconut milk. Stir well; return chicken to pot. Add cardamom. Simmer 10–15 minutes.

5. Add cilantro and salt. Serve with steamed rice.

CHAPTER 10

Stew to You

Classic Beef Stew

This is the rich, brown beef stew of your childhood. The alcohol in the red wine dissipates during cooking, so no need to worry about serving this to children.

INGREDIENTS | SERVES 6–8

2½ pounds bottom round roast

1 teaspoon kosher salt

1 teaspoon black pepper

1 teaspoon cayenne pepper

½ teaspoon garlic powder

¼ teaspoon paprika

⅓ cup flour

5 tablespoons olive oil

1 medium onion, diced

4 cups beef broth

2 cloves garlic, minced

1 rib celery, sliced

6 ounces mushrooms, sliced

1 teaspoon Worcestershire sauce

1 cup dry red wine

3 pounds red potatoes, peeled and quartered

2 cups baby carrots

Salt and pepper to taste.

¼ cup minced fresh parsley

What Is Stew Beef?

Supermarkets and meat markets often sell beef cubes labeled as "stew meat." Depending on the market, stew beef can be leftover bits from cutting pot roasts or from preparing ground beef. Usually, the meat sold as stew beef is chuck, shoulder, or arm meat. Occasionally, stew beef is rump or round roast. Both chuck and round cuts are flavorful and both require slow cooking; however, the round cuts generally have less gristle and fat.

1. Trim fat from roast; cut into 1½ cubes. Combine salt, black and cayenne peppers, garlic powder, and paprika; stir well. Liberally sprinkle seasoning mixture over beef; toss. (You may not use all of it. Reserve leftover spice mix for later use.) Sprinkle small amount of flour over beef, just enough to coat cubes lightly.

2. In a heavy Dutch oven over medium-high heat, brown beef in oil. Working in batches, remove browned cubes to bowl using slotted spoon. Add ½ of onion to oil; sauté 3 minutes.

3. Sprinkle oil and onion with remaining flour; stir until flour begins to brown. Whisk in 1 cup broth; continue stirring until browned bits have been pulled from bottom and sauce is smooth. Add remaining onion, garlic, celery, and mushrooms; return beef to pot. Reduce heat to medium; simmer 2 minutes.

4. Add remaining broth, Worcestershire sauce, and wine; simmer uncovered 2 hours, stirring occasionally.

5. Add potatoes and carrots; cook until potatoes are tender, about 20–30 minutes.

6. Remove from heat. Add salt, pepper, and parsley.

Slow-Cooker Beef Stew

If you prefer to cook all of the ingredients at once, just cut potatoes in half instead of quarters.

INGREDIENTS | SERVES 6–8

2½ pounds bottom round roast

1 teaspoon kosher salt

1 teaspoon black pepper

1 teaspoon cayenne pepper

½ teaspoon garlic powder

¼ teaspoon paprika

⅓ cup flour

5 tablespoons olive oil

1 medium onion, diced

4 cups beef broth

2 cloves garlic, minced

1 rib celery, sliced

1 (14-ounce) can diced tomatoes

1 teaspoon Worcestershire sauce

3 pounds red potatoes, peeled and quartered

2 cups baby carrots

¼ teaspoon thyme

Salt and pepper to taste

1. Trim fat from roast; cut into 1½ cubes. Combine salt, black and cayenne peppers, garlic powder, and paprika; stir well. Liberally sprinkle over beef; toss. (You may not use all of it. Reserve leftover spice mix for later use.) Sprinkle small amount of flour over beef, just enough to coat lightly.

2. In a heavy skillet over medium-high heat, brown beef in oil. Working in batches, remove cubes to slow cooker using slotted spoon. Add ½ of onion to oil; sauté 3 minutes.

3. Sprinkle oil and onion with remaining flour; stir until flour begins to brown. Whisk in 1 cup broth; continue stirring until browned bits have been pulled from bottom and sauce is smooth. Pour over beef in slow cooker. Add remaining onion, garlic, celery, tomatoes, and Worcestershire sauce; cover and set on high. Cook 2 hours on high.

4. Add remaining ingredients. Reduce heat to medium high; continue cooking 6 hours.

5. Turn heat to low to keep stew warm until ready to serve.

Spring Pork Stew with Orange Gremolata

*Orange gremolata—a blend of minced parsley, garlic, and orange peel—
gives this stew a fresh, light flavor.*

INGREDIENTS | SERVES 6–8

3 pounds boneless pork loin
¼ cup sauce and gravy flour
1 teaspoon kosher salt
½ teaspoon coarsely ground
black pepper
½ teaspoon garlic powder
⅓ cup olive oil
1 (14-ounce) can diced tomatoes
1 cup pork or chicken broth
1 cup white wine
2 bay leaves
2 cups julienned carrots
2 cups sugar snap peas
1 cup cioppolini onions, quartered
1 cup loosely packed flat parsley leaves
4 cloves garlic, peeled
Zest of 1 large orange
Freshly ground black pepper

1. Trim roast; cut into rectangular pieces 1 thick. Combine flour with salt, pepper, and garlic powder dredge pork pieces until well coated. Heat oil in a heavy Dutch oven over medium-high heat. Brown pork, working in batches if necessary; remove to a bowl.

2. Add tomatoes to Dutch oven, stirring up any browned bits from bottom of pan. Add broth and wine; bring to a boil. Add bay leaves; cook 5 minutes.

3. Remove from heat. Arrange a layer of pork on bottom of pot, followed by carrots, sugar snap peas, and onions. Place remaining pork on top layer; cover. Place in 350°F oven 1½ hours.

4. Make gremolata by combining parsley, garlic, and orange zest in a food processor fitted with a metal blade; pulse until finely minced.

5. Carefully open Dutch oven; stir in gremolata. In process, draw pork from bottom of pan to top. Cover; return to oven 30 minutes, or until pork is fork tender. Serve with saffron rice or mashed potatoes. Top with freshly ground black pepper.

Beef Cholent

The secret to this whole meal in a pot is long, slow cooking.
Resist the urge to stir things up while it is baking.

INGREDIENTS | SERVES 8

⅓ cup vegetable oil

2 pounds boneless chuck roast, cut in large pieces

2 pound flank steak, cut in pieces

2 large onions, sliced

2 cloves garlic, minced

1 cup dry kidney beans

1 cup dry lima beans

6 cups beef broth

⅓ cup ketchup

1 cup dry pearl barley

6 white potatoes, peeled and cut in large chunks

Salt and pepper to taste

1. Heat vegetable oil in a Dutch oven. Brown beef pieces; set aside. Add onions; sauté until onion softens, about 3 minutes.

2. Add garlic and beans; sauté 3–5 minutes.

3. Stir in broth, ketchup, and barley. Return beef to pot; stir. Add potatoes, salt, and pepper; adjust liquid to make sure beef is covered. Bring to a boil; remove from heat. Cover Dutch oven tightly.

4. Place Dutch oven in 200°F oven 10–15 hours. Check occasionally to make sure broth hasn't been absorbed or evaporated. Serve in bowls.

Savoring the Sabbath

Cholent is a traditional Saturday noon meal for many Jewish families. The dish originated from the desire to have a hot entrée on the Sabbath, without breaking religious laws that forbid lighting a fire between sundown Friday and sundown Saturday. All the preparation for the dish, including turning on the oven, can be done Friday afternoon and the cholent can be left to cook until the family is ready to eat on Saturday. Those who are squeamish about leaving an oven on all night can use a slow cooker instead.

Irish Lamb Stew

This stew freezes well and is a great way to introduce lamb to friends and family who think they don't like lamb.

INGREDIENTS | SERVES 6–8

6 strips bacon

3 pounds boneless lamb shoulder

⅓ cup flour

1 teaspoon kosher salt

1 teaspoon black pepper

½ teaspoon garlic powder

¼ teaspoon paprika

2 medium onions, diced

2 cloves garlic, minced

4 cups beef or lamb broth

1 teaspoon sugar

1 cup stout ale

2 bay leaves

½ teaspoon thyme leaves

1 large leek, trimmed and sliced

3 pounds white potatoes, peeled and cut into chunks

3 cups thickly sliced carrots

1½ cups green peas, frozen or shelled fresh

Salt and pepper to taste

⅓ cup minced fresh parsley

1. In a large, heavy frying pan, cook bacon until crisp; set aside. Trim fat from lamb; cut into 1½ cubes. Combine flour, salt, pepper, garlic powder, and paprika. Dredge lamb pieces; shake off excess flour. Brown in bacon fat over medium-high heat; remove to Dutch oven.

2. Sauté ½ of onions in skillet over medium-high heat until browned. Add garlic; stir well. Pour 1 cup of broth in skillet; stir to scrape browned bits from bottom of pan. Pour broth, onions, and garlic over lamb in Dutch oven. Add remaining broth, sugar, ale, bay leaves, thyme, and bacon.

3. Place Dutch oven over high heat; bring to a boil. Reduce heat to medium; cook, stirring occasionally, 1½ hours. Add additional stock or water if needed.

4. Add leek, potatoes, carrots, and peas; cover and cook until potatoes are tender, about 20–30 minutes.

5. Remove from heat; add salt, pepper, and parsley. Serve in shallow bowls with broth.

Lamb by Mail

Supermarket meat counters in North America generally stock lamb from New Zealand, Australia, or the Western United States. What winds up in the store may have as much to do with seasonal availability and pricing as anything else. However, lamb aficionados often prefer lamb from one venue over another, citing flavor and texture differences. Mail-order sources—easy to find on the Internet—can provide lamb from specific countries as well as from small farms and organic providers.

Chicken Stew a la Bonne Femme

This recipe can be made with 3 pounds of bone-in chicken-breast halves or pieces of your choice.

INGREDIENTS | SERVES 4–6

1 pound bacon

1 (3-pound) chicken, cut into pieces

3 pounds white potatoes, peeled and cut in chunks

2 large onions, chopped

1 large green bell pepper, cored and chopped

2 ribs celery, sliced

3 cloves garlic, minced

2 green onions, sliced

¼ cup minced parsley

Salt, pepper, and cayenne to taste

3 cups chicken broth

1. In a Dutch oven, fry bacon over medium-high heat; remove to platter. Using bacon fat, brown chicken pieces; remove to platter. In remaining fat, brown potato pieces; remove to platter. In a bowl, combine onions, bell pepper, celery, garlic, green onions, and parsley; mix well.

2. Carefully remove all but 1 or 2 tablespoons of fat. Layer ingredients in pan in following order: chicken, potatoes, bacon, vegetable mixture, potatoes, bacon, chicken, and vegetable mixture. Sprinkle salt, pepper, and cayenne between layers.

3. Pour broth into Dutch oven; cover tightly. Place in 350°F oven 2½ hours.

4. Let stand 10 minutes before serving.

Chicken Fricassee

Chicken fricassee tops many folks comfort-food lists. This version smells heavenly while cooking.

INGREDIENTS | SERVES 4–6

1 large chicken, cut into 8 pieces
1 teaspoon salt
½ teaspoon black pepper
½ teaspoon cayenne pepper
½ teaspoon garlic powder
½ cup vegetable oil
⅔ cup granulated flour
1 large onion, diced
6 cups chicken broth
1 green bell pepper, cored and diced
Pinch thyme
3 green onions, minced

1. Rinse chicken; pat dry. Combine salt, pepper, cayenne, and garlic powder; sprinkle liberally over chicken. In large Dutch oven over medium-high heat, brown chicken pieces in oil; remove to platter.

2. Stir granulated flour into hot oil; cook, stirring constantly, until flour turns dark brown. Add ½ of onion; cook, stirring, 1 minute.

3. Carefully add broth; stir until roux is dissolved in broth. Return chicken to pot along with remaining onion, bell pepper, and thyme. Reduce heat to medium; cook, stirring occasionally, 1½ hours, or until chicken is tender and sauce is thick. Stir in green onions. Serve over rice.

Dumplings Anyone?

Chicken-and-dumpling lovers will find this stew a perfect foil for white clouds of dough. Just remove the chicken pieces from the sauce and keep warm. Bring the sauce to a boil. Add a little more broth if it seems too thick. Prepare your favorite dumpling recipe (biscuit mix packages often have easy recipes printed on the back) and drop dumplings into the boiling broth. Reduce heat to medium, cover the pot, and simmer dumplings 12–15 minutes. Return chicken to the pot and serve.

Osso Bucco

Veal shanks should be tied with kitchen twine to keep them from falling apart in the pot.
Do it yourself or ask your butcher to do it for you.

INGREDIENTS | SERVES 6–8

4 veal shanks
Salt and pepper to taste
¼ cup flour
⅓ cup olive oil
1 medium onion, diced
1 large carrot, diced
1 rib celery, diced
2 tablespoons tomato paste
1 cup white wine
2 sprigs fresh thyme
2 bay leaves
2 garlic cloves, pressed
3 cups veal or chicken broth
⅓ cup minced parsley
Grated zest of 1 lemon

1. Rinse veal shanks; pat dry. Sprinkle with salt and pepper; coat lightly with flour. In Dutch oven over medium-high heat, brown shanks well in olive oil, turning to brown on all sides; remove from pan.

2. Add onion, carrot, and celery to oil; sauté, stirring constantly, 3 minutes.

3. Add tomato paste; cook, stirring, 1 minute. Add wine, thyme, bay leaves, and garlic. Bring to a boil; simmer 3 minutes.

4. Reduce heat to medium. Return veal shanks to pan; add broth. Cover; simmer 1½ hours. Check veal often, basting and keeping the lower ⅔ of the shank height covered with liquid.

5. When shanks are almost falling apart, carefully remove to serving dish; cut strings. Ladle sauce and vegetables around shanks; sprinkle parsley and lemon zest over all. Serve with saffron rice.

Rabbit Stew with Spinach Dumplings

These dumplings are delicious, but have an extra step. If you don't have the time or inclination to make spinach dumplings, you can always serve the stew with mashed potatoes.

INGREDIENTS | SERVES 4–6

For stew:

3 pounds rabbit, cut in serving pieces

Salt and pepper to taste

⅓ cup flour

⅓ pound pancetta, diced

1 onion, diced

1 pound white mushrooms, sliced

1 (14-ounce) can diced tomatoes with roasted garlic

1 teaspoon mixed dried Italian herbs

1 cup dry red wine

2 cups chicken broth

1 tablespoon cornstarch

2 tablespoons cold water

¼ cup minced fresh parsley (for garnish)

For dumplings:

1 pound spinach

1 clove garlic, minced

1 tablespoon butter

1 pound ricotta cheese

2 cups flour

¼ teaspoon salt

3 eggs

Bunny on the Menu

Rabbit stew is a traditional, popular dish throughout much of Europe and parts of the United States. Farm-raised rabbit, already cut in serving pieces, can be purchased in specialty markets and some supermarkets. Rabbit meat has the texture of stewing chicken, with a slightly sweeter, gamier flavor. If you can't bring yourself to eat rabbit, you can always substitute chicken or duck in recipes.

1. Rinse rabbit pieces; pat dry. Sprinkle with salt and pepper; coat with flour. In Dutch oven, cook pancetta over medium-high heat until meat browns and fat is released. Brown rabbit in pancetta fat; remove to platter.

2. Add onion and mushrooms to Dutch oven; sauté 3–5 minutes, until vegetables soften.

3. Add tomatoes, herbs, and wine. Bring mixture to a boil; reduce heat to medium. Return rabbit to pot; add broth. Cover; simmer 1½ hours, adding water occasionally to maintain liquid level.

4. Uncover pot; cook 15 minutes longer. Dissolve cornstarch in cold water. Carefully remove rabbit pieces to platter. Turn heat to high; bring sauce to a boil. Stir in cornstarch; cook, stirring, until sauce is smooth and no longer cloudy. Remove from heat; return rabbit pieces to pot. Keep warm.

5. To make dumplings, cook spinach and garlic in butter; let cool. Press as much liquid as possible from spinach and garlic; finely chop. Mix spinach with ricotta, ⅔ of flour, salt, and eggs; work together until well blended. Add additional flour to make a soft dough, reserving small amount of flour. Shape into 16 small ovals. Bring large pot of water to gentle boil; add dumplings. Reduce heat to a simmer; cook 15 minutes.

6. Drain. Place rabbit pieces and dumplings in deep serving dish or casserole. Ladle sauce over all; sprinkle with parsley. Serve immediately.

Beef Shortrib Stew

For a cold-weather variation on this dish, substitute parsnips and sweet potatoes for the russet potatoes.

INGREDIENTS | SERVES 6

4 pounds beef shortribs
Salt and pepper to taste
½ cup flour
½ cup olive oil
2 onions, diced
1 rib celery, diced
1 carrot, diced
4 fresh tomatoes, diced
1 teaspoon sugar
2 garlic cloves, minced
1 cup red wine
2 bay leaves
1 teaspoon thyme leaves
6 cups beef broth
6 medium russet potatoes, peeled and sliced
¼ cup minced fresh parsley

1. Rinse short ribs; pat dry. Season with salt and pepper; dust liberally with flour. In large Dutch oven, heat olive oil over high heat; brown ribs on all sides; remove to platter.

2. Add onions, celery, and carrot; sauté 3–5 minutes, or until carrot begins to soften.

3. Add tomatoes, sugar, and garlic; cook, stirring, until tomatoes begin to soften and release juice. Add wine; stir, scraping up any browned bits from bottom of pot. Add bay leaves, thyme, and broth; bring to a boil.

4. Reduce heat to medium; return ribs to pot. Cover and cook, checking liquid levels periodically, 1½ hours.

5. Add potatoes, moving ribs to allow potatoes to settle in broth. Add more broth or water if necessary; cook, covered, 20–30 minutes.

6. Remove from heat; add parsley. Let stand 5 minutes before serving.

Mixed Game Stew

Serve this aromatic stew with mashed sweet potatoes or simple boiled red potatoes. The game can be replaced with beef, pork, or chicken.

INGREDIENTS | **SERVES 6**

1 pound bacon

1 pound venison or elk roast, cut in 1½ cubes

1 pound boneless rabbit, cut in chunks

Salt and pepper to taste

1 pound duck sausage, sliced

2 onions, sliced

1 cup sliced fennel

1 cup red wine

2 cups chicken broth

3 whole cloves

2 bay leaves

6 tart apples, cored and sliced

1 large red cabbage, cored and cut in 6 wedges

1. In a Dutch oven over high heat, cook bacon until crisp; remove to platter. Season venison and rabbit with salt and pepper. Working in batches, brown venison and rabbit in bacon fat. Brown duck sausage; set aside meats.

2. Carefully remove all but 3 tablespoons of fat from Dutch oven. Add onions and fennel; sauté 3 minutes.

3. Add wine; stir, scraping up any browned bits from bottom. Bring mixture to a boil. Reduce heat to medium; add broth, cloves, and bay leaves.

4. Return meat, sausage, and bacon to pot; cover. Simmer 1½ hours, adding water as needed to maintain liquid level.

5. Add apples and cabbage; cover, cooking until cabbage is tender. Serve in shallow bowls.

Crawfish Stew

Every Cajun family has a favorite recipe for crawfish stew.
Crawfish stew is not to be confused with étouffée, which has a more delicate sauce.

INGREDIENTS | SERVES 4

1 cup vegetable oil

1 cup granulated flour

2 large onions, diced

3 cups hot seafood broth or water

1 green bell pepper, cored and diced

1 rib celery, diced

3 cloves garlic, minced

2 fresh tomatoes, diced

1 tablespoon tomato paste

1 teaspoon Tabasco sauce

2 pounds peeled crawfish tails

¼ cup sliced green onion

¼ cup minced parsley

Salt, pepper, and cayenne pepper
to taste

1. In a large, heavy saucepan, combine oil and flour. Cook over medium-high heat, stirring constantly, until mixture reaches a deep brown. Turn off heat; carefully add ½ of onions to roux; stir until onions have begun to caramelize. Whisk broth or water into roux a small amount at a time; whisk well to incorporate. If mixture seems too thick, add additional liquid.

2. Return to medium-high heat; add remaining onion, bell pepper, celery, and garlic. Bring to a boil; stir in tomatoes, tomato paste, and Tabasco. Reduce heat to medium; cook, stirring occasionally, 30 minutes.

3. Add crawfish tails; cook additional 30–40 minutes.

4. Remove from heat; stir in green onion, parsley, salt, and peppers. Serve over steamed rice.

Les Ecrivesse Est Arrivé! (Crawfish Have Arrived!)

Throughout Louisiana Cajun country, the arrival of crawfish in the springtime was heralded with signs outside markets and seafood stands. Crawfish is still a seasonal product, but with the advent of modern farm-raised crawfish, there are now two seasons: one in the fall and one in the springtime. In between, blanched, vacuum-sealed packs of peeled crawfish tails can be found at many supermarkets and fish markets. If you can't find crawfish, it's fine to substitute peeled shrimp.

Cioppino Seafood Stew

Some purists insist that anchovies must be part of the cioppino broth. If you like, add two or three drained anchovies to the oil and butter and sauté briefly before adding veggies.

INGREDIENTS | SERVES 4

2 tablespoons olive oil

1 tablespoon butter

1 onion, finely diced

1 small bell pepper, cored and diced

2 garlic cloves, minced

1 jalapeño pepper, minced

1 (28-ounce) can tomatoes

1 (8-ounce) can tomato sauce

1 cup red wine

1 tablespoon red wine vinegar

3 cups shellfish or fish broth

2 bay leaves

1 teaspoon fresh oregano leaves

1 sprig fresh rosemary

Salt to taste

12 large shrimp, peeled

12 small clams, scrubbed

12 mussels, scrubbed

8 cracked stone crab claws or 4 cleaned blue crab halves

⅓ cup minced parsley

Freshly ground black pepper to taste

1. In a large, heavy soup pot or Dutch oven, combine olive oil and butter. Over medium-high heat, sauté onion, bell pepper, garlic, and jalapeño pepper until vegetables are crisp-tender, about 3 minutes.

2. Add tomatoes, tomato sauce, wine, vinegar, broth, bay leaves, oregano, and rosemary. Bring to a boil; reduce heat and simmer 20 minutes.

3. Remove bay leaves and rosemary sprig; add salt, shrimp, clams, mussels, and crab. Cover and simmer just until clams and mussels open and shrimp turn opaque, about 2 to 3 minutes.

4. Add parsley and pepper. Divide shrimp and other shellfish over 4 bowls; ladle over broth. Serve with hot crusty bread.

Make It Your Own

Cioppino is a simple seafood stew and can be made from whatever is fresh and available. Many cooks add fillets of firm white fish, scallops, or shelled lobster tail to the mix. Traditionally, the dish has in-the-shell mussels or clams in it, but if you prefer not to pick shells from your food, just steam the clams or mussels in a separate pot, strain the resulting broth into the stew, and add the shelled clams or mussels to the stew at the last minute.

Carolina Frogmore Stew

*This low-country seafood boil showcases the fresh ingredients of the region.
It's often prepared in a backyard boiling pot for casual get-togethers.*

INGREDIENTS | SERVES 6

1 gallon water

1 lemon, halved

3 tablespoons crab boil seasoning

1 pound kielbasa sausage, cut in thick slices

1 onion, peeled and quartered

6 cloves garlic, peeled

18 small red potatoes, trimmed but not peeled

6 ears corn, shucked and halved

2 pounds washed, shell-on shrimp

Melted butter

Cocktail sauce

1. Bring water to a boil in a large soup pot; squeeze lemon juice into water. Add lemon halves, crab boil, kielbasa, onion, and garlic; stir well. Add potatoes; cook over medium-high heat 20 minutes.

2. Add corn; boil an additional 10 minutes.

3. Turn off heat; add shrimp. Cover pot; let stand 5–10 minutes, or until shrimp turn pink.

4. Use a long-handled strainer to remove ingredients from pot. Place shrimp, sausage, and vegetables on large platter or baking sheet. Serve with butter and cocktail sauce for dipping on a table covered with newspaper.

Seafood Feasts

The Frogmore Stew recipe—which is named after a tiny hamlet in South Carolina—can be used to boil crabs or crawfish as well as shrimp. Live crabs must be added while the water is still boiling, allowed to boil for 15 minutes, then left to steep for 5. Crawfish should boil 5 minutes and steep for 10.

Vindaloo Chicken Curry

If you prefer, this dish can be made with boneless chicken breasts instead of thighs.

INGREDIENTS | SERVES 6–8

2 onions, chopped

4 plum tomatoes, chopped

4 cloves garlic, peeled

1 slice peeled ginger root

1 tablespoon tomato paste

1½ teaspoons cumin

½ teaspoon coriander

½ teaspoon black pepper

¼ teaspoon cardamom

¼ teaspoon cayenne

¼ teaspoon paprika

¼ teaspoon turmeric

2 tablespoons olive oil

8 boneless chicken thighs, cut in 1½ pieces

8 russet potatoes, diced

2 cups chicken broth or water

Salt and pepper to taste

1. Place onion, tomatoes, garlic, ginger root, tomato paste, cumin, coriander, pepper, cardamom, cayenne, paprika, and turmeric in work bowl of food processor. Pulse until puréed.

2. Heat olive oil in a large, heavy saucepan; add purée. Fry over medium-high heat, stirring constantly, 3–5 minutes.

3. Add chicken and potatoes; stir to coat. Sauté an additional 5 minutes; add broth. Bring to a boil; reduce heat to medium and simmer 20 minutes, adding liquid if needed. Add salt and pepper to taste. Serve with soft flatbread or steamed basmati rice.

Thai Red Curry with Shrimp

Packaged Thai curry pastes, containing galangal, lemongrass, kafir lime leaves, and chilies, are available at most supermarkets.

INGREDIENTS | SERVES 4

2 tablespoons vegetable oil
1 tablespoon Thai red curry paste
2 cups coconut milk
1 teaspoon sugar
1 tablespoon fish sauce
1 onion, cut into eight wedges
2 cloves garlic
1 cup julienned carrots
1 red bell pepper, cored and cut in strips
1 cup snow pea pods or green beans
1½ pounds shrimp, peeled and deveined
1 teaspoon grated lime zest
¼ cup fresh basil leaves, cut in strips

1. In a large, heavy saucepan, heat oil over medium-high heat. Add curry paste; stirring, cook 3 minutes. Whisk in coconut milk, sugar, and fish sauce. Reduce heat to medium; simmer 3 minutes.

2. Add onion, garlic, carrots, bell pepper, and snow pea pods; simmer 15 minutes.

3. Add shrimp and lime zest. Continue cooking until shrimp turn opaque, about 3 minutes; add basil. Serve over jasmine rice.

Ratatouille

This savory vegetable stew makes a great vegetarian entrée when served over whole-wheat couscous or rice. Or serve it as a side with roasted meats.

INGREDIENTS | SERVES 4–6

1 medium eggplant, diced
1½ teaspoons salt
2 tablespoons olive oil
1 small onion, diced
1 green bell pepper, cored and diced
3 cloves garlic, minced
1 large zucchini, diced
2 yellow squash, diced
4 ounces white mushrooms, quartered
1 (28-ounce) can crushed tomatoes
1 teaspoon dried Italian seasoning mix
Salt and pepper to taste
¼ cup fresh basil leaves, chopped

1. Sprinkle eggplant with salt; leave in colander 1 hour.

2. Rinse eggplant well; pat dry with paper towels. In a large, heavy saucepan, heat olive oil over medium-high heat. Add onion, bell pepper, and garlic; sauté 3 minutes.

3. Add eggplant, zucchini, squash, and mushrooms to pot. Pour in crushed tomatoes and Italian seasoning; reduce heat to medium. Simmer 10–15 minutes, or until eggplant is tender.

4. Season with salt and pepper; stir in fresh basil. Remove from heat; let stand a few minutes before serving.

Caribbean Pork and Pumpkin Stew

Acorn or other winter squash can be used in place of pumpkin.
For garnish, toasted pumpkin seeds make a nice touch.

INGREDIENTS | SERVES 6

2 pounds pork shoulder, cut in 1½ cubes

1 teaspoon Jamaican jerk seasoning

⅓ cup flour

2 tablespoons olive oil

1 onion, diced

1 green bell pepper, cored and diced

1 rib celery, diced

1 (28-ounce) can crushed tomatoes

2 cups pork or chicken broth

Juice and zest of 1 orange

Pinch thyme

2 small sugar pumpkins, peeled, seeded, and diced

Salt and pepper to taste

1. Sprinkle pork cubes with jerk seasoning; dust with flour until well coated. Heat oil in a Dutch oven over medium-high heat. Brown pork in batches; remove to a platter. Sauté onion, pepper, and celery until crisp-tender, about 3–5 minutes.

2. Add tomatoes, broth, orange juice, and zest; bring to a boil. Lower heat to medium. Return pork to pan; add thyme. Cover; simmer 45 minutes. Stir occasionally; add more liquid if needed.

3. Add pumpkin; cook until tender, about 1 hour. Add salt and pepper to taste.

Pick a Pumpkin

Giant pumpkins may be great for Jack-o-Lanterns and centerpieces, but they aren't the best choice for cooking. Look for smaller, meatier pie pumpkins or sugar pumpkins for stews and pies. Where giant pumpkins are hollow and filled with fibrous strings, "eating" pumpkins have thick walls and smaller seed cores. As with acorn squash, small pumpkins can be scooped out, stuffed, and baked for a tempting fall dish.

Country Captain

Country Captain isn't meant to be a heavily curried dish, but as with all stews, the spices can be adjusted to suit the cook.

INGREDIENTS | SERVES 4

1 (3-pound) chicken, cut in serving pieces
Salt and pepper
⅓ cup flour
2 tablespoons oil or bacon fat
1 onion, diced
1 green bell pepper, cored and diced
1 rib celery, diced
2 cloves garlic
1 (14-ounce) can petite-dice tomatoes
1 cup chicken broth
2 teaspoons curry powder
½ teaspoon paprika
⅔ cup golden raisins
Salt and pepper to taste
⅓ cup sliced toasted almonds

1. Rinse chicken pieces; pat dry. Sprinkle with salt and pepper; coat with flour. Place oil or bacon fat in Dutch oven over medium-high heat. Brown chicken; remove to platter. Add onion, bell pepper, celery, and garlic; sauté 3 minutes.

2. Add tomatoes and broth; bring to a boil. Stir in curry powder and paprika. Return chicken to pan; reduce heat to medium. Cover; cook 15 minutes.

3. Add raisins; continue cooking, covered, 25 minutes. Check liquid occasionally. Add salt and pepper to taste. Serve over rice with toasted almonds sprinkled on top.

Chicken Corn Stew

Familiar flavors merge in this comforting stew, making it a great choice for family weeknight suppers.

INGREDIENTS | SERVES 4

3 strips bacon

2 tablespoons oil or butter

4 boneless, skinless chicken breast halves

1 medium onion, finely diced

1 small green bell pepper, finely diced

2 plum tomatoes, diced

4 cups fresh or frozen corn kernels

1 teaspoon sugar

1½ cups chicken broth

4 large red potatoes, peeled and diced

¼ teaspoon cumin

1½ teaspoons cornstarch

2 tablespoons cold water

1 green onion, sliced

¼ cup minced fresh parsley

Salt and pepper to taste

1. Cut bacon strips into 1 pieces. In a deep skillet or Dutch oven, fry bacon over medium-high heat until browned; remove and reserve.

2. Add oil or butter to the pot. Cut chicken breast halves in half crosswise, into 8 pieces; fry until browned on each side. Remove to platter. Add onion, green pepper, and tomatoes; sauté, stirring constantly, 3 minutes.

3. Add corn and sugar; continue cooking over medium-high heat. Stir and scrape any browned bits from bottom of pan. When corn mixture begins to brown slightly, after about 10 minutes, add broth; return chicken and bacon to pan.

4. Add potatoes and cumin; cover with tight-fitting lid. Reduce heat to medium low; simmer 20 minutes.

5. Dissolve cornstarch in water; add to pan, stirring well. Raise heat to medium high; bring mixture to a boil. Add green onion, parsley, salt, and pepper. Stir well; remove from heat.

Okra, Corn, and Tomato Stew

*For best flavor, make this dish during the summer with corn cut
from the cob and just-picked tomatoes and okra.*

INGREDIENTS | SERVES 4

3 tablespoons oil or butter

1 medium onion, finely diced

1 small green bell pepper, finely diced

1 rib celery, finely diced

2 cloves garlic, minced

2 cups sliced okra

2 cups diced ripe tomatoes

2 cups fresh corn kernels

1 cup water or chicken broth

¼ teaspoon cayenne

1 green onion, sliced

2 tablespoons minced fresh parsley

Salt and pepper to taste

1. In a deep skillet or Dutch oven, heat oil or butter over medium-high heat. Add onion, green pepper, celery, and garlic; sauté 5 minutes.

2. Add okra; cook, stirring constantly, 3 minutes, or until okra begins to release thick liquid.

3. Add tomatoes, corn, and water; bring to a boil. Reduce heat to medium low. Simmer, stirring often and adding more liquid if needed, 20 minutes, or until corn is tender.

4. Stir in cayenne, green onion, parsley, salt, and pepper; remove from heat. Serve as a side dish or over rice as an entrée.

Creamy Shrimp and Grits

This classic South Carolina brunch dish can be prepared with a creamy sauce or shrimp sauté over cream-infused grits. This is the creamy stew version.

INGREDIENTS | SERVES 4

4 strips bacon
1 tablespoon butter
1 small onion, finely chopped
2 tablespoons flour
1 cup shrimp or chicken broth
1½ pounds shrimp, peeled and deveined
1 cup heavy cream
¼ teaspoon thyme
¼ teaspoon cayenne
¼ teaspoon lemon zest
2 green onions, sliced
2 tablespoons minced fresh parsley
Salt and pepper to taste
4 cups cooked stone-ground grits or cheese grits

1. In a deep skillet, fry bacon strips over medium-high heat until crisp; remove to plate and reserve. Add butter and onion to bacon fat; sauté onion 5 minutes.

2. Sprinkle flour over skillet; stir well to blend. Slowly add broth; stir until mixture is smooth and thickened. Reduce heat to medium; cook 5 minutes, stirring frequently.

3. Add shrimp; cook just until shrimp turn pink. Stir in cream, thyme, cayenne, lemon zest, green onions, and parsley. Crumble bacon into sauce; add salt and pepper. Remove from heat.

4. Divide grits over 4 shallow soup plates. Ladle shrimp sauce over grits; serve immediately.

Glorified Grits

First the definitions: Grits are ground hominy; that is, the dried corn kernel from which the hull and germ have been removed. Corn grits are ground dried corn kernels with the hull and germ still intact. Southerners love both, but insist the best grits are stone ground and slow cooked. Although one can make grits by boiling the grains in water, grits are often augmented with butter, cream, and cheese. Oh, and there's an ongoing debate as to whether the term grits is singular or plural, as in "grits are" versus "grits is."

CHAPTER 11

Soups and Stews
by Any Other Name

Short-Crust Beef Pot Pie

Make a double batch of beef stew and freeze half.
A week or a month later, you'll be able to whip this pie up for a potluck.

INGREDIENTS | SERVES 8

1 recipe Classic Beef Stew (Page 178)
2¼ cups flour
1 teaspoon salt
1 cup chilled lard
¼ cup water

The Lowdown on Lard

It's just a little pig fat, but the way people carry on, you'd think lard was a four-letter word. Fact is, pure lard is actually better for you than hydrogenated vegetable shortening. It's also lower in saturated ("bad") fat and higher in monounsaturated ("good") fat than butter and contains more helpful omega-3 fatty acids. Of course, lard is still a very high-calorie food—but it does make fabulous pie crusts.

1. Spoon beef stew into a large, buttered casserole dish. (If frozen, thaw first.) Preheat oven to 350°F.

2. In a large bowl, combine flour and salt; whisk to blend. Cut cold lard into pieces; add to flour. Cut in with knives or a pastry blender until mixture resembles coarse meal. Add water; work together to make dough.

3. With floured hands, roll out dough to fit top of casserole. Cut a few ovals in dough to vent steam; place dough over stew. Press into place around dish; remove excess.

4. Bake 30–40 minutes, or until dough is browned and filling is bubbling through vents. Remove from oven; let stand 10 minutes before serving.

Chicken under a Bread Crust

Thawed frozen bread dough works perfectly well with this recipe and eliminates a lot of time and mess.

INGREDIENTS | SERVES 4

½ pound bread dough
2 tablespoons butter
1 small onion, diced
1 rib celery, diced
1 carrot, diced
1 pound mushrooms, sliced
2 tablespoons flour
1½ cups chicken broth
1 cup heavy cream
¼ cup chopped fresh herbs
2 cups diced cooked chicken
Salt and pepper to taste

1. Place bread dough in a bowl; cover loosely and allow to rise once. Punch dough down; set aside.

2. In a heavy saucepan over medium-high heat, melt butter. Add onion, celery, and carrot; sauté 1 minute. Add mushrooms; continue to sauté 5 minutes.

3. Sprinkle flour over mixture; stir to blend. Add broth; bring mixture to a boil. Simmer 15 minutes, allowing broth to reduce by one third.

4. Add cream, herbs, and chicken; simmer an additional 5 minutes.

5. Season with salt and pepper; pour into buttered casserole dish.

6. Preheat oven to 350°F. Lightly butter hands; shape bread dough into roll-sized balls. Place dough over chicken, spacing dough evenly. Bake until bread crust is browned and firm, about 30 minutes.

Easy Turkey Cobbler

In a hurry? Sometimes the easiest sauce comes from a can in your pantry.

INGREDIENTS | SERVES 4

1 (10-ounce) can condensed cream of mushroom soup

2 cups whole milk

1–1½ cups shredded turkey meat

1 cup frozen mixed vegetables

½ teaspoon Worcestershire sauce

¼ teaspoon cayenne or curry powder

¼ cup minced parsley

Salt and pepper to taste

2¼ cups biscuit mix

Next-Day Turkey

Lean roasted turkey makes a beautiful centerpiece on any table. Properly cooked, it's also tender and juicy. But even the best baked turkey dries out by the second or third day in the refrigerator. Instead of foisting dry turkey sandwiches on friends, freeze leftover turkey meat in a little broth. Use it later in saucy casseroles and quick-fix stews where a little moisture loss won't be a factor.

1. Preheat oven to 350°F. In a saucepan or oven-safe skillet, combine soup, 1⅓ cups of the milk, turkey, vegetables, Worcestershire sauce, and cayenne or curry powder. Cook over medium heat, stirring, until hot and bubbly. Sprinkle with parsley and add salt and pepper to taste.

2. In a bowl, combine biscuit mix and remaining milk; stir until mixture forms a soft dough.

3. Spoon turkey mixture into a small casserole—if you're not already using an oven-safe skillet—and top with spoonfuls of biscuit dough, evenly spaced. Bake just until biscuits are browned, about 12–15 minutes. Let stand 10 minutes before serving.

Cassoulet

The authentic version of this dish is made with duck confit.
This recipe uses ingredients you might have on hand.

INGREDIENTS | SERVES 8

2 tablespoons olive oil

½ pound Italian sausage, cut in a few pieces

1 pound boneless chicken breast, cubed

½ pound lean beef, lamb, or pork, finely diced

1 tablespoon herbes de Provence

1 large onion, diced

1 red bell pepper, cored and diced

3 cloves garlic, minced

2 cups chicken or beef broth

1 (28-ounce) can plum tomatoes, crushed

1 cup white wine

1 teaspoon salt

2 bay leaves

10 cups cooked cannellini beans

½ cup fine bread crumbs

¼ cup minced parsley

1 tablespoon melted butter

1. In a medium Dutch oven, heat 1 tablespoon of olive oil over medium heat. Add sausage; cook, stirring, until sausage is no longer pink. Remove to a platter.

2. Sprinkle chicken and meat cubes with half of herbes de Provence. Working in batches, brown chicken and meat in sausage drippings, adding 1 tablespoon of olive oil if necessary. Remove to a platter.

3. Add onion, bell pepper, and garlic to fat; sauté 3 minutes.

4. Remove vegetables to a platter. Add broth, tomatoes, wine, salt, bay leaves, and remaining herbes de Provence. Stir well; scrape up any bits from bottom of pot. Raise heat to high; bring mixture to a boil. Boil until liquid is reduced by one third.

5. Remove casing from sausage; chop. Mix sausage, chicken, meat, and vegetables together. Ladle ½ of liquid from Dutch oven into another container; reserve. Layer one third of beans in bottom of pot; top with ½ of meats and vegetables. Layer another ⅓ of beans, followed by remainder of meats and vegetables. Top with remaining beans. Pour rest of liquid over beans. (Liquid should not be higher than level of beans.)

6. Mix bread crumbs with parsley; sprinkle over beans. Drizzle butter over crumbs. Bake at 350°F for 1 hour. Remove from oven; let stand 15 minutes before serving.

Shepherd's Pie

The mashed potatoes used for Shepherd's Pie should be a little on the stiff side.
Potatoes that are too creamy make a flat topping.

INGREDIENTS | SERVES 4

1 pound ground lamb or beef

1 small onion, minced

2 cloves garlic, minced

1 tablespoon minced parsley

1 tablespoon vegetable oil

1 tablespoon flour

1 cup lamb or beef broth

1 tablespoon tomato paste

1 teaspoon Tabasco

Pinch thyme

1 cup frozen peas and carrots

Salt and pepper to taste

3 cups mashed potatoes

⅓ cup shredded Cheddar cheese

Cottage Versus Shepherd

In most of the world, a Shepherd's pie is any mixture of seasoned ground or chopped meat and gravy topped with a mashed potato crust. However, in England—where the dish originated—cooks usually distinguish shepherd's pie as a recipe that contains lamb. The beef version of it is called cottage pie. In either case, the dish is most often made from leftover roast and gravy, rather than just-cooked ground meat.

1. In a heavy saucepan over medium heat, combine beef or lamb with onion, garlic, and parsley; sauté until meat is no longer pink and vegetables are tender. With a slotted spoon, remove to a bowl. Discard fat.

2. Put 1 tablespoon of oil in saucepan; heat over medium-high heat. Add flour; stir until mixture is lightly browned. Add broth; stir until well blended. Stir in tomato paste, Tabasco, and thyme; bring mixture to a boil. Add peas and carrots. Reduce heat; simmer, stirring frequently, 10 minutes, or until gravy is thick and veggies are hot.

3. Return meat mixture to saucepan; stir to blend. Add salt and pepper; pour into medium casserole dish. Spoon mashed potatoes over top; sprinkle shredded cheese over potatoes. Bake in 350°F oven for 15 minutes, or until potatoes are nicely browned. Let stand briefly before serving.

Steak and Kidney Pie

*This dish is an acquired taste, but if you don't like organ meats,
you can always substitute more beef or chopped sausage.*

INGREDIENTS | SERVES 4

1 pound round steak
¼ pound lamb kidneys
3 tablespoons butter
1 shallot, minced
2 cloves garlic, minced
4 ounces mushrooms, sliced
2 tablespoons flour
3 cups beef broth
1 tablespoon tomato paste
1 teaspoon Worcestershire sauce
¼ teaspoon thyme
¼ teaspoon cayenne
Salt and pepper to taste
Pastry for single-crust pie

1. Thinly slice round steak. Trim kidneys; cut into small dice. In a large, heavy saucepan, melt butter over medium-high heat. Working in batches, brown kidney and steak; remove to platter. Add shallot, garlic, and mushrooms; sauté 5 minutes.

2. Sprinkle flour over vegetables; stir to blend. Add broth; stir until flour is dissolved. Add tomato paste, Worcestershire, thyme, and cayenne; bring to a boil, then reduce heat to medium. Return steak and kidneys to pot; simmer 2 hours, or until meat is very tender. Add salt and pepper to taste.

3. Spoon meat, vegetables, and enough gravy to cover into a deep-dish pie plate. Cover top with pie crust pastry; cut slits to vent. Place pie plate on foil-covered baking sheet; bake at 375°F for 40 minutes, or until pie crust is browned and filling is bubbly. Let stand 10 minutes before serving.

Tamale Pie

This is a great weeknight supper. The chili can be made a day or two ahead to save time.

INGREDIENTS | SERVES 8

1 double batch Easy Homestyle Chili
(Page 139)

2 cups shredded Cheddar cheese

2 cups self-rising cornmeal

1 (10-ounce) can cream-style corn

2 eggs, beaten

½ cup melted butter

1 cup milk

Pinch cumin

1. Preheat oven to 350°F. Spoon chili into a lightly greased casserole; sprinkle cheese over top.

2. In a large bowl, combine cornmeal, corn, eggs, butter, milk, and cumin; whisk together until smooth.

3. Pour cornmeal mixture evenly over chili. Place in oven, uncovered; bake 40–45 minutes, or until crust is firm and browned. Remove from oven; let stand 10 minutes before serving.

Pie Possibilities

Some cooks make this dish with a cornmeal-mush crust, while others use taco-seasoned beef as the filling. This version combines chili and cornbread in one dish, for a nearly complete meal. Another variation—barbecue pie—combines a filling of shredded or chopped pork, barbecue sauce, and a cornbread crust.

Spicy Pork and Apricot Tajine

This dish can be made with boneless lamb or chicken in place of pork.

INGREDIENTS | **SERVES 6–8**

2 pounds boneless pork roast

1 teaspoon cinnamon

½ teaspoon ginger

½ teaspoon cumin

½ teaspoon cayenne

1 teaspoon paprika

1 teaspoon kosher salt

¼ teaspoon cardamom

2 tablespoons olive oil

1 large onion, diced

3 garlic cloves, minced

¼ teaspoon saffron

¼ cup hot water

1 (16-ounce) can diced tomato

1 tablespoon brown sugar

2 cups chicken or pork broth

8 dried apricots, quartered

¼ cup minced fresh cilantro

1. Cut pork into 2 cubes. Combine cinnamon, ginger, cumin, cayenne, paprika, kosher salt, and cardamom; sprinkle half of mixture over pork cubes.

2. In a Dutch oven, heat oil over medium-high heat. Brown pork on all sides; remove to platter. Add onion and garlic; sauté 5 minutes.

3. Dissolve saffron in hot water. Add saffron, tomatoes, and brown sugar to the pot; stir well. Return pork to pot; add broth and apricots. Stir in remaining spices; bring to a boil. Reduce heat to medium low; cover and simmer 2 hours, adding more liquid if necessary.

4. Stir in cilantro. Remove from heat; let stand 10 minutes. Serve over steamed couscous.

Crawfish Pie

If you happen to have leftover crawfish étouffée, you can always use that as a crawfish pie filling.

INGREDIENTS | SERVES 6

3 tablespoons butter

2 tablespoons flour

1 medium onion, finely diced

1 cup hot shellfish broth or water

½ small green bell pepper, cored and finely diced

½ rib celery, finely diced

1 medium tomato, peeled, seeded, and chopped

1 teaspoon Tabasco

Pinch cayenne

1 pound crawfish tails, fresh or thawed

¼ cup heavy cream

Salt and pepper to taste

2 refrigerated or homemade 9-inch pie crusts

C'est Si Bon!

In many Louisiana kitchens, crawfish pies are often prepared as crawfish-filled fried turnovers. To make this type of pie, skip the tomato in the baked pie filling recipe and remove the crawfish and vegetables from the sauce with a slotted spoon. Finely chop the filling in a food processor, then place spoonfuls on half of several small pie-crust circles. Fold the dough over, seal the edges well, and deep fry until the pie is golden.

1. In a heavy saucepan, melt butter over medium-high heat. Add flour; stir until a paste forms. Cook, stirring, until mixture turns light brown. Add half of onions; stir until translucent. Carefully add hot broth or water; stir until roux dissolves and mixture is thickened. Reduce heat to medium; add remaining onion, green pepper, celery, and tomato. Simmer 10 minutes, or until vegetables are tender, stirring often.

2. Add Tabasco, cayenne, and crawfish tails; simmer 10 minutes longer.

3. Add cream, salt, and pepper. Remove from heat; allow to cool to lukewarm. Mixture should be very thick.

4. Press 1 pie crust into a buttered 9 pie plate; spoon in crawfish mixture. Place remaining crust on cutting surface; cut out circle, star, or diamond shape. Top crust should sit on top of filling without touching sides.

5. Bake at 350°F for 40–45 minutes, or until crust is browned. Let stand 10 minutes before serving.

Italian Sausage and Peppers over Polenta

This dish uses quick-cooking instant polenta to save time and stirring.

INGREDIENTS | SERVES 6

6 cups water

2 cups instant polenta

2 tablespoons butter

½ cup shredded Parmesan cheese

Salt and pepper to taste

1 pound hot Italian sausage

1 pound sweet Italian sausage

⅓ cup olive oil

3 garlic cloves, minced

1 pound sliced mushrooms

1 medium onion, cut in strips

1 red bell pepper, cored and cut in strips

1 green bell pepper, cored and cut in strips

Splash white wine

1. In a large saucepan, bring water to a boil. Whisk in polenta; cook over medium heat, stirring constantly, 5 minutes.

2. Remove from heat; whisk in butter, Parmesan, salt, and pepper. Pour into buttered oblong baking dish. When firm, cut into 6 pieces.

3. In a deep skillet, place sausages with just enough water to cover; bring to a boil over high heat. Reduce heat; simmer 20 minutes, occasionally pricking sausages to release fats.

4. Remove sausage to a platter; discard cooking liquid. Rinse and dry skillet. Add half of olive oil to skillet; heat over medium-high heat. Add garlic, mushrooms, and onion; sauté 5 minutes. With a slotted spoon, remove to bowl.

5. Add peppers to skillet; sauté 3 minutes. Remove to bowl.

6. Slice sausages diagonally into disks; raise heat to high and fry sausage until browned, about 3 minutes. Remove to a bowl.

7. Discard oil in pan. Return pan to stove; add remaining olive oil. Heat oil over medium heat. Return sausage and vegetables to pan; cook, stirring often, 5 minutes.

8. Raise heat to high 2 minutes. Add a splash of wine; stir to scrape up bits from pan. Remove from heat. Spoon sausage and peppers over polenta; serve.

Buffalo Chicken in a Bread Bowl

This fiery-hot dish isn't for the squeamish. Serve with plenty of extra bread and drinks.

INGREDIENTS | SERVES 4

4 round, ½-pound loaves of pumpernickel or honey wheat bread

4 boneless chicken breasts

2 tablespoons flour

1 teaspoon salt

½ teaspoon cayenne

1 teaspoon chili powder

½ cup butter

1 small onion, minced

3 jalapeño peppers, minced

2 garlic cloves, minced

2 tablespoons tomato paste

¼ cup white vinegar

¼ cup hot sauce

1 teaspoon sugar

1½ cups water or chicken broth

½ cup beer

2 ribs celery, sliced

½ cup sour cream

¼ cup ranch or bleu cheese dressing

1. Slice tops off bread loaves; set aside. Carefully hollow out insides, leaving at least ½ thick shell. (Reserve bread for bread crumbs.) Place each bread loaf on plate or in shallow bowl.

2. Dice chicken breasts. Combine flour, salt, cayenne, and chili powder; coat chicken in flour mixture. In a large saucepan, melt butter over medium-high heat. Brown chicken in butter; remove to platter. Add onion, jalapeño peppers, and garlic; sauté 3 minutes.

3. Add tomato paste; cook, stirring, 1 minute. Add vinegar, hot sauce, sugar, water or broth, and beer; bring to a boil. Cook 10 minutes, allowing sauce to reduce.

4. Add celery and chicken; reduce heat to medium and continue cooking 10 minutes. Remove from heat; let stand 5 minutes.

5. Spoon hot chicken and celery into bread bowls with some of the sauce. Combine sour cream and dressing; place a dollop over each bread bowl and serve with bread tops on the side.

Chicken Pot Pie

Frozen puff pastry makes it possible for anyone to add a haute touch to their homey comfort dishes.

INGREDIENTS | SERVES 4

2 tablespoons butter

1 small onion, diced

1 rib celery, diced

1 carrot, diced

4 ounces mushrooms, chopped

2 tablespoons flour

1½ cups chicken broth

½ teaspoon curry powder

¼ cup cream

1 cup peas

¼ cup minced fresh parsley

2 cups chopped cooked chicken

Salt and pepper to taste

1 sheet frozen puff pastry, thawed

1. In a heavy saucepan over medium-high heat, melt butter. Add onion, celery, and carrot; sauté 1 minute. Add mushrooms; continue to sauté 5 minutes.

2. Sprinkle flour over mixture; stir to blend. Add broth and curry powder; bring to a boil. Simmer 15 minutes, allowing broth to reduce by one third.

3. Add cream, peas, parsley, and chicken; simmer an additional 5 minutes.

4. Season with salt and pepper; pour into a buttered oblong casserole dish. Lightly score top of puff pastry sheet; place over chicken filling. Bake at 375°F for 20 minutes, or until pastry is nicely browned.

Pure Puff

If you're comfortable making your own puff pastry—and devoting hours to rolling, folding, and rechilling the dough—you probably already know how delicate puff pastry can be. Even if you use premade or frozen pastry sheets, you should know that puff pastry becomes very soft and hard to handle at room temperature. Work quickly, and return the dough to the refrigerator if necessary. Also, excessive handling builds up gluten that can flatten the "puff" out of the pastry.

Chicken à la King

Several venues claim to be the point of origin for Chicken à la King.
There are two things we know: It is an American dish, and it first shows up in cookbooks in 1898.

INGREDIENTS | SERVES 4

2 tablespoons butter
1 green onion, chopped
4 ounces mushrooms, quartered
1 small red bell pepper, cored and diced
2 tablespoons flour
1½ cups chicken broth
1 cup light cream
2 cups diced cooked chicken
Salt and pepper to taste

1. In a heavy saucepan, melt butter over medium-high heat. Add green onion, mushrooms, and bell pepper; sauté 5 minutes.

2. Add flour; stir to coat. Add broth; stir until flour dissolves. Bring mixture to a boil; cook, stirring often, 10 minutes, or until liquid is reduced by one third.

3. Reduce heat to medium low. Stir in cream and chicken; add salt and pepper. Simmer 5 minutes; remove from heat. Serve in puff pastry shells or over toast.

White Chili Pie

Aged Manchego is a firm, dry cheese similar to good Parmesan.
Find it in the imported cheese case at your supermarket.

INGREDIENTS | SERVES 4

1 recipe White Chicken Chili (Page 150)
1 egg, beaten
2 refrigerated pie crusts
1 cup crumbled aged Manchego cheese

1. Heat chicken chili over medium low heat; stir until most of broth has evaporated. Pour egg into chili; stir quickly to distribute egg evenly.

2. Preheat oven to 350°F. Press 1 pie crust into a greased deep-dish pie pan. Using a slotted spoon, fill pie crust with chili. Sprinkle cheese over filling; cover with second crust. Cut slits into top crust; place on foil-covered baking sheet. Bake 40 minutes, or until crust is brown and pie is bubbling. Let stand 10 minutes before serving.

Tuna Cups

This easy luncheon dish offers a lot of flavor without a lot of expensive ingredients.

INGREDIENTS | SERVES 6–8

1 tablespoon vegetable oil
1 onion, finely diced
1 small green pepper, cored and diced
1 rib celery, diced
2 cloves garlic, minced
1 (10-ounce) can condensed cream of mushroom soup
½ cup cream
2 (6-ounce) cans tuna, drained
¼ teaspoon cayenne pepper
¼ cup minced parsley
Salt and pepper to taste
12 slices white bread

Something Fishy

Canned tuna may not be everybody's idea of gourmet fare, but it is quite popular. In the United States, it's the second most popular seafood dish, after shrimp. Chunk, light-meat tuna packed in water is the best seller. Although canned tuna contains heart-healthy omega-3 fatty acids, it also contains traces of mercury—a heavy metal found in the tissues of many oily fish. Some health advocates advise limited tuna consumption for pregnant women and small children.

1. In a large saucepan, heat oil over medium-high heat. Add onion, pepper, celery, and garlic; sauté 5 minutes.

2. Add cream of mushroom soup and cream; cook, stirring, until mixture is hot and bubbly.

3. Reduce heat; add drained tuna, cayenne, and parsley. Stir to break up tuna. Simmer 3–5 minutes.

4. Add salt and pepper; remove from heat.

5. Butter bread on one side. Carefully press each slice into a greased muffin-tin cup. Bread corners should rise over sides of cups in 4 points. Bake at 350°F for 10 minutes.

6. Carefully remove from oven; fill each cup with tuna mixture. Return pan to oven; bake an additional 10–15 minutes.

7. Place cups on luncheon plates and serve with green salad.

Corned Beef and Cabbage Pie

Think corned beef hash with layers of cabbage between.
Serve this dish at a St. Patrick's Day brunch with a garnish of sliced boiled eggs.

INGREDIENTS | **SERVES 4–6**

1 leafy cabbage head
1 tablespoon butter
1 medium onion, minced
2 cups heavy cream
1 tablespoon coarse mustard
2 cups shredded corned beef
2 cups finely diced boiled potatoes
Salt and pepper to taste
2 plum tomatoes, sliced

1. Boil whole cabbage in large soup pot about 15 minutes, or just until leaves are tender and pliable. Set aside to cool.

2. In a large, heavy saucepan over medium-high heat, combine butter and onion; sauté 5 minutes.

3. Stir in cream and mustard. Bring to a boil; reduce heat to medium. Add corned beef and potatoes; stir gently to blend into sauce. Simmer 3 minutes. Remove from heat; add salt and pepper.

4. Drain cabbage; carefully remove leaves from core. In a well-buttered ceramic or glass casserole, make a layer of several cabbage leaves. Top with half of corned beef mixture, followed by another layer of cabbage. Spoon remaining corned beef mixture into casserole and top with cabbage. Cover with foil; bake at 350°F for 30 minutes.

5. Remove foil; layer tomatoes over top layer of cabbage. Bake uncovered 10 minutes to roast tomatoes. Let stand 10 minutes before serving.

Pork Pie

This is a very basic French-Canadian dish.
Some cooks like to doctor it with a bit of crumbled bacon or a tablespoon of tomato paste.

INGREDIENTS | SERVES 4

1 pound ground pork
1 onion, minced
¼ teaspoon thyme
¼ teaspoon cayenne pepper
½ teaspoon salt
3 white potatoes, peeled and boiled
2 refrigerated pie crusts

Meat Pies

Instead of baking meat pies in traditional pie plates, try making tartlets for individual servings. Or skip the pie plates altogether. Instead, spoon filling onto half of a round pie crust and fold the crust over the filling, making a half-moon. Place this turnover onto a nonstick foil–lined baking sheet and bake at 350°F for 30 minutes. Another alternative is to make small stuffed crescents, seal the edges tightly, and deep fry the little pies until nicely browned. Drain on paper towels.

1. In a heavy skillet, combine pork and onion. Cook over medium-high heat, stirring, until meat is browned. Drain off fat; stir in thyme, cayenne, and salt.

2. In a large bowl, mash boiled potatoes with potato masher. Fold in cooked pork and onion mixture; adjust seasonings to taste.

3. Place 1 crust in a buttered deep-dish pie plate; fill with pork and potato mixture. Cut slits in second crust; arrange on top of filling. Bake at 350°F for 40–50 minutes, or until crust is nicely browned. Let stand 10 minutes before serving.

Fajita Casserole

*This can easily become a seafood dish by substituting firm fish, shrimp,
or scallops for the beef and chicken.*

INGREDIENTS | SERVES 6–8

1 pound sirloin steak

1 pound boneless chicken breast

3 tablespoons olive oil

1 large onion, cut in strips

1 red bell pepper, cored and cut in strips

1 green bell pepper, cored and cut in strips

2 cloves garlic, minced

2 tomatoes, seeded and diced

½ cup sliced black olives

1 (1-ounce) packet taco seasoning

1 cup water

¼ cup minced fresh cilantro

6 large flour tortillas

4 cups shredded Mexican-blend cheese

1 cup chunky salsa

Sour cream

Avocado slices

1. Thinly slice steak and chicken. In a large skillet or flat-bottomed wok, heat oil over high heat. Quickly sear beef and chicken; remove to platter. Add onion, bell peppers, and garlic sauté 3 minutes. Add tomatoes, olives, taco seasoning, and water; bring to a boil. Simmer 10 minutes.

2. Remove sauce from heat. Return beef and chicken to pan; stir to mix with sauce. Add cilantro.

3. Lightly grease an oblong casserole dish. Place 3 large tortillas, overlapping, on bottom of dish. Spoon chicken and beef mixture over tortillas; top with ½ of shredded cheese. Layer remaining tortillas; top with salsa and remaining cheese.

4. Bake at 350°F for 20 minutes, or until cheese is lightly browned. Remove from oven; let stand 10 minutes before cutting with a sharp knife. Serve with sour cream and avocado slices.

Hunter's Pie

This is the game version of the classic Shepherd's pie.
Sweet potatoes complement the rich flavor of the venison.

INGREDIENTS | SERVES 4

1 pound ground venison
1 small onion, minced
2 cloves garlic, minced
1 tablespoon minced parsley
1 tablespoon vegetable oil
1 tablespoon flour
1 cup beef or venison broth
1 tablespoon tomato paste
1 teaspoon Tabasco
Pinch thyme
1 cup sliced mushrooms
Salt and pepper to taste
3 cups mashed sweet potatoes
Pinch cinnamon

1. In a heavy saucepan over medium heat, combine venison with onion, garlic, and parsley; sauté until meat is no longer pink and vegetables are tender. With a slotted spoon, remove to a bowl. Discard fat.

2. Put 1 tablespoon oil in saucepan; heat over medium-high heat. Add flour; stir until mixture is lightly browned. Add broth; stir until well blended. Stir in tomato paste, Tabasco, and thyme; bring to a boil. Add mushrooms. Reduce heat; simmer, stirring frequently, 10 minutes, or until gravy is thick and mushrooms are tender.

3. Return meat mixture to saucepan; stir to blend. Add salt and pepper.

4. Pour into medium casserole dish. Spoon mashed sweet potatoes over top; sprinkle cinnamon over potatoes. Bake in 350°F oven 15 minutes, or until potatoes are nicely browned. Let stand briefly before serving.

CHAPTER 12

Dessert Soups and Fruit Stews

Key Lime Floating Island

This very basic liquid custard dessert never fails to make an impressive entrance.

INGREDIENTS | SERVES 4

Floating Island:

4 egg whites

½ cup sugar

Pinch cream of tartar

1 tablespoon key lime juice

Custard:

4 egg yolks

2 tablespoons flour

Pinch salt

⅔ cup sugar

3 cups milk

2 teaspoons vanilla

1 tablespoon key lime zest

Meringue Tips

Egg whites turn into meringue when air is beaten into the whites and trapped in air bubbles formed by egg proteins. Sugar strengthens meringues, making the bubbles more stable. Any impurities or fats—in the egg whites, the bowl, or beaters used—will cause the air bubbles in the beaten whites to collapse. Even oils from your fingers can affect the end result. Make sure everything touching the eggs is dry and spotless; use fresh eggs at room temperature and add sugar gradually after egg whites have started to foam.

1. To make meringues, in a chilled glass or metal bowl, combine egg whites, sugar, cream of tartar, and key lime juice. Beat on low speed to blend; beat at high speed until meringue is very stiff. Fill a large Dutch oven with water; bring to a boil over high heat. Reduce heat to medium. When water is simmering, spoon 8 mounds of meringue into water; simmer 3–5 minutes, turning once, until meringues are firm. Remove with slotted spoon; set aside.

2. To make sauce, in a bowl, whisk together egg yolks, flour, salt, and sugar until well blended. Scald milk in top of double boiler. Ladle a cup of hot milk into egg mixture, whisking constantly. Immediately pour tempered egg mixture into top of double boiler; whisk to blend. Cook, stirring constantly, until sauce coats the back of a spoon. Remove from heat; beat in vanilla and lime zest.

3. Pour custard sauce in a shallow serving bowl. Place meringues on top of sauce, turning once to coat. Chill dessert until ready to serve. Drizzle with caramel or raspberry sauce if desired.

Mango-Nectarine Yogurt Soup

This easy soup makes a great brunch or breakfast dish. Experiment with other types of fruit.

INGREDIENTS | SERVES 4

1½ cups peeled and diced mango, chilled

1 cup peeled and diced nectarines, chilled

1 cup cold peach nectar

2 cups vanilla yogurt

Mint sprigs

1. Combine mango, nectarines, peach nectar, and vanilla yogurt in a blender; pulse until smooth.

2. Pour into soup mugs; garnish with mint sprigs.

Watermelon Soup with Frozen Grapes

If you can cut fruit and boil water, you can make this fun summer soup.

INGREDIENTS | SERVES 4

1 cup sugar

1 cup water

5 cups diced watermelon, seeds removed

½ teaspoon lemon juice

1 cup green grapes, rinsed and frozen

1. In a saucepan, combine sugar and water. Bring mixture to a boil, stirring until sugar is dissolved. Remove from heat to cool to room temperature. Place in refrigerator; chill 2 hours.

2. In a blender, combine chilled sugar syrup, watermelon, and lemon juice. Pulse until puréed; pour through a fine strainer into a bowl.

3. Ladle cold soup into bowls; place several frozen grapes in each bowl.

Great Grapes

Grapes freeze into perfect little iced treats. Rinse grape bunches under running water, then place still-wet grapes in a freezer-safe resealable plastic bag. Freeze for two hours or longer, then pull a few frosty grapes from the bag as needed. Frozen grapes can be used in place of ice in cold drinks and in punch bowls. Or bunches of frozen grapes can be part of a summer party hors d'oeuvre table. Finally, frozen seedless grapes make wonderful sweet soup and salad garnishes.

Creamy Mocha Soup with Chocolate Muffins

Serve this soup warm for an experience that resembles hot chocolate in Heaven!

INGREDIENTS | SERVES 4

Muffins:

1 egg

½ cup sugar

⅓ cup butter, softened

½ cup flour

⅛ teaspoon salt

¼ cup cocoa powder

1 teaspoon baking powder

⅓ cup milk

Soup:

3 egg yolks

2 tablespoons flour

Pinch salt

4 teaspoons instant coffee crystals

¾ cup sugar

3 cups half-and-half

½ cup dark chocolate sauce

Muffin Magic

Muffins make people smile. Round out your menus with a repertoire of both sweet and savory muffins. Muffins have a more open, coarse grain than cupcakes, making them perfect little breads to go with soups, salads, and stews. Corn muffins with bacon bits, whole-grain muffins with chopped sun-dried tomatoes, and buttermilk muffins with minced herbs are all great complements to simple dishes.

1. To make muffins, preheat oven to 350°F. In a bowl, combine egg and sugar; beat at high speed until light and fluffy. Beat in butter. In a small bowl, whisk together flour, salt, cocoa powder, and baking powder. Add to butter and sugar mixture alternately with milk. Pour batter into 12 buttered mini-muffin cups. Bake until done, about 10 minutes.

2. To make soup, in a bowl, whisk together egg yolks, flour, salt, coffee crystals, and sugar until well blended. Scald half-and-half in top of a double boiler. Ladle 1 cup of hot half-and-half into egg mixture, whisking constantly. Immediately pour tempered egg mixture into top of double boiler; whisk to blend. Cook, stirring constantly, until sauce coats back of a spoon.

3. Remove from heat; ladle into shallow bowls. Drizzle a bit of chocolate sauce into each bowl; use a knife to create a swirl pattern. Serve with muffins.

Margarita Soup

This is an adults-only treat, the equivalent of drinking a frozen margarita.

INGREDIENTS | SERVES 4

1 (6-ounce) can frozen limeade
6 ounces tequila
4 cups cracked ice
⅓ cup cherry syrup
Sliced limes
Coarse sugar
Whipped cream

1. Combine limeade, unthawed, and tequila in a blender with a strong motor. Add cracked ice; pulse to chop. Add cherry syrup; blend to a smooth purée.

2. Rub rims of 4 large martini glasses with a lime slice. Pour coarse sugar onto a plate; dip wet-rimmed glasses into sugar. Pour margarita mix into each glass. Garnish with remaining lime slices and whipped cream.

Peanut Butter Soup with Chocolate Swirl

This dessert soup is a kids' favorite.
You can also make it with a swirl of fruit preserves or jelly instead of chocolate.

INGREDIENTS | SERVES 4

1 cup creamy peanut butter
1 pint dulce de leche ice cream
2 cups milk
⅓ cup sugar
1 teaspoon vanilla
Pinch cinnamon
8 ounces dark or milk chocolate
½ cup heavy cream

1. In a food processor or blender, combine peanut butter, ice cream, and 1 cup of milk; process until smooth. Add remaining milk, sugar, vanilla, and cinnamon; process until well blended.

2. Break up chocolate in a dry, heat-safe bowl. Pour cream over chocolate; microwave in 30-second bursts until chocolate is melted and can be stirred into cream, making a smooth sauce. Ladle soup into shallow bowls and drizzle chocolate over each portion.

Peaches and Cream Soup

Make this soup from super-ripe peaches.
Dice peaches over a bowl to catch any sweet juice that drips from the fruit.

INGREDIENTS | SERVES 4

1 cup water
1 cup sugar
3 cups diced fresh peaches
1 teaspoon vanilla
1 cup heavy cream
1 cup whipped cream

1. In a saucepan, combine water and sugar. Bring to a boil, stirring until sugar is dissolved. Remove from heat; allow to cool. Add peaches and collected peach juice to sugar syrup; chill 2 hours.

2. Combine sugar syrup and peaches in a blender with vanilla; pulse to purée. Slowly add heavy cream; blend. Pour into bowls and garnish with whipped cream.

Spiced Orange Soup with Gingersnaps

This is a slightly tart, aromatic soup that's also light and refreshing.

INGREDIENTS | SERVES 4

½ cup sugar
½ cup water
2 cinnamon sticks
3 whole cloves
1 slice fresh ginger
3 cups fresh orange juice with pulp
1 cup orange juice, frozen in ice cube trays
½ cup buttermilk
Orange slice candies
8 large gingersnap cookies

1. In a saucepan, combine sugar and water. Bring to a boil, stirring until sugar is dissolved. Add cinnamon sticks, cloves, and ginger; set aside to cool. Place in refrigerator 1 hour to cool.

2. Strain sugar syrup into blender. Add orange juice and frozen orange juice cubes' pulse until well blended. Add buttermilk. Ladle into bowls; garnish with orange slice candies. Serve with gingersnaps.

Norwegian Sweet Soup

Some cooks augment this Christmas soup with Mandarin orange slices.
Serve warm soup as is or with a scoop of vanilla ice cream.

INGREDIENTS | SERVES 6

6 cups water

½ cup sugar

1 tablespoon quick-cooking tapioca

1 cinnamon stick

1 cup halved dried apricots

½ cup diced dried apples

½ cup diced dried pears

1 cup dry-packed prunes

1 cup golden raisins

1 cup fresh or frozen pitted cherries

1 teaspoon grated lemon zest

1 teaspoon vanilla

1. In a large saucepan, combine water, sugar, and tapioca. Bring to a boil, stirring constantly. Add cinnamon stick, apricots, apples, pears, prunes, and raisins. Reduce heat to medium; cover and simmer 20 minutes, or until fruit is plump and tender.

2. Stir in cherries, lemon zest, and vanilla. Continue to simmer for 5 minutes; remove from heat. Remove cinnamon stick; serve warm.

Dried Harvest

Fresh fruit can be dried under a hot sun, in an oven, or in a food dehydrator. Regardless of the method, the result is a concentration of sugars and flavors that makes the best dried fruit an intense pleasure. Dried fruit can be used as is in recipes or it can be partially rehydrated by soaking or boiling in liquids. However, once dried, the texture of the fruit is permanently altered; it can never replace fresh fruit in dishes.

Stone Fruit Stew with Shortbread

*Although you can serve this stew as a dessert in its own right,
it really works well as a sauce for pound cake or ice cream.*

INGREDIENTS | **SERVES 6–8**

1 cup seeded diced plums

1 cup seeded diced peaches

1 cup seeded diced nectarines

1 cup seeded diced apricots

1 cup seeded cherries

1 cup sugar

1 cup water

¼ cup orange juice

1. Combine all fruits in a heavy saucepan; sprinkle with sugar. Let stand 20 minutes.

2. Add water and orange juice. Over medium-high heat, bring to a boil, stirring constantly. Reduce heat to medium low; simmer 15 minutes, stirring frequently.

3. Remove from heat. Serve warm with shortbread wedges.

Shortbread Shortcuts

Shortbread is about the simplest cookie to make. Recipes abound, but you can't go wrong by combining 2 cups of cold butter with 4 cups of flour and 1 cup of brown sugar. Just work the mixture together as you would a pie crust. Sprinkle up to ½ cup more flour over the soft dough to make it easy to handle, then roll it into a rectangle. Score the shortbread diagonally, then bake at 325°F for 20 minutes. Cool, break apart, and serve.

Warm Apple Cranberry Stew

Think of this stew as apple cobbler without the crust.
The sugar can be replaced with an equivalent amount of artificial sweetener.

INGREDIENTS | SERVES 4

2 Granny Smith apples, peeled, cored, and diced

2 Fuji or McIntosh apples, peeled, cored, and diced

1 cup dried cranberries

½ cup sugar

1 teaspoon cinnamon

1 cup apple or cranapple juice

1. Combine all ingredients in a large saucepan. Stirring constantly, bring to a boil over medium-high heat. Reduce heat to low; simmer 20 minutes, or until apples are tender.

2. Let stand at least 10 minutes. Serve warm with cookies, ice cream, or cake.

Warm Ambrosia

Fresh fruit makes all the difference in this new take on an old classic.

INGREDIENTS | SERVES 4

1 cup diced fresh pineapple

1 cup fresh Clementine orange slices, pith removed

½ cup maraschino cherries

¼ cup flaked coconut

1 cup coconut milk

1 cup miniature marshmallows

Whipped cream

1. Combine pineapple, oranges, cherries, coconut, and coconut milk in a saucepan. Gently warm ingredients over medium heat, just until fruit is heated through, about 5 minutes.

2. Serve in bowls; top with miniature marshmallows and whipped cream.

Heavenly Fare

In Greek mythology, ambrosia was the magical food of the gods on Mount Olympus. Although ambrosia fruit salad pays homage to the Olympian treat, the popular dessert actually originated in the American south sometime in the late nineteenth century. Food historians credit the availability of dried coconut with inspiring the orange-pineapple-coconut dish. Later recipes added cream, marshmallows, bananas, cherries, and even gelatin to the mix.

Stewed Cherries with Almonds

This super-simple stewed fruit dish tastes best with fresh cherries, but frozen will do in a pinch.

INGREDIENTS | SERVES 4

½ cup water
½ cup sugar
1 teaspoon almond extract
3 cups cherries
1 tablespoon cherry brandy
⅓ cup toasted slivered almonds

Cheer for Cherries

Sweet or tart cherries contain powerful, disease-fighting antioxidants. In fact, the stone fruit's red color comes from anthocyanins, compounds that may protect against heart disease by lowering cholesterol and triglycerides. Cherries also have been shown to reduce arthritis inflammation, and the fruit is a natural source of melatonin, which promotes good sleep. Not bad for only 60 calories a cup.

1. Combine water and sugar in a saucepan; bring to a boil over medium-high heat, stirring constantly until sugar is dissolved.

2. Remove from heat; carefully add almond extract and cherries. Return to medium-high heat; bring cherries to a boil. Reduce heat to medium low; simmer 5 minutes.

3. Stir in cherry brandy; remove from heat. Sprinkle with toasted almonds; serve over ice cream or pound cake.

Blackberry Stew with Sweet Biscuits

This easy-to-assemble dessert is a cross between shortcake and cobbler.
For a dramatic presentation, cut the biscuits into decorative shapes.

INGREDIENTS | **SERVES 6**

1 cup sugar

½ cup water

6 cups blackberries

1 teaspoon lemon juice

2 cups flour

½ teaspoon salt

1 tablespoon baking powder

1 cup confectioners' sugar

½ cup very cold unsalted butter

¾ cup light cream

1. In a large saucepan, combine sugar and water. Bring to a boil over medium-high heat, stirring constantly. Remove from heat; carefully add blackberries and lemon juice. Return to medium-high heat; bring mixture to a boil. Immediately reduce heat to medium low; simmer 15 minutes.

2. In a large bowl, combine flour, salt, baking powder, and confectioners' sugar; stir with whisk to blend. Add butter; cut in with a pastry blender or 2 knives. Work until mixture resembles coarse meal. Stir in cream to make a soft dough.

3. Coat hands and a work surface with additional flour. Knead dough briefly; roll out to 1 thick. Using a biscuit or cookie cutter, cut into 8 biscuits. Place on a baking sheet covered with nonstick foil, at least 1 apart. Bake at 400°F for 10–12 minutes, or until biscuits are light brown on top.

4. Ladle blackberry stew into shallow bowls; top each bowl with a hot biscuit.

Slushy Raspberry Soup

This recipe can be used with other berries or fruits to make a light summer dessert.

INGREDIENTS | SERVES 4

1 cup sugar

1 cup water

4 cups frozen raspberries

⅓ cup heavy cream

1 tablespoon brandy (optional)

Whipped cream

Fresh raspberries

Berry Smooth

Straining raspberry purée removes the hard, beady little seeds that can add unwanted texture to recipes. The combination of simple sugar syrup and puréed raspberries, strained, is the base for both raspberry sauces and raspberry sorbet. Keep a bag of raspberries in your freezer and you'll always be able to whip up a dessert sauce worthy of fancy restaurants.

1. In a heavy saucepan, combine sugar and water. Bring to a boil over high heat, stirring until sugar dissolves. Remove from heat; let come to room temperature.

2. Combine frozen raspberries and sugar syrup in a blender; pulse until smooth. Pour through a sieve into a bowl to remove seeds; discard seeds. Pour into ice cube trays; freeze 2 hours, or until firm.

3. When ready to serve, put frozen raspberry cubes, cream, and brandy in a food processor. Pulse until mixture is slushy, adding more cream if needed. Ladle into bowls; garnish with whipped cream and whole raspberries.

Bobbing Blueberries

*Instead of a rich crème Anglaise drizzled over fresh blueberries,
this recipe offers a bowl of creamy sauce covered by fruit.*

INGREDIENTS | SERVES 4

4 egg yolks

2 tablespoons flour

Pinch salt

⅔ cup sugar

3 cups milk

2 teaspoons vanilla

2 tablespoons lemon zest

2 cups fresh blueberries

1. In a bowl, whisk together egg yolks, flour, salt, and sugar until well blended. Scald milk in top of double boiler. Ladle 1 cup of hot milk into egg mixture, whisking constantly. Immediately pour tempered egg mixture into top of double boiler; whisk to blend.

2. Cook, stirring constantly, until sauce coats back of a spoon. Remove from heat; beat in vanilla and lemon zest. Pour sauce into a bowl; cover and refrigerate until well chilled. When ready to serve, pour sauce into 4 bowls; float ½ cup of blueberries over each bowl.

Minted Cantaloupe Soup

This is a summer classic. If you prefer a thinner soup, just add more orange juice.

INGREDIENTS | SERVES 4

1 ripe cantaloupe, peeled, seeded, and diced

1 cup orange juice

2 tablespoons lime juice

¼ teaspoon grated fresh ginger

¼ cup chopped fresh mint

1 cup vanilla frozen yogurt (optional)

1. Place diced cantaloupe, orange juice, lime juice, and ginger in a blender; process until smoothly puréed.

2. Pour into 4 bowls. Sprinkle with chopped mint; place 1 scoop of frozen yogurt in center of each bowl.

White Chocolate Strawberry Soup

This recipe can be used with other berries or fruits to make a light summer dessert.

INGREDIENTS | SERVES 4

1 cup sugar
1 cup water
4 cups frozen strawberries
6 ounces white chocolate
1 tablespoon Frangelico (optional)
⅓ cup heavy cream
Whipped cream
Fresh strawberries

1. In a heavy saucepan, combine sugar and water. Bring to a boil over high heat, stirring until sugar dissolves. Remove from heat; let come to room temperature.

2. Combine frozen strawberries and sugar syrup in a blender; pulse until smooth. Pour through a sieve into a bowl to remove seeds; discard seeds. Pour into ice cube trays; freeze 2 hours, or until firm.

3. Break up white chocolate into small pieces. Combine with half the cream in a heat-safe dish. Microwave on high for 30 seconds. Stir to combine. If chocolate is still hard, microwave in 10-second bursts to melt completely. Set aside chocolate and cream mixture to cool to room temperature.

4. When ready to serve, put frozen strawberry cubes, remaining cream, and Frangelico in a food processor. Pulse until mixture is slushy. With processor motor running, pour white chocolate and cream mixture into the food processor in a steady stream until completely combined. Ladle into bowls; garnish with whipped cream and whole strawberries.

CHAPTER 13

Soups and Stews for Kids

Vegetable Alphabet Soup

Frozen vegetables in resealable bags make it easy to add variety to this soup without waste. For a quicker fix, substitute 3 cups frozen mixed veggies for the carrot, peas, beans, and corn.

INGREDIENTS | SERVES 6

1 small onion, minced
1 large white potato, peeled and diced
1 large carrot, peeled and finely diced
½ cup green peas
½ cup green beans
1 cup corn
1 (14-ounce) can tomato sauce
3 cups beef broth
2 cups water
1 cup alphabet-shaped pasta
Salt and pepper to taste

1. Combine vegetables, tomato sauce, broth, and water in a large soup pot. Bring mixture to a boil over high heat; reduce heat to medium. Simmer 20 minutes, stirring occasionally.

2. When vegetables are all tender, bring soup to a boil; stir in alphabet-shaped pasta. Cook, stirring often, 5–10 minutes, or until pasta is tender. Season with salt and pepper; serve.

Cooking with Kids

Making soup is a great way to introduce children to cooking. Instead of working at the kitchen counter, bring the empty soup pot and precut ingredients to the table or a child-level surface. Show kids how to measure the vegetables and liquids to be added to the pot. Let them put the mixture together and give it a stir before you carry it to the stove. Then remind them never to touch anything on a hot stove without a grownup present.

Chicken and Stars Soup

This super-simple soup is a great way to use up bits of chicken from a roasted chicken dinner. Plus, the basic ingredients will appeal to the fussiest eaters.

INGREDIENTS | SERVES 4

7 cups chicken broth
1 clove garlic, pressed
½ cup finely chopped cooked chicken
2 tablespoons minced fresh parsley
1 cup uncooked star-shaped pasta
Salt and pepper to taste

1. Bring broth to a boil in a large soup pot over medium-high heat. Add garlic, chicken, and parsley; cook 5 minutes.

2. Add star-shaped pasta; stir well and reduce heat to medium. Cook, stirring often, 5–10 minutes, or until pasta is tender. Add salt and pepper to taste. Ladle into bowls to cool before serving.

Macaroni and Ham Soup

This homemade soup is almost as easy as opening a can. If you don't have leftover ham in the fridge, you can buy packaged, diced ham in the supermarket meat department.

INGREDIENTS | SERVES 4

6 cups chicken broth
1 (15-ounce) can small-diced tomatoes
1 cup diced ham
⅔ cup uncooked elbow macaroni
Salt and pepper to taste
Grated cheese for garnish

1. In a soup pot, combine broth, tomatoes, and ham; bring to a boil. Reduce heat; simmer 10 minutes.

2. Over high heat, return to a boil; stir in macaroni. Reduce heat to medium high; simmer until macaroni is tender, about 8–10 minutes.

3. Add salt and pepper to taste. Ladle into bowls; allow to cool slightly. Sprinkle on grated cheese; serve.

Tomato Soup with Broken Spaghetti

*This vegetarian soup is very satisfying and goes perfectly with
a grilled cheese sandwich or veggies and dip.*

INGREDIENTS | SERVES 6

1 green onion, chopped

1 clove garlic, chopped

4 piece celery, chopped

3 baby carrots, chopped

2 tablespoons olive oil

1 (15-ounce) can diced tomatoes, with liquid

1 teaspoon sugar

1 (15-ounce) can tomato sauce

4 cups water or vegetable broth

1 cup uncooked spaghetti, broken into 2 lengths

Salt and pepper to taste

1. In a large soup pot, combine green onion, garlic, celery, carrots, and olive oil; sauté over medium-high heat until vegetables begin to soften. Add diced tomatoes and sugar; bring to a boil. Reduce heat; simmer 5 minutes.

2. Carefully ladle tomato-vegetable mixture into blender or food processor; pulse until mixture is puréed. Return to soup pot. Add tomato sauce and water or broth; simmer 10 minutes over medium heat.

3. Turn heat to high; bring to a boil. Add spaghetti; stir. Cook just until pasta is tender, about 6–8 minutes. Add salt and pepper to taste; cool slightly and serve.

Veggie Loading

Sneak vegetables into soups by puréeing or cutting them into tiny pieces. Tomato soup, bean soup, and creamed soups all make great vehicles for slipping a little spinach, cabbage, or other leafy greens into children's daily menus.

Baked Potato Soup

This soup takes a bit of effort, but kids absolutely love it. To make an adult version, stir sour cream into the soup before serving and add a minced jalapeño pepper to the mix.

INGREDIENTS | SERVES 6

3 baking potatoes
6 strips bacon
½ cup butter
½ cup flour
6 cups milk
1 green onion, chopped
1 cup shredded mild Cheddar cheese
Salt and pepper to taste
Sour cream and chives for garnish

1. Bake potatoes until tender. Remove from oven; pierce with a fork. Allow to cool; peel and dice. Cook bacon until crisp; drain and crumble.

2. In a heavy soup pot, melt butter over medium heat. Add flour; whisk until well blended and bubbly. Slowly add milk while continuing to whisk. Simmer, stirring often, 10 minutes.

3. Ladle 1 cup of milk broth into blender container with ⅓ of potato cubes and green onion; blend until smooth. Pour back into soup pot; stir well.

4. Add remaining diced potatoes, bacon, and Cheddar cheese; simmer 10 minutes, stirring often.

5. Add salt and pepper; cool slightly before serving. Ladle into bowls or soup mugs; add a dollop of sour cream and chives on top.

Vegetable Barley Soup

Barley adds mild-tasting whole grain to this soup. For a heartier dish, add diced or shredded leftover pot roast or turkey to the soup in the last 10 minutes of cooking.

INGREDIENTS | SERVES 8

12 cups beef or vegetable broth

1 cup shredded cabbage

1 small onion, diced

3 cups frozen mixed vegetables

1 cup diced tomatoes

½ cup pearl barley

Salt and pepper to taste

1. Combine broth, cabbage, onion, frozen vegetables, and tomatoes in a large soup pot; bring to a boil over medium-high heat. Reduce heat to medium; simmer 10 minutes.

2. Stir in barley; cook 1 hour, stirring often.

3. When barley is tender, add salt and pepper. Let stand 10 minutes before serving.

Warming Up to Whole Grain

Nutritionists generally agree that whole grains are better for long-term health and weight management than refined flours. But how to sell kids—many of whom find the crust on white bread objectionable—on fiber-laden grains? Slipping barley, quinoa, brown rice, and whole-grain couscous into soups and stews is one way to start. The grains become part of a flavorful whole and don't command as much individual attention. Gradually increase the whole grains in your child's foods until it isn't such a big deal.

Macaroni and Cheese Soup

For a meat-free soup, substitute drained beans or diced tofu for the sausage.
Diced chicken or ham can be substituted for a milder-tasting soup.

INGREDIENTS | SERVES 4

1 (14-ounce) package macaroni and cheese
½ cup pre-packaged broccoli slaw
4 cups evaporated milk
2 cups water
2 cups shredded mild Cheddar cheese
Pinch cumin
½ cup finely diced smoked sausage
Salt and pepper to taste

1. In a large saucepan, bring 6 cups water to a boil over high heat; stir in uncooked macaroni only (not powdered cheese) and broccoli slaw. Cook until macaroni is just tender, about 9 minutes.

2. Drain macaroni and broccoli; discard water. Pour evaporated milk and water into saucepan. Cook over medium-high heat, stirring, until milk begins to bubble around edges of pan. Whisk in powdered cheese; stir in shredded Cheddar cheese. Simmer until shredded cheese has melted; add cumin.

3. Add sausage, macaroni, and broccoli slaw to pan; turn heat to medium low. Stir and simmer 5 minutes; add salt and pepper. Cool in pan a few minutes; serve.

Croquette Soup

These golden croquettes can be floated in homemade or ready-to-serve tomato soup or beef soup, in addition to chicken broth.

INGREDIENTS | SERVES 6

1½ cups seasoned mashed potatoes
½ cup shredded Colby cheese
1 egg
2 tablespoons flour
½ cup minced ham or corned beef
1 green onion, minced
1 tablespoon ranch dressing
1 cup fine bread crumbs
Vegetable oil for frying
10 cups chicken broth

Do the Mash

Leftover mashed potatoes can be recycled in a variety of ways, all delicious. Thinned with milk, mashed potatoes can become the base for creamy herb-flavored soups. Recipes for many croquettes, fritters, and seafood cakes use mashed potatoes instead of bread for fillers. Mashed potato mounds can top a savory pie. And, you can always press cold mashed potatoes into a pie pan, brush with butter or top with cheese and breadcrumbs, and bake until browned. Ladle your favorite thick stew into the crust for a clever entrée.

1. In a large bowl, combine mashed potatoes, cheese, and egg; mix until well blended. Sprinkle flour over top of potatoes; work into mixture. Fold in minced ham or corned beef, green onion, and dressing.

2. Roll potato mixture into 2 long ovals. (If mixture seems too soft, add a little more flour.) Roll ovals in bread crumbs to coat. Pour vegetable oil into a heavy skillet to a depth of 1. Over medium-high heat, brown croquettes on all sides. Remove to a plate covered with paper towels.

3. Heat broth. Place several croquettes in each of 6 shallow soup bowls. Ladle broth over croquettes; serve.

Three-Bean Soup

This slow-cooking soup can be made in a double batch and frozen in individual portions in resealable plastic bags. When it's time to pack a school lunch, just heat one portion in the microwave and pour it into a Thermos jar.

INGREDIENTS | SERVES 8

2 cups dry white beans

2 cups dry red beans

2 cups dry lima beans

1 (10-ounce) can mild tomatoes and green chilies

1 small onion, diced

1 rib celery, diced

2 ham hocks, rinsed

1 teaspoon mild chili powder

Salt and pepper to taste

1. Rinse beans well; place in a large glass or ceramic bowl. Add water until beans are covered by a few inches. Cover bowl; place in a cool spot and let beans soak for 6 hours, or overnight.

2. Drain beans. Place soaked beans, tomatoes and green chilies, onion, celery, and ham hocks in a large soup pot; add 10 cups water. Stir in chili powder. Bring to a boil over high heat; reduce heat to medium low and cook, stirring occasionally, 2 hours. As soup cooks, skim off foam that rises to top.

3. When beans reach desired tenderness, remove from heat; season with salt and pepper. Let stand 10 minutes; serve.

Creamy Corny Soup

This soup can be turned into an entrée with the addition of shredded chicken or diced smoked turkey.

INGREDIENTS | SERVES 6

1 (15-ounce) can creamed corn

1½ cups frozen corn

1 small zucchini, diced

1 medium tomato, diced

4 cups vegetable or chicken broth

1 cup cream

Salt and pepper to taste

Croutons (optional)

1. In a large saucepan, combine creamed corn, frozen corn, zucchini, tomato, and broth. Stirring frequently, cook soup 15 minutes over medium-high heat.

2. Remove soup from heat; stir in cream. Add salt and pepper to taste. Serve with croutons.

Mild Cheesy Chili

Serve this chili with baked tortilla chips for a healthy lunch that feels like fun food. Feel free to substitute your favorite chili seasoning packet for the chili powder.

INGREDIENTS | SERVES 6

1 pound lean ground beef

1 medium onion, diced

1 small bell pepper, diced

2 tablespoons mild chili powder

1 (14-ounce) can red kidney beans

1 (15-ounce) can tomato sauce

1 (15-ounce) can diced tomatoes

1 cup water

Salt and pepper to taste

3 cups shredded Colby cheese

Chili Powder Versus Chili Seasoning Mixes

Chili powder is a blend of dried and powdered peppers, plus cumin, oregano, and other seasonings. Some spice companies bottle single-source powders made from specific types of chilies, and many carry powders in mild or hot versions. Packets of chili seasoning usually contain finely ground chili powder, plus salt and thickeners.

1. In a large, heavy saucepan combine ground beef, onion, and bell pepper; cook over medium-high heat, stirring to break up beef. When ground beef is completely browned, drain fat. Sprinkle with chili powder; stir well.

2. Add beans, tomato sauce, tomatoes, and 1 cup water; cook over medium heat 30 minutes, stirring often. When chili is thick and most of water has cooked out, season with salt and pepper.

3. Remove from heat; stir in Colby cheese until melted. Let cool slightly; ladle into bowls.

Chili Dog Soup

Serve this dish with corn muffins or old-fashioned corn chips for a fun rainy-day lunch.

INGREDIENTS	SERVES 8

1 recipe Mild Cheesy Chili (page 241)
1½ cups beef broth
24 cocktail-sized wieners
Sweet relish for garnish

1. Prepare Mild Cheesy Chili, but don't add cheese yet. Stir in broth and cocktail wieners. Over medium-high heat, bring to a boil; simmer 10 more minutes.

2. Ladle soup into bowls; sprinkle cheese over top. Put a dab of sweet relish in the center of each; serve.

Edamame Ramen Soup

Children love crisp, green edamame (fresh soy) beans. They have a mild flavor and are packed with protein and disease-fighting phytochemicals. Let the kids help you shell them.

INGREDIENTS	SERVES 4

4 cups water
2 packages chicken or vegetarian ramen noodles
1 cup shelled edamame beans
Dash soy sauce

1. Bring water to a boil in a large saucepan; add ramen noodles. Stir, separating noodles as they soften. In 3 minutes, remove from heat.

2. Stir in seasoning mix packet from ramen and edamame; stir until seasoning powder has dissolved. Add a dash of soy sauce; let stand 1 minute before serving.

Fishy Fish Soup

This is a great introduction to seafood soup for kids who normally eschew anything from the sea. For older kids, try adding a couple of tablespoons of chopped steamed clams to the mix.

INGREDIENTS | SERVES 4

8-ounce fillet of mild white fish

6 cups chicken or seafood broth

2 cups Clammato juice

1 cup diced potato

1 cup corn

4 rib celery, sliced

1 cup uncooked fish-shaped noodles

Pinch dried mixed Italian herbs

Salt and pepper to taste

Best Catch

Fish offers flavorful, high-quality protein, along with some beneficial fatty acids. However, some varieties of fish harbor high levels of mercury and other toxins and should not be fed to children. Shark, swordfish, king mackerel, and tilefish are among the ocean fish with high mercury levels, and heavy metals have been found in some freshwater fish like bass and catfish. Most varieties of fish—like cod, tuna, salmon, wild trout, haddock, grouper, and sablefish—are safe to eat once a week.

1. Cut fish into 1 cubes; return to refrigerator. In a heavy saucepan, bring broth and Clammato to a boil; add potatoes, corn, and celery. Reduce heat to medium; cook until veggies are tender, about 10 minutes.

2. Turn heat on high; when soup begins to boil, stir in fish-shaped noodles. Cook until noodles are almost soft, about 5 minutes.

3. Add diced fish; turn heat to medium low. Simmer 3 minutes, or until fish turns opaque. Stir in dried herbs, salt, and pepper. Cool slightly; serve.

Chicken Nugget Parmesan Stew

If you have children, chances are you have some sort of "nugget" in the freezer.
Breaded fish nuggets or vegetarian nuggets can be substituted for the chicken.

INGREDIENTS | SERVES 6

1 pound frozen breaded chicken nuggets

2 tablespoons olive oil

2 cups diced zucchini

1 cup diced yellow squash

½ cup sliced baby carrots

1 small onion, diced

1 (26-ounce) jar ready-to-serve pasta sauce

1 cup chicken broth or water

2 cups shredded Italian cheese blend

1. Place nuggets on a baking sheet lined with nonstick foil. Bake according to package directions, until nuggets are browned and crisp. Remove from oven; set aside.

2. In a heavy saucepan, heat olive oil over medium-high heat. Add zucchini, squash, carrots, and onion; sauté until vegetables are crisp-tender, about 3 or 4 minutes.

3. Add pasta sauce and broth or water. Reduce heat to medium; simmer 15 minutes.

4. Pour stew into a baking dish. Carefully drop chicken nuggets over sauce in a single layer; sprinkle cheese over all. Bake in 350°F oven for 10 minutes, or until cheese is melted and lightly browned. Let stand 5 minutes before serving.

Campfire-Style Hamburger Stew

Anyone who ever went Girl Scout or Boy Scout camping has eaten a version of this stew,
prepared in a pan over a campfire. It isn't gourmet, but it's fun and filling.

INGREDIENTS | SERVES 4

1 pound ground beef

2 (10-ounce) cans condensed vegetable soup

1 soup-can water

Salt and pepper to taste

1. Brown ground beef in large skillet; carefully drain fat. Add soup and water; stir well.

2. Bring to a boil over medium-high heat. Reduce heat to medium; simmer 10 minutes. Add salt and pepper to taste. Serve in bowls or soup mugs with bread and crackers.

Pizza Stew

Favorite pizza flavors make this stew an easy sell to kids and even pizza-loving adults.
Buy ready-to-bake pizza dough in your supermarket bakery department.

INGREDIENTS | SERVES 6

1 pound mild bulk sausage

1 cup sliced mushrooms

⅓ cup diced green bell pepper

1 cup quartered pepperoni slices

2 cups prepared pizza sauce

1 (14-ounce) can diced tomatoes

½ cup grated Parmesan cheese

1 pound ready-to-bake pizza dough

2 cups shredded mozzarella cheese

Grab the Dough

One of the greatest convenience foods to become available in supermarkets is ready-to-bake pizza dough, usually sold in one-pound bags in the bakery or deli refrigerator case. In addition to using the dough for pizza, you can also roll it out to serve as a bottom or top crust for pot pies and savory cobblers. Or just roll it out and brush with olive oil, garlic, and herbs. Bake, and serve in wedges with your favorite soup.

1. In a large saucepan, brown sausage; drain fat. Add mushrooms, peppers, pepperoni, pizza sauce, and tomatoes; bring to a boil over medium-high heat. Reduce heat to medium; simmer 10 minutes. Stir in Parmesan cheese.

2. Lightly grease deep baking dish; press pizza dough over bottom and up sides of dish. Pour stew mixture into crust; top with mozzarella. Bake at 350°F for 25 minutes, or until crust and cheese have browned.

3. Let stand 10 minutes before serving.

Chicken Wagon Wheel Stew

This boneless chicken stew can be served over rice or flat noodles. Just omit the pasta from the recipe.

INGREDIENTS | SERVES 6

6 chicken breast halves

4 tablespoons olive oil

4 tablespoons flour

1 medium onion, diced

2 cups chicken broth

½ teaspoon poultry seasoning

1 cup baby carrots

1 cup frozen green beans

½ cup half-and-half

3 cups cooked wagon wheel-shaped pasta

Salt and pepper to taste

1. Trim any fat from chicken; cut each fillet in half crosswise to make 12 pieces. In a large, heavy saucepan over medium-high heat, brown chicken pieces in olive oil; remove to a plate.

2. Add flour to oil; cook, stirring constantly, until mixture is smooth and lightly browned. Add onion; cook 1 more minute. Slowly whisk in broth. Bring mixture to a boil; add poultry seasoning, carrots, and green beans.

3. Reduce heat to medium; return chicken to pot. Simmer, uncovered, 20 minutes, or until chicken is cooked through and carrots are tender.

4. Stir in half-and-half and cooked pasta. Simmer 2 minutes, stirring to coat pasta with sauce. Season with salt and pepper to taste. Let stand 5 minutes before serving.

Turkey Stew with Stuffing

This is a quick-fix recipe that kids love.
Use Thanksgiving leftovers or just buy a turkey breast half and grab a box of instant stuffing.

INGREDIENTS | SERVES 4

4 cups diced cooked turkey

2 (10-ounce) cans condensed cream of mushroom soup

1 cup water

Dash soy sauce

1 cup green peas

Salt and pepper to taste

4 cups prepared bread or cornbread stuffing

1. In a heavy saucepan, combine turkey, cream of mushroom soup, water, soy sauce, and peas; cook over medium-high heat until mixture begins to bubble, about 5 minutes. Reduce heat to medium low; simmer, stirring often, 10 minutes.

2. Season with salt and pepper; remove from heat.

3. Divide stuffing into 4 portions. Press each portion into bottom and up sides of an oven-safe bowl or tart pan or oversized muffin cups. Bake in 350°F oven 10 minutes.

4. Remove from oven; place 1 baked stuffing shell in each plate or bowl. Ladle turkey stew into stuffing shell; serve.

Turkey Taco Stew

Serve this low-fat stew over rice or in bowls with corn muffins on the side for a quick weeknight supper.
For variety, substitute a can of black beans for the potatoes.

INGREDIENTS | SERVES 6

1 pound ground turkey

1 (1¼-ounce) packet taco seasoning

1 (14-ounce) can diced tomatoes with onion

2 cups diced potatoes

2 cups corn

1 cup water

Salt and pepper to taste

1. In a nonstick saucepan, cook turkey until meat is no longer pink.

2. Add taco seasoning, tomatoes, potatoes, corn, and water. Stir well; simmer over medium heat until potatoes are tender, about 15 minutes.

3. Remove from heat; season with salt and pepper. Let stand 5 minutes; serve.

Meatball Stew

Kids love meatballs, so this basic stew is sure to delight. Add any vegetables you like to make it a one-dish meal or serve the stew over noodles with a side of raw veggies and dip.

INGREDIENTS | SERVES 6

1½ pounds ground beef
¼ cup minced parsley
¼ cup minced green onion
1 egg
¼ cup commercial barbecue sauce
1 cup bread crumbs
½ cup vegetable oil
½ cup flour
1 large onion, diced
3 cups beef broth
¼ cup ketchup
8 ounces sliced white mushrooms
Salt and pepper to taste

Meatball Mania

Virtually every culinary tradition has some form of meatballs, some of which may be made with beef, pork, lamb, or even a combination of meats and grains. These versatile creations can add substance to virtually any sauce or broth. Better still, they freeze exceptionally well. Get in the habit of making large batches of meatballs and freezing a dozen or more in plastic bags for later use.

1. In a large bowl, combine ground beef, parsley, green onion, egg, and barbecue sauce; mix well, distributing all ingredients evenly through beef. Add bread crumbs a little at a time, mixing well after each addition. Roll into 24 firm meatballs.

2. In a large saucepan or Dutch oven, heat oil over medium-high heat. Brown meatballs a few at a time; remove to a platter lined with paper towels.

3. When all meatballs have been browned, add flour to oil; stir until mixture forms a smooth roux. Cook, stirring constantly, until roux turns medium brown. Turn off heat; carefully add onions. Continue stirring until onions begin to brown around edges.

4. Turn burner to medium-high heat; whisk in broth. Stir in ketchup and mushrooms; bring to a boil. Reduce heat to medium; simmer 10 minutes.

5. Return meatballs to pan; cook 20 minutes, or until meatballs are cooked through and sauce is thick. Season with salt and pepper; serve.

Barbecue Stew

This mild, quick-fix version of Brunswick Stew is designed to make use of leftovers and convenience foods from the supermarket. If you don't have leftover pot roast, substitute ready-to-heat shredded barbecue beef or pork.

INGREDIENTS | SERVES 6

1 cup diced rotisserie chicken

2 cups shredded leftover pot roast or brisket

1 (14-ounce) can fire-roasted tomatoes

1 cup hickory-flavored barbecue sauce

1 medium onion, diced

1 cup frozen corn

1 cup frozen lima beans

1 (14-ounce) can barbecue-flavored baked beans

1 cup water or chicken broth

Salt and pepper to taste

1. Combine chicken, pot roast, tomatoes, barbecue sauce, onions, corn, lima beans, and baked beans in a large saucepan. Stir well to combine; add water or broth.

2. Over medium-high heat, bring to a boil. Reduce heat to medium low; simmer 15 minutes.

3. Season with salt and pepper. Serve in bowls or over wedges of cornbread.

CHAPTER 14

Dinner Party Fare

Beef Stroganoff

This is a classic version of a 100-year-old Russian dish that first hit the dinner party circuit in the 1950s. More economical family dinner recipes exist, but top-quality sirloin or even tenderloin distinguishes true Stroganoff from pretenders.

INGREDIENTS | SERVES 6

1½ pounds top sirloin, 1 thick

½ cup flour

Salt and pepper to taste

8 tablespoons unsalted butter

2 shallots, minced

1 pound white or cremini mushrooms, cleaned and sliced

1 cup water

1 tablespoon tomato paste

¼ cup sherry

1½ cups sour cream, room temperature

Menu Planning

Friends may like to congregate in your kitchen, but nobody wants to watch you slaving over a complicated meal during a dinner party. Soups, stews, and exotic chilies are great dinner-party fare because most of the prep work, and even a good bit of the cooking, is done well in advance. All you have to do is put finishing touches on the dish or turn on the stove for a few minutes and you're ready to ladle up some excitement.

1. Thinly slice beef across the grain. Toss slices in flour to coat lightly; sprinkle with salt and pepper. Place butter in a heavy skillet over high heat; quickly brown beef on each side. Work in batches; remove beef to plate when browned.

2. Add shallots to pan; sauté 1 minute, stirring up pan drippings as you stir. Add mushrooms; sauté an additional 2 minutes.

3. Stir in water and tomato paste. Bring to a boil; add sherry. Reduce heat to medium; simmer 10 minutes.

4. Return beef to pan; cook 1–2 minutes. Whisk sour cream into pan; stir. Continue cooking just until sour cream is warm, about 30 seconds; do not allow sauce to bubble or boil. Serve immediately over cooked noodles.

Crawfish Stew in Eggplant Shells

The trickiest part of this recipe is scooping out the eggplant to make a shell.
Try using a melon baller or serrated-edge grapefruit spoon to make the task easier.

INGREDIENTS | SERVES 4

1 recipe Crawfish Stew (page 189)
2 large eggplants
Salt
1 egg, beaten with 1 tablespoon water
1 cup seasoned bread crumbs
⅓ cup olive oil
⅔ cup finely diced plum tomatoes

Eggplant Savvy

The best eggplants are blemish free, feel heavy for their size, and have soft, pale seeds. Young, small purple or white eggplants and long Asian-style eggplants usually can be used as is. Larger Italian-style eggplant may need to be lightly salted and drained before using; the salt draws out the bitterness in mature eggplants.

1. Prepare Crawfish Stew in advance; allow to come to room temperature.

2. Wash eggplants; cut in half lengthwise. Scoop pulp from center, leaving ½ thick shell; discard pulp or reserve for other use. Lightly salt inside of eggplant; place cut side down on paper towels to drain. Let stand 10 minutes.

3. Rinse salt from eggplant; pat dry with paper towel. Brush beaten egg and water mixture over insides and rims of shells; sprinkle evenly with bread crumbs.

4. Heat olive oil in a large, nonstick skillet over high heat. Place eggplant shells, cut side down, in skillet; cook 5 minutes, until edges become browned.

5. Carefully remove shells; place cut-side up in a baking dish. Place baking dish in 350°F oven 10 minutes.

6. Carefully remove pan from oven. Using a slotted spoon, fill each shell with Crawfish Stew. Return to oven; bake 15–20 minutes.

7. Remove from oven; garnish with finely diced plum tomatoes. Let stand 2–3 minutes before serving.

Shrimp and Chanterelle Stroganoff

This dish looks impressive and it's very easy to make. The sauce can be prepared up to a day in advance; just reheat it and add the shrimp and sour cream the day of your party.

INGREDIENTS | SERVES 8

4 tablespoons butter

2 shallots, minced

2 cloves garlic, minced

4 plum tomatoes, diced

1 pound chanterelle mushrooms, separated

4 ounces portobello mushrooms, finely chopped

1 cup dry white wine

1 cup heavy cream

3 pounds shrimp, peeled and deveined

1 tablespoon chopped fresh tarragon

1 cup sour cream, room temperature

Salt and pepper to taste

1. Melt butter in a heavy saucepan over medium-high heat. Add shallots and garlic; sauté 2 minutes.

2. Add diced tomatoes; cook an additional 2 minutes. Add mushrooms; cook, stirring frequently, until mushrooms soften.

3. Add white wine and heavy cream to mushroom mixture. Bring to a boil; stir well. Add shrimp; cook just until shrimp begin to turn opaque, about 2 minutes.

4. Remove from heat; stir in chopped tarragon, sour cream, salt, and pepper. Serve immediately over wild rice pilaf or basmati rice.

Grilled Ratatouille under a Fontina Crust

Serve this dish as a first course or a vegetarian entrée.
The best part is, the grilled ratatouille can be prepared in advance.

INGREDIENTS | SERVES 4

2 cups baby zucchini

1 cup baby yellow squash

1 cup white mushrooms, halved

2 cups grape tomatoes

½ cup olive oil

1 tablespoon balsamic vinegar

2 cloves garlic, pressed

Salt and pepper to taste

⅓ cup fresh basil ribbons

8 ounces Fontina cheese slices

1. Combine zucchini, squash, mushrooms, and grape tomatoes in a large bowl. Whisk together oil, vinegar, and garlic. Pour over vegetables; toss to coat. Sprinkle with salt and pepper to taste. Let stand 10 minutes.

2. Place vegetables in a grill basket; grill over medium heat 10 minutes, or until tender.

3. Divide vegetables over 4 lightly oiled individual soufflé or tart pans; sprinkle with basil ribbons. Divide Fontina slices evenly over pans. Bake in 350°F oven 10 minutes, or until cheese is browned and bubbly. Allow to cool slightly before serving.

Beef, Chicken, and Shrimp Fajita Stew

This homey stew turns into a dish fit for company with the addition of chicken, shrimp, and fajita fixings. Yellow rice and black beans are the best side choices.

INGREDIENTS | SERVES 8

2 pounds top round steak

¼ cup flour

¼ cup vegetable oil

1 large onion, halved and sliced

1 (16-ounce) can diced roasted tomatoes

2 (1-ounce) envelopes fajita seasoning mix

1 cup water

1 yellow bell pepper, cored and sliced

1 green bell pepper, cored and sliced

1 pound boneless, skinless chicken breast halves

1 pound shrimp, peeled and deveined.

⅓ cup minced cilantro

Sour cream, salsa, and avocado slices for garnish

Upgrade Ingredients

Food for company doesn't have to mean wandering into uncharted culinary territory. Instead of reaching for a double boiler and assorted hollandaise-sauce recipes, just peruse your list of family favorites. Then, upgrade the profile of your favorite comfort dish by adding "luxury" ingredients like beef tenderloin, shrimp, or lobster. Or just provide an impressive, colorful array of garnishes and side dishes and set a beautiful table.

1. Trim steaks; cut into 4 pieces. Dredge in flour. In a large Dutch oven, heat oil over medium-high heat. Brown beef; remove to a plate. Add onion; sauté for 3 minutes.

2. Add tomatoes, fajita seasoning, and water; stir well. Return beef to pot.

3. Reduce heat to medium and cover. Simmer, stirring occasionally, 20 minutes. Add more water to the pot if additional liquid is needed.

4. Add bell peppers and chicken. Cover; cook 15 minutes longer.

5. Add shrimp; adjust liquid and cook just until shrimp turn opaque, about 5 minutes.

6. Sprinkle cilantro over all. To serve, carefully remove beef to a cutting board; slice across grain. Arrange beef in one area of a deep serving platter or baking dish. Slice chicken breasts; arrange next to beef. Remove shrimp from pot; arrange next to chicken. Ladle sauce over beef, chicken, and fish; pile onions and peppers together. Serve with sour cream, salsa, and avocado slices.

Cajun Jambalaya Stew

Don't let the length of the ingredients list deter you.
This dish is simple to make and rewards you and your guests with layers of bold flavors.

INGREDIENTS | SERVES 8

1 tablespoon vegetable oil
1 pound andouille sausage, sliced
1 large onion, diced
1 rib celery, sliced
1 bell pepper, cored and diced
2 garlic cloves, minced
½ pound diced ham
1 pound boneless skinless chicken, diced
2 pounds shrimp, peeled and deveined
1 (14-ounce) can diced tomatoes
3 (14-ounce) cans tomato sauce
2 cups chicken broth
1 teaspoon Tabasco sauce
2 bay leaves
1 teaspoon rubbed sage
½ teaspoon dried thyme leaves
⅓ cup sliced green onions
⅓ cup minced fresh parsley
Salt and pepper to taste

1. In a heavy soup pot over medium-high heat, combine oil and sliced andouille. Sauté, stirring constantly, until sausage begins to brown. Add onion, celery, and bell pepper; continue to sauté 3–5 minutes, until vegetables are crisp-tender.

2. Add garlic, ham, chicken, and shrimp. Stir well to blend; cook 1 minute. Add tomatoes, tomato sauce, broth, Tabasco, bay leaves, sage, and thyme; stir to combine. Bring to a boil.

3. Reduce heat to medium low; cover. Simmer 40 minutes, stirring occasionally.

4. Remove cover; continue cooking an additional 20 minutes, or until mixture reaches desired thickness.

5. Turn off heat; add green onions, parsley, salt, and pepper. Cover; let stand 5 minutes before serving. Serve with steamed white rice.

Corned Beef and Cabbage Soup in Rye Bowls

This dish is perfect for game-day parties when the gang gathers around the TV.
Oven-simmered homecooked corned-beef brisket gives this soup the best taste and texture.

INGREDIENTS | SERVES 6

1½ pounds cooked corned beef, trimmed and shredded

1 small head cabbage, cored and diced

1 medium onion, diced

10 cups chicken broth

Dash ground cloves

Salt and pepper to taste

6 round ½-pound loaves rye or pumpernickel bread

1 cup sour cream mixed with ¼ cup coarse mustard

1. In a large soup pot over high heat, combine shredded corned beef, cabbage, onion, broth, and cloves; bring mixture to a boil. Reduce heat to medium; simmer 20 minutes, until cabbage is tender and broth is reduced. Soup should be thick. Add salt and pepper.

2. Slice off top quarter of each bread loaf; reserve. Remove some of soft interior of loaves, creating a hollow bowl. Place each bread bowl on a plate or in a shallow bowl; fill with soup. Place a dollop of mustard-laced sour cream at top of each bowl; serve with bread top on side.

The Gang's All Here

When it comes to good friends, sometimes getting together is more important than putting out a fancy spread. Don't let time or budget concerns keep you from enjoying good times. Prepare a main-dish soup, chili, or stew, stock the cooler with drinks, then ask everyone to bring a dish. You'll wind up with a fun smorgasbord and great memories.

Deep-Dish Pepperoni Pie

*At first glance, this looks like a pizza recipe, but a deep-dish pizza this saucy
is really just an oven-simmered cheesy stew with a bread base.*

INGREDIENTS | SERVES 6

1 pound ready-to-bake pizza dough

2 cups thick marinara sauce

1 (16-ounce) container ricotta cheese

2 cups cooked fresh spinach

4 cups sliced pepperoni

1 bell pepper, cored and sliced

2 cups shredded Asiago cheese

2 cups shredded mozzarella cheese

2 cups shredded provolone cheese

1. Press dough into bottom and partway up sides of lightly oiled deep 13 × 9 baking pan. Ladle ½ cup of sauce onto dough; spread to coat. Dot dough with ricotta cheese. Press as much liquid as possible from cooked spinach; spread half over ricotta, followed by half of pepperoni and all of bell pepper.

2. Ladle 2 cups of sauce over peppers; use a fork to move ingredients slightly so sauce can penetrate. Combine all shredded cheeses; distribute ½ over dish. Top with remaining pepperoni, remaining spinach, and remaining sauce. Spread remaining cheese mixture over dish.

3. Cover loosely with foil; bake in 325°F oven 30 minutes. Remove foil; bake an additional 10–15 minutes, or until cheese is browned and bubbly.

Grilled Chicken in Warm Salsa

The trick to this dish is warming, but not cooking, the salsa.
The ingredients meld together and give the chicken a take-notice, fresh backdrop.

INGREDIENTS | SERVES 6

6 chicken breast halves
½ cup olive oil
½ cup balsamic vinegar
Salt and pepper to taste
6 cups diced ripe tomatoes
1 cup finely diced onions
2 cloves garlic, minced
3 jalapeño peppers, minced
⅓ cup fresh lime juice
⅓ cup minced cilantro

1. Place chicken breast halves in resealable plastic bag. Whisk together oil and vinegar; pour over chicken. Seal bag; refrigerate 2–4 hours.

2. Half an hour before dinner time, remove chicken from marinade; add salt and pepper. Heat an indoor or outdoor grill; grill chicken over medium-high heat 6–8 minutes per side. Remove to deep serving platter.

3. After placing chicken in marinade, prepare salsa. In a glass or ceramic bowl, combine tomatoes, onions, garlic, jalapeño peppers, lime juice, and cilantro. Mix well; cover and refrigerate.

4. While chicken is grilling, use a slotted spoon to transfer salsa to a deep skillet. Heat, stirring often, over medium-high heat. As soon as it is heated through, spoon around grilled chicken breasts on serving platter.

Wild Mushroom Pot Pies

The term "wild mushrooms" is a bit of a misnomer, since most mushrooms are cultivated these days. Many supermarkets sell prepackaged mushroom mixes in the produce section. Otherwise, put together any combination of oyster mushrooms, chanterelles, shiitakes, straw mushrooms, enokis, and morels.

INGREDIENTS | SERVES 4

2 pounds wild mushrooms

4 tablespoons butter

2 shallots, minced

2 cloves garlic, minced

¼ cup granulated flour

½ cup white wine

1 cup heavy cream

Salt and pepper to taste

1 teaspoon truffle oil

1 sheet frozen puff pastry, thawed

1 egg beaten with 1 tablespoon water

1. Wash mushrooms; separate any clusters. Set on paper towels to dry. In a large, heavy saucepan over high heat, melt butter; sauté shallots 3 minutes.

2. Add garlic and mushrooms; sauté until mushrooms are tender, about 5 minutes.

3. Sprinkle mushrooms with flour; stir to coat. Slowly add wine to mushrooms, stirring to dissolve flour. Bring to a boil; reduce heat to medium. Slowly add heavy cream, salt, and pepper; simmer until mixture thickens slightly. Remove from heat; stir in truffle oil.

4. Divide mushrooms into 4 buttered individual soufflé or tart pans. Cut 4 circles from puff pastry sheet; circles should just fit over mushroom mixture in pans. Lightly brush pastry caps with egg and water mixture.

5. Bake in 375°F oven 15 minutes, or until pastry caps turn flaky and light brown. Remove from heat; cool slightly and serve.

New England Lobster Chowder

Clean lobster shells can be boiled to make lobster stock for this recipe,
or you can buy lobster base in the gourmet section of your supermarket.

INGREDIENTS | SERVES 8

4 slices bacon, cut into 1 strips

1 small onion, finely diced

1 small green pepper, finely diced

1 small rib celery, finely chopped

2 cloves garlic, minced

1 carrot, finely diced

4 tablespoons butter

⅓ cup flour

8 cups hot lobster stock

4 russet potatoes, peeled and diced

2 cups corn kernels

2 cups cooked lobster, in small chunks

2 cups heavy cream

Salt and pepper to taste

Dash sherry

1. In a tall soup pot over medium heat, cook bacon until tender. Add onion, bell pepper, celery, garlic, and carrot; sauté with bacon until vegetables are crisp-tender, about 5 minutes.

2. Add butter; when melted, add flour and stir well. Add hot stock, potatoes, and corn; bring to a boil, stirring frequently. Simmer 20 minutes, until mixture is slightly reduced and potatoes are cooked.

3. Add lobster meat, heavy cream, salt, and pepper; simmer 10 minutes. Add sherry to individual servings as desired.

Maine Versus Florida Lobsters

New Englanders can rest assured that their indigenous crustaceans have the sweetest meat and fattest claws. But that doesn't mean Florida spiny lobsters—which are really a kind of ocean crawfish—aren't also delicious. Depending on the season, they're also less expensive than Maine lobsters and work very well in seafood soups and stews.

Gazpacho with Lump Crabmeat

Very ripe tomatoes give this soup a sweet, bright flavor.
For a beautiful presentation, serve this soup in oversized martini glasses.

INGREDIENTS | SERVES 6

4 large ripe tomatoes, chopped

1 small red onion, chopped

1 cucumber, peeled and chopped

½ green pepper, seeded and chopped

1 clove garlic, peeled and chopped

½ rib celery, chopped

¼ cup fresh parsley

¼ cup red wine vinegar

¼ cup extra-virgin olive oil

1 teaspoon Worcestershire sauce

1 teaspoon sugar

2 cups tomato juice

1 large avocado, cut into 6 wedges

1 pound chilled lump crabmeat

1. Combine all ingredients except tomato juice, avocado, and crabmeat in a blender or food processor; pulse until puréed.

2. Strain mixture through coarse strainer into glass bowl or pitcher; press to extract all juices. Stir in tomato juice; cover and refrigerate until well chilled.

3. Just before serving, slice avocado. Pour gazpacho into bowls or stemmed glasses; garnish each with a wedge of avocado. Spoon crabmeat into center of each serving.

Pork Tenderloin in Roasted Root Vegetable Stew

*Serve this hearty, colorful dish in the fall just as the leaves are beginning to turn.
For best results, vegetables should be diced 1 or smaller.*

INGREDIENTS | SERVES 6

¼ cup plus 1 tablespoon olive oil

1 tablespoon balsamic vinegar

1 medium onion, diced

8 large cloves garlic, peeled

1 cup diced parsnips

1 cup diced rutabaga

1 cup diced turnips

1 cup diced beets

1 cup diced carrots

1 cup diced potatoes

1 cup diced sweet potatoes

Salt and pepper to taste

2 tablespoons fresh rosemary leaves

1½ pounds pork tenderloin

1 tablespoon soy sauce

2 tablespoons orange zest

½ cup orange juice

1. Whisk together ¼ cup olive oil and balsamic vinegar. In a heavy roasting pan, combine onion, 6 cloves garlic, and all diced vegetables; toss with oil and vinegar to coat. Season with salt and pepper; sprinkle rosemary leaves over. Bake in 350°F oven 1 hour, stirring occasionally.

2. In another baking dish, place pork tenderloins; coat with remaining olive oil and sprinkle with soy sauce. Put remaining 2 garlic cloves through press; spread evenly over pork. Pat orange zest evenly over pork. Bake in 350°F oven 15–20 minutes. Add orange juice in last 5 minutes of cooking to deglaze the pan.

3. Remove tenderloin to a heated serving platter; let stand 5 minutes. Slice thickly; ladle pan drippings over slices. Spoon veggies around pork; serve.

Creamy Cucumber Dill Soup with Caviar

This brunch or lunch soup can be extravagant—with pricey imported beluga caviar—or just tasty. For a non-budget-busting alternative, explore American farmed sturgeon caviar or the many inexpensive nonsturgeon roes.

INGREDIENTS | SERVES 4

5 cucumbers, peeled and seeded

1½ cups plain yogurt

1 cup sour cream

1 teaspoon sugar

¼ teaspoon Dijon mustard

1 tablespoon fresh lemon juice

¼ cup fresh dill

Salt and pepper to taste

2 tablespoons black or red caviar

1 tablespoon lemon-zest strips

1. Coarsely chop 4 peeled and seeded cucumbers; combine in a food processor with yogurt, ⅔ cup of sour cream, sugar, mustard, lemon juice, and dill. Process until smooth and creamy. Add salt and pepper to taste.

2. Refrigerate until well chilled. Dice remaining cucumber; divide over 4 glass bowls. Ladle soup into bowls; top each serving with a dollop of remaining sour cream. Carefully spoon ½ tablespoon of caviar onto sour cream. Garnish with a few lemon-zest strips. Serve immediately.

Strong Flavors, Big Impact

Cool, refreshing cucumber soup gets a burst of salty ocean flavor from caviar. Even if you don't like fish eggs, which are admittedly an acquired taste, you can use the same culinary principle by topping a subtle soup with a sliver of smoked salmon, a teaspoon of olive tapenade, or just a dollop of wasabi-laced sour cream. This technique works especially well with cold fruit and vegetable soups.

Roasted Salmon with Scallop and Mushroom Ragout

Oven-roasted salmon is simple to prepare and lends itself to a wide variety of embellishments. This dish pays homage to the French classic Coquilles St. Jacques.

INGREDIENTS | SERVES 8

2 pounds salmon fillet
1 tablespoon olive oil
Salt and pepper to taste
3 tablespoons butter
2 shallots, minced
1 pound quartered white mushrooms
½ pound quartered crimini mushrooms
2 plum tomatoes, diced
2 tablespoons flour
1½ cups heavy cream
2 tablespoons brandy
1 pound bay scallops
Pinch dried thyme
Chopped fresh parsley for garnish

1. Place salmon skin-side down in a shallow roasting pan lined with nonstick foil; rub top with olive oil and sprinkle with salt and pepper. Place in 400°F oven 12–15 minutes, depending on thickness of salmon; do not overcook.

2. In a large, heavy saucepan, melt butter over high heat. Add shallots; sauté 2 minutes.

3. Add mushrooms; sauté 5 minutes.

4. Add tomatoes; continue to sauté until tomatoes begin to release liquid. Sprinkle in flour; stir to blend.

5. Slowly add cream to saucepan, stirring constantly. Bring mixture to a boil; reduce heat to medium. Add brandy; simmer 10 minutes.

6. Add scallops; cook just until scallops are opaque, about 3–4 minutes. Remove from heat; season with salt and pepper and stir in thyme.

7. To serve, cut salmon crosswise into 8 pieces. Using a sharp spatula, carefully separate salmon from skin. Place portions on plates; ladle ragout around salmon. Sprinkle with parsley; serve immediately.

Thai Shrimp Curry

Packaged Thai curry pastes, available in most supermarket Asian-food sections, bring the exotic flavors of galangal root, Kaffir lime leaves, lemongrass, and chilies to your kitchen without all the shopping and chopping.

INGREDIENTS | SERVES 8

2 tablespoons olive oil

3 tablespoons Thai green curry paste

2 (14-ounce) cans coconut milk

1 tablespoon fish sauce

1 medium sweet onion, cut into 8 wedges

1 medium red bell pepper

2 small Asian eggplants, diced

3 pounds shrimp, peeled and deveined

1 tablespoon lime juice

½ cup fresh sweet basil leaves

Salt and pepper to taste

Chopped peanuts or cashews for garnish

1. In a heavy soup pot or Dutch oven, heat oil over medium-high heat. Add curry paste; cook, stirring constantly, 1 minute.

2. Slowly add coconut milk and fish sauce; reduce heat to medium. Whisk to incorporate curry paste in coconut milk.

3. When sauce is simmering, add onion, pepper, and eggplants; cook 15 minutes.

4. Add shrimp; continue cooking until shrimp turn opaque, about 3 minutes.

5. Stir in lime juice, basil leaves, salt, and pepper. Serve with steamed jasmine rice and chopped peanuts or cashews.

Spiced Wild Boar with Prunes

Sweet prunes make a nice foil for rich wild boar meat in this fall favorite.
If you don't have access to wild boar, you can substitute pork or even venison.

INGREDIENTS | SERVES 6

1½ cups dried pitted prunes

1½ cups red wine

1 small orange, quartered

4 tablespoons butter

3 pounds wild boar loin, cut into 1 cubes

½ cup flour

Salt and pepper to taste

1 small onion, diced

3 cloves garlic, minced

4 cups beef or chicken broth

2 bay leaves

¼ cup brandy

⅓ cup heavy cream

Pinch thyme

1. In a small bowl, combine prunes, wine, and orange quarters. In a heavy Dutch oven, melt 3 tablespoons butter over medium-high heat. Toss boar cubes in flour; season with salt and pepper. Working in batches, brown meat on all sides; remove to a bowl. Add remaining butter to pot along with onion and garlic; sauté 3 minutes.

2. Add broth; stir well, scraping up browned bits from bottom. Add bay leaf; bring mixture to a boil. Reduce heat to medium; return boar to pot. Remove orange quarters; pour prune and wine mixture into pot. Stir well; simmer 1 hour, or until boar is tender.

3. Add brandy, cream, and thyme; cook an additional 5 minutes. Serve with boiled sliced potatoes.

This Little Piggy Went to Market

Boar, a type of pig, are not native to North America; they were brought to the continent by early Spanish settlers. Escapees made themselves quite at home in low-lying coastal brush and forests, and today their descendents are considered an invasive species. They're a favorite target for hunters, both for sport and meat. For non-hunters, boar is now farmed at various locations in the U.S. Wild boar meat can be found at specialty stores and through some online purveyors. In general, boar can be used in place of pork in any recipe.

Pumpkin Bisque

Serve this rich soup in mugs for a casual game-night supper or in place of salad at a fall holiday meal.

INGREDIENTS | SERVES 4

3 cups pulp from baked pie pumpkins
1 cup chicken or vegetable stock
1 cup heavy cream
1 green onion, chopped
⅓ cup fresh parsley
Dash ground ginger
Salt and pepper to taste
Crème fraîche or sour cream for garnish

1. Combine pumpkin pulp, stock, heavy cream, green onion, and parsley in a blender container. Pulse to combine; process until puréed.

2. Pour in a saucepan; cook over medium heat until hot. Stir in ginger, salt, and pepper to taste. Serve with a dollop of crème fraîche or sour cream for garnish.

Peaches and Champagne Soup

Serve this soup as a summer aperitif or palate cleanser. To make it an elaborate dessert, place a scoop of rich vanilla ice cream in the center of each bowl and drizzle with raspberry coulis.

INGREDIENTS | SERVES 4

6 ripe peaches
1 teaspoon sugar
Pinch salt
1 cup dry Champagne

1. Peel and seed peaches; chop and mix with sugar and salt. Cover; place in freezer 2 hours.

2. Spoon peach mixture into blender container; pulse until puréed.

3. Pour ½ cup of Champagne into each of 4 bowls or large martini glasses. Stir an equal amount of peach purée into each glass; serve.

Gnocchi with Fennel, Sausage, and Peppers in Broth

Gnocchi are tender little potato dumplings that make a tasty alternative to pasta.
Always cook gnocchi in boiling water before adding to soups or sauces.

INGREDIENTS | SERVES 4

2 cups frozen or vacuum-packed gnocchi

1 tablespoon olive oil

½ pound Italian sausage

6 cups strong chicken broth

1 cup thinly sliced fennel

1 medium red bell pepper, cored and sliced

Salt and pepper to taste

½ cup freshly grated Parmesan cheese

1. Bring a large kettle of water to a boil over high heat. Add gnocchi; cook until dumplings float to surface. (This should only take a few minutes.) Cook about 1 minute longer; remove to bowl with slotted spoon. Drizzle hot gnocchi with olive oil; gently turn to coat.

2. Brown Italian sausage in a skillet over high heat, piercing casing to let fat escape. When cooked, set aside to cool slightly. Remove casing; chop into small pieces.

3. Bring broth to a boil in a soup pot. Add fennel; cook 3 minutes.

4. Reduce heat to medium. Add pepper and sausage; let simmer 5 minutes.

5. Add gnocchi, salt, and pepper; remove from heat. Cover pot; let stand 1 minute. Ladle into bowls; serve with freshly grated Parmesan.

CHAPTER 15

Quick-Fix Soups and Stews

Blender Potato-Garlic Soup

This easy, satisfying soup can be varied with the addition of crumbled bacon or a dash of nutmeg. For a thicker soup, just use more potatoes or less milk.

INGREDIENTS | SERVES 2

1½ cups leftover mashed potatoes

2 cloves garlic

1 green onion, minced

1½ cups hot milk

Salt and pepper to taste

½ cup shredded Cheddar cheese

Cooking with Leftovers

Recycling leftovers into soups or stews is a great way to eliminate waste in the kitchen while keeping meals fresh and interesting. Most leftovers will keep for two or three days in the refrigerator, and up to six months in the freezer.

1. Warm mashed potatoes in microwave on high 1 minute; spoon into blender container.

2. Add garlic, green onion, and hot milk; pulse several times to combine. Blend on high speed 30 seconds; add salt and pepper and pulse once more.

3. Ladle soup into 2 bowls; garnish with shredded cheese. Serve immediately.

Egg Drop Soup

The secret to this recipe is adding the eggs to the boiling broth very slowly, resulting in smooth ribbons of egg throughout the soup.

INGREDIENTS | SERVES 4

6 cups chicken broth

¼ teaspoon grated fresh ginger or dash ground ginger

2 eggs, beaten

1 tablespoon minced green onion or chives

1 tablespoon cornstarch dissolved in 2 tablespoons cold water

Salt and pepper to taste

1. In a soup pot, bring broth and ginger to a rolling boil. With a fork, drizzle in beaten eggs. While egg streams drip into pot, gently stir broth with your other hand. Continue until all egg is in soup.

2. Stir in green onion or chives and cornstarch dissolved in water. Stir and continue to cook until soup is slightly thickened, about 1–2 minutes. Season with salt and pepper; serve.

Cream of Broccoli Soup

Fresh broccoli gives this soup a superb flavor. However, frozen broccoli can be used in a pinch.

INGREDIENTS | SERVES 4

1 small head broccoli
1 tablespoon butter
1 small onion, diced
4 cups chicken or vegetable broth
1 teaspoon sugar or sugar substitute
2 cups heavy cream
⅛ teaspoon nutmeg
Salt and pepper to taste

1. Trim off woody exterior of broccoli stalk and cut off stalk; chop coarsely. Separate florets into individual pieces. Bring a soup pot of water to a boil; cook 2–3 minutes, until crisp-tender. Drain and set aside; discard cooking liquid.

2. Add butter to soup pot, along with onion and broccoli stems and florets. Reserve 4 florets for garnish. Sauté mixture over high heat, stirring constantly, 3 minutes.

3. Add broth; reduce heat to medium. Simmer 20 minutes.

4. Purée broccoli and broth mixture in blender or food processor; add sugar. Return to soup pot; heat until just bubbling around edges. Turn off heat; stir in heavy cream, nutmeg, salt, and pepper.

5. Ladle into 4 bowls; garnish each with a reserved broccoli floret.

Saucy Minestrone

Ready-to-eat spaghetti sauce gives this soup an instant infusion of Italian seasoning. Leftover diced pot roast or cooked sausage can be added to make a heartier minestrone.

INGREDIENTS | SERVES 6

1 (26-ounce) can or jar spaghetti sauce
1 (15-ounce) can red kidney beans
1 (15-ounce) can white cannellini beans
2 cups frozen or canned green beans
1 cup sliced carrots
1 cup diced zucchini
3 cups water or chicken broth
1 cup dry digitalini or elbow macaroni
Salt and pepper to taste

1. Combine sauce, beans, vegetables, and broth in a large soup pot; bring to a boil over high heat, stirring often.

2. Add pasta; reduce heat to medium. Simmer, stirring occasionally to keep pasta from sticking to bottom of pot, until pasta is cooked and carrots are tender, about 10–15 minutes. Add salt and pepper to taste.

Tortellini in Chicken Broth

If you don't have homemade chicken stock in the freezer, substitute canned. In small portions, this soup makes a nice first course to a winter-night supper of roast beef or chicken and vegetables.

INGREDIENTS | SERVES 4

3 cups frozen meat or cheese tortellini
6 cups strong chicken stock
½ cup frozen peas
Salt and pepper to taste
¼ cup fresh basil ribbons

Veggie Confetti

Frozen peas add color to broth-based soups, but carrots, lima beans, or even diced red peppers will work as well. Just because a dish is quick fix, doesn't mean it shouldn't be pleasing to the eye. Don't be afraid to doctor your soups with chopped leftover vegetables or a handful of frozen veggies.

1. Fill a large saucepan or soup pot with water; bring to a boil. Add frozen tortellini; cook according to package directions until just done—do not overcook. Carefully drain tortellini; discard water.

2. Add stock and peas; bring to a boil over high heat. Reduce heat to medium; carefully add cooked tortellini. Simmer 3 minutes.

3. Season with salt and pepper; stir in basil. Serve immediately.

Spicy Black Bean Bisque

Jalapeño peppers carry most of their heat in the seeds and inner ribs.
If you want a milder soup, split the pepper in half and remove the seeds before using.

INGREDIENTS | SERVES 3–4

2 (15-ounce) cans black beans

1 jalapeño pepper, chopped

1 cup half-and-half

1 teaspoon cumin

Salt and pepper to taste

⅓ cup sour cream or crème fraîche

Chopped fresh cilantro or green onion

A Bounty of Beans

Legumes are among the few vegetables that taste almost as good canned as home cooked. Take advantage of these inexpensive, complex carbs to make meals heartier and healthier. Puréed beans can be used as thickeners for soups and chilies or as sauces for meats and chicken.

1. Drain and rinse black beans; reserve ½ cup for later use. Place remaining beans, jalapeño pepper, and half-and-half in blender; pulse until blended. Add cumin; blend until puréed.

2. Pour purée into saucepan; cook over medium heat until just bubbling at sides of pan. Stir in reserved beans; add salt and pepper. Ladle into bowls; garnish with sour cream or crème fraîche and chopped herbs.

Shrimp and Cod with Grape Tomatoes

This super-easy dish gets a burst of fresh flavor from the tiny, sweet grape tomatoes. Adding the tomatoes whole at the end of cooking time warms the tomatoes but keeps them from getting too soft.

INGREDIENTS | SERVES 6

1 pound fresh or thawed frozen shrimp, peeled and deveined

½ pound cod fillet, cut into strips

1 cup water or shrimp broth

1 cup yellow bell pepper strips

1 cup green peas

1½ cups ready-to-serve Alfredo sauce

1½ cups grape tomatoes

Salt and pepper to taste

1. In a large saucepan, combine shrimp, cod strips, and water or broth. Bring to a boil over high heat; reduce heat to medium. Add pepper and peas; cover and simmer 3 minutes.

2. Remove cover. When seafood turns opaque, stir in Alfredo sauce; cook until sauce is bubbly. Remove from heat; add tomatoes, salt, and pepper. Cover and let stand 5 minutes before serving. Serve over rice or pasta.

Cooking Times for Shrimp

Nobody likes tough shrimp. To avoid serving too-chewy crustaceans, you have two options. Either cook your shrimp just until the flesh turns opaque or cook the shrimp over low heat for 30 minutes or more. The longer cooking time breaks down the fibers, making the shrimp less plump, but more tender.

Chicken and Chickpea Stew

Rotisserie chicken from the supermarket deli works perfectly in this recipe. You can also plan ahead for this stew by roasting an extra chicken next time you make a chicken dinner.

INGREDIENTS | SERVES 6–8

4 cups diced, cooked chicken
1 teaspoon hot curry powder
½ teaspoon cumin
¼ cup flour
¼ cup olive oil
1 medium onion, diced
1 cup water or chicken broth
1 (10-ounce) can tomatoes and chilies
3 (15-ounce) cans chick peas, drained
Salt and pepper to taste

1. Sprinkle chicken with curry powder and cumin. In a large, heavy skillet or saucepan, combine flour and oil; cook over medium-high heat, stirring constantly, until mixture turns light brown. Add diced onion; continue to cook, stirring, until onion begins to brown around edges.

2. Add water or broth; stir until mixture is well blended. Add tomatoes and chilies, chicken, and chickpeas; stir well. If mixture is too thick, add a little more liquid. Simmer 15 minutes.

3. Add salt and pepper. Serve over couscous.

Sausage Barley Stew

This recipe takes an hour to cook, but it's so easy to put together it qualifies as a quick fix.

INGREDIENTS | SERVES 4

2 tablespoons oil
1 large onion, chopped
½ pound spicy Italian sausage
½ pound presliced mushrooms
1 cup baby carrots, halved
2 cups preshredded cabbage
½ cup raw pearl barley
6 cups chicken broth
Salt and pepper to taste

1. In a large Dutch oven with a tight-fitting lid, heat oil. Add chopped onion; sauté over medium-high heat until onion begins to brown.

2. Cut sausage into 1 pieces; add to pan. Cook, stirring often, until well browned. Add mushrooms; continue to sauté 3 minutes.

3. Add remaining ingredients; stir well. Bring to a boil; reduce heat to medium low. Cover and simmer 1 hour, or until barley is tender. Stir well before serving.

Ramen with Broccoli Slaw

Ramen noodle soup is the preferred sustenance of many cash-strapped college students. This recipe adds a serving of vegetables to the mix. For a healthier soup, use homemade chicken broth or pick a lower-sodium brand.

INGREDIENTS | SERVES 2

4 cups water

1 cup broccoli slaw

2 packages vegetarian or chicken-flavored ramen

1 green onion, trimmed and sliced

Dash soy sauce

1. In a medium soup pot, bring water to a boil. Add broccoli slaw; cook 1 minute.

2. Add ramen noodles; cook, stirring to separate noodles, 3 minutes.

3. Add green onion and soy sauce; serve immediately.

Fab Fast Barbecue Stew

Different brands of prepared shredded BBQ pork offer different levels of spice, sweetness, and tanginess. Experiment to find the brand that suits your taste.

INGREDIENTS | SERVES 4

2 sweet potatoes, peeled and diced

1 (18-ounce) tub prepared shredded BBQ pork

1 (15-ounce) can chili-seasoned pinto beans

1 cup corn kernels

½ cup water

1 teaspoon honey mustard

1 cup shredded Cheddar cheese

1. Place sweet potatoes in a heavy saucepan with enough water to cover. Bring to a boil; cook just until tender, about 10 minutes.

2. Drain; return potatoes to pan. Add pork, beans, corn, and water; stir in honey mustard. Cook over medium heat, stirring occasionally, 10 minutes.

3. Pour into bowls; sprinkle with cheese. Serve with cornbread.

Corn, Roasted Tomato, and Chicken Chowder

*Any combination of fresh herbs—parsley, green onion, cilantro, basil, oregano, or tarragon—
can be used to give this soup a unique flavor profile.*

INGREDIENTS | SERVES 6

6 cups chicken broth
1 (15-ounce) can fire-roasted diced
tomatoes
3 cups corn kernels
1 cup shredded cooked chicken
1 cup half-and-half
⅓ cup minced fresh herbs
Salt and pepper to taste

1. In a large saucepan, bring broth to a boil; add tomatoes and corn. Reduce heat to medium; simmer 10 minutes.

2. Stir in cooked chicken; continue cooking 5 minutes.

3. Add half-and-half and fresh herbs; cook just until heated through. Add salt and pepper to taste. Serve immediately.

Quick Cioppino

*If you have access to fresh clams, firm white fish fillets, or any
other favorite seafood, feel free to make substitutions.*

INGREDIENTS | SERVES 4

2 cups clam juice
2 cups tomato and basil spaghetti sauce
1 cup red wine
1 cup water or chicken broth
½ teaspoon red pepper flakes
1 pound shrimp, peeled and deveined
2 dozen mussels in the shell, scrubbed
1 pound sea scallops
Salt and pepper to taste
Fresh basil ribbons

1. Combine clam juice, spaghetti sauce, wine, and water or broth in Dutch oven; Bring to a boil over high heat. Add red pepper flakes; continue cooking 5 minutes.

2. Carefully add shrimp, mussels, and scallops; reduce heat to medium and cover. Cook 5–10 minutes, or until mussels pop open. Season with salt and pepper; sprinkle with basil. Serve with crusty bread.

Turkey Pipperade

Buy ready-to-cook thin-sliced turkey cutlets at your supermarket meat counter.
For a splurge, veal cutlets can be used in this recipe as well.

INGREDIENTS | **SERVES 4**

1 pound turkey breast cutlets
⅓ cup flour
1 teaspoon seasoned salt
2 tablespoons butter
1 medium onion
1 small red bell pepper, cored
1 small green bell pepper, cored
1 cup turkey or chicken broth
1 cup white wine
Salt and pepper to taste

1. Lightly pound turkey cutlets with a meat mallet. Combine flour and salt in a shallow bowl; dredge turkey in mixture.

2. Heat butter in a deep skillet over medium-high heat. Place cutlets in butter; brown on each side. Thinly slice onion and peppers by hand or in food processor; spread evenly over top of cutlets. Carefully add broth and wine to skillet.

3. Cover and cook until turkey is done and veggies are crisp-tender, about 10 minutes. Season with salt and pepper; serve over rice.

Chicken Stroganoff

Adding cream of mushroom soup to a dish may seem retro, but it works.
Doctored, condensed soup can make a thick, creamy sauce without the need for a roux.

INGREDIENTS | **SERVES 4**

1 tablespoon butter
1 tablespoon olive oil
4 boneless skinless chicken breast halves
Salt and pepper to taste
2 green onions, minced
½ pound sliced mushrooms
1 cup water or chicken broth
1 (10-ounce) can cream of mushroom soup
1 cup sour cream
Chopped parsley

1. In a large, heavy skillet, heat butter and olive oil over high heat. Cut chicken breast halves crosswise, to get 8 pieces; sprinkle with salt and pepper. Brown in butter and olive oil.

2. Add green onions and mushrooms along with 1 cup water or broth. Bring to a boil; reduce heat to medium. Cover and simmer 12 minutes.

3. Remove chicken pieces to a plate. Add cream of mushroom soup to skillet; whisk to blend with mushrooms and pan juices. Bring to a boil. Remove skillet from heat; whisk in sour cream.

4. Return chicken to skillet; sprinkle with parsley. Serve over noodles.

Meatball Curry

Frozen, ready-to-heat meatballs make this dish a quick fix.
To make it child friendly, substitute sweet bell pepper for the jalapeños.

INGREDIENTS | SERVES 4

2 tablespoons butter
1 large onion, sliced
2 jalapeño peppers, chopped
2 cloves garlic, minced
2 teaspoons curry powder
2 (15-ounce) cans diced tomatoes
½ cup water
24 prepared meatballs

1. In a large, heavy saucepan, heat butter over medium-high heat; add onion, peppers, and garlic. Sauté 5 minutes, or until onion begins to turn translucent.

2. Sprinkle curry powder over onion mixture; stir well. Add tomatoes, water, and meatballs. Bring to a boil; reduce heat to medium.

3. Stir to coat meatballs with sauce. Cover; simmer 15 minutes, or until meatballs are heated through. Serve with basmati rice.

A World of Curries

Curry is both a dish—a stew—and a spice mix. Just as curry recipes differ from country to country, so do the recipes for curry spice blends. The curry powders available in most supermarkets reflect ingredients common to Indian curries, such as turmeric, cumin, cardamom, fenugreek, coriander, and peppers. Caribbean curry powders usually contain an extra shot of pepper as well as cloves, cinnamon, and nutmeg. Thai and Chinese curry seasonings are often sold in paste form and reflect the blend of aromatic roots, herbs, and peppers common to dishes in those countries.

Thai Vegetable Stew

Feel free to substitute pattypan squash, cauliflower, or other vegetables for those in the recipe.

INGREDIENTS | SERVES 6

1 tablespoon oil
2 tablespoons Thai red curry paste
2 cans coconut milk
1 small onion, diced
1 cup sliced mushrooms
1 cup snow peas or sugar snap peas
1 zucchini, sliced
2 yellow squash, sliced
1 Japanese eggplant, sliced
1 cup broccoli florets
½ teaspoon grated lime zest
1 cup chopped peanuts

1. In a heavy soup pan or Dutch oven, heat olive oil over medium heat. Add curry paste; stir with wooden spoon 1 minute.

2. Slowly whisk in coconut milk. Add vegetables; simmer, stirring occasionally, 15 minutes.

3. Stir in lime zest; garnish with chopped peanuts. Serve over jasmine rice.

White Bean and Bacon Soup

Cut this recipe in half for a fast, filling lunch for one. Or you can freeze half for later.

INGREDIENTS | SERVES 2–3

2 cups chicken broth
2 (15-ounce) cans white beans
1 (15-ounce) can tomatoes with oregano and garlic
4 strips cooked bacon
Salt and pepper to taste

1. In a saucepan, combine broth, beans, and tomatoes; bring to a boil over medium-high heat. Crumble in bacon; reduce heat to medium. Simmer 5 minutes.

2. Season with salt and pepper. Serve in soup mugs with breadsticks or muffins.

Creamsicle Dessert Soup

Serve this icy soup with chocolate cookies or sugar wafers for a refreshing summer dessert.

INGREDIENTS | **MAKES 4 SERVINGS**

1 pint orange sorbet

1 cup heavy cream

½ cup orange juice

1 teaspoon vanilla

1. Place all ingredients in a blender pitcher; purée until well blended.

2. Pour into glass bowls; serve immediately.

Piña Colada Soup

Serve this soup in place of fruit at breakfast. On weekend mornings,
a splash of brandy will add another layer of flavor to the mix.

INGREDIENTS | **SERVES 4**

1 cup fresh pineapple chunks

1 (14-ounce) can coconut milk, chilled

2 cups cold pineapple juice

1 teaspoons vanilla

1 tablespoon sugar

4 mint sprigs

1. Divide pineapple chunks evenly over 4 small bowls.

2. Combine coconut milk, pineapple juice, vanilla, and sugar in a blender; pulse until well blended. Pour over pineapple in bowls; garnish with mint sprigs.

Glossary

Base: Concentrated pastes created from meats, poultry, fish, or vegetables. Mixed with boiling water, can be used to create broths instantly.

Bisque: Creamy soups thickened with roux, cream, or both. Often the solids have been puréed for a smooth dish.

Braise: Cooking method that involves long, slow cooking over low heat in a small amount of liquid. Well suited to poultry or tough cuts of meat, usually browned in butter or oil before simmering in liquid.

Broth: Thin, clear soup made by simmering bones, skin, and flesh of red meats, poultry, or seafood in water to extract flavor and nutrients. Meatless broth can be made from a mix of vegetables.

Chili powder: Mixture of dried, powdered chili peppers, cumin, oregano, and other spices. Single-source chili powders contain only the dry powder of one type of chili pepper.

Chipotle: Smoked, dried jalapeño peppers. Can be purchased whole as well as canned, powdered, or as a paste.

Cholent: Slow-cooked stew traditionally including tough but flavorful cuts of beef, dried legumes, potatoes, and aromatic vegetables. Can be cooked overnight in an oven on low heat or in a slow cooker.

Confit: Duck or other meat preserved in fat. Meat is salted then cooked slowly in its own fat. After cooking, meat is packed in the cooking fat and refrigerated.

Courtbouillon: Term used to refer to two different but related dishes: a flavored liquid, often made with aromatic herbs and vegetables, used for poaching ingredients such as meat, poultry, fish, or eggs; and a thick, spicy tomato-based soup or stew in which fish or shellfish have been poached.

Curry: Stew made with customary mix of aromatic spices. Curry seasonings and ingredients vary widely from one region to another. Often can be purchased already blended as powder or paste.

Étouffée: French for "smothered," referring to cooking method by which ingredients are braised and slowly simmered in a rich, seasoned sauce. Staple of south Louisiana cooking, usually made with crawfish or shrimp.

Fricassee: Stew of chicken, rabbit, or other light meats cut into serving pieces but not deboned and simmered in a roux-thickened gravy that may or may not include mushrooms and other vegetables.

Gnocchi: Small dumplings made from a dough of eggs, flour, and either mashed potatoes or ricotta cheese. Can be served with butter and cheese as pasta course or in broth for a hearty soup.

Gremolata: Aromatic mix of finely minced or ground fresh garlic, parsley, and lemon zest. Variations use different herbs and orange or lime zest. A traditional seasoning for Milanese-style braised veal shanks.

Gumbo: Thick soup that can include spicy sausage, poultry, shellfish, and vegetables. Served over rice, often as a main-dish soup.

Jerk: Slow-grilled or smoked meats seasoned with a hot-and-sweet mixture of dry or wet spices including hot chili peppers, cinnamon, ginger, allspice, garlic, nutmeg, and brown sugar. Served throughout the Caribbean; recipes vary from island to island, cook to cook.

Purée: Vegetables, fruits, or other ingredients combined with liquid and blended into a uniformly smooth soup or sauce. Can be seasoned and served as a soup or become a sauce or ingredient in another dish.

Raft: A combination of ground meat, egg whites, and sometimes eggshells. Added to simmering strained broth, will coagulate into a floating mass, taking solids and impurities from the broth with it.

Roux: Mixture of fat and flour, cooked to a desired shade ranging from white to dark brown, used to thicken soups, stews, and sauces.

Spaetzle: Thick, free-form egg noodle or dumpling that can be served as a side dish or addition to soups and stews. Frequently found in German cuisine.

Stock: Term often used interchangeably with broth; most chefs define stock as the liquid from simmering meat or poultry bones. Stock is usually an ingredient in another dish, whereas broth can be an ingredient or eaten as is.

Velouté: Classic sauce made from light broth and blonde roux; velouté-based soups may also include heavy cream and eggs. Can be served as a smooth cream soup or contain small amounts of vegetable purée, chopped vegetables, minced poultry, or seafood.

Dry Soup Mixes

Use these recipes to give the gift of nonperishable soup to friends and family. Top jars with a square of fabric and a bow and attach seasoning packets and a recipe card for preparing the soup.

Six-Bean Soup

INGREDIENTS | SERVES 4

⅓ cup dried calico beans
⅓ cup dried navy beans
⅓ cup dried kidney beans
⅓ cup dried lima beans
⅓ cup green split peas
⅓ cup yellow split peas
1 tablespoon granulated chicken bouillon
½ teaspoon dried oregano
½ teaspoon garlic powder
½ teaspoon onion powder
½ teaspoon paprika
1 teaspoon kosher salt
½ teaspoon black pepper

1. To assemble: Layer beans and peas in a clean, dry pint jar. Seal tightly. Combine chicken bouillon and other seasonings and spoon into a small resealable plastic bag. Store together until ready to use.

2. To prepare: Rinse beans in a colander. Combine beans and seasonings with 8 cups water and a ham hock in a soup pot. Cook over medium low heat 3 hours, stirring often.

Chili Bean Soup

INGREDIENTS | SERVES 6–8

1 cup kidney beans
1 cup pinto beans
1 cup white beans
½ cup calico beans
½ cup black beans
3 tablespoons chili powder
1 teaspoon cumin
½ teaspoon oregano
1½ teaspoons kosher salt
½ teaspoon cayenne pepper
1 teaspoon dehydrated onion flakes
½ teaspoon garlic powder

1. To assemble: Layer beans in a clean, dry quart jar. Seal tightly. Combine seasonings and spoon into a resealable plastic bag. Store together until ready to use.

2. To prepare: Rinse beans in a colander. Combine beans and seasonings with 12 cups water in a large soup pot. Add 1 (28-ounce) can tomatoes, crushed. Bring to a boil; reduce heat and simmer over medium low heat 3 hours. Add cooked shredded or ground beef if desired.

Mediterranean Bean Soup

INGREDIENTS | SERVES 6–8

1 cup dry cannellini beans
1 cup dry kidney beans
1 cup dry garbanzo beans
½ cup dried fava beans
½ cup dried cranberry beans
1 tablespoon mixed dried Italian herbs
1 teaspoon dehydrated onion flakes
1 teaspoon dehydrated celery flakes
1 tablespoon granulated chicken bouillon
1 teaspoon kosher salt
½ teaspoon black pepper
½ teaspoon red pepper flakes
2 tablespoons chopped dried tomatoes

1. To assemble: Layer beans in a clean, dry quart jar. Seal tightly. Combine seasonings and spoon into a resealable plastic bag. Store together until ready to use.

2. To prepare: Rinse beans in a colander. Combine beans and seasonings with 12 cups water in a large soup pot. Add 1 (32-ounce) can tomato sauce. Bring to a boil; reduce heat and simmer over medium low heat 3 hours. Add ½ pound sliced sausage or diced ham during cooking if desired.

Hoppin' John Soup

INGREDIENTS | SERVES 4

3 cups dried black-eyed peas
1 cup short-grain brown rice
1 tablespoon granulated chicken bouillon
1 tablespoon dehydrated onion flakes
1 teaspoon dehydrated celery flakes
1 bay leaf
½ teaspoon garlic powder
½ teaspoon kosher salt
½ teaspoon black pepper
¼ teaspoon dried thyme leaves

1. To assemble: Alternate peas and rice in a pint jar. Combine bouillon and other seasonings and spoon into a small resealable plastic bag. Store together until ready to use.

2. To prepare: Rinse beans and rice in a colander. Combine beans and rice with seasonings and 8 cups water in a large soup pot. Add 1 (16-ounce) can diced tomatoes and one ham hock. Bring to a boil; reduce heat and simmer over medium low heat 3 hours, stirring often. Stir in 1 cup chopped greens during the last hour of cooking if desired.

Hearty Fifteen-Bean Soup

INGREDIENTS | MAKES 8 BATCHES
EACH BATCH SERVES 4

1 cup dried black beans

1 cup dried small red beans

1 cup dried kidney beans

1 cup dried great northern beans

1 cup dried navy beans

1 cup dried pinto beans

1 cup dried calico beans

1 cup dried baby lima beans

1 cup dried black-eyed peas

1 cup dried garbanzo beans

1 cup dried green split peas

1 cup dried yellow split peas

1 cup dried brown lentils

1 cup dried field peas

1 cup pearled barley

½ cup granulated chicken bouillon

3 tablespoons dried Italian herbs

2 tablespoons dehydrated onion flakes

1 tablespoon dehydrated celery

1½ tablespoons kosher salt

1 tablespoon red pepper flakes

2 teaspoons garlic powder

2 teaspoons black pepper

1 teaspoon cumin

1. To assemble: Mix all beans and barley together in a very large salad bowl. Scoop well-mixed beans and barley into 8 pint jars. Cover tightly. Combine chicken bouillon and seasonings together and scoop into 8 small resealable plastic bags.

2. To prepare: Pour 1 pint jar of mixed beans and barley into a strainer; Rinse well. Combine with 1 packet seasonings and 8 cups water in a large soup pot. Add ½ pound smoked sausage or diced ham; bring to a boil. Reduce heat to medium low; simmer 3 hours. Add ⅓ cup minced fresh herbs, if desired.

The Cabbage Soup Diet

The Cabbage Soup Diet has been around for decades, promoted as a temporary, quick weight-loss tool. No dietitians or food historians claim to know exactly where it originated, but everyone does agree on this: It did not come from Sacred Heart Medical Center, Mayo Clinic, the U.S. military, or any of the other institutions to which it is sometimes attributed.

The diet is designed to last for one week only. While the Cabbage Soup Diet is not a well-rounded program, nutritionists say most healthy people can easily withstand it for a short period.

And, it does encourage consumption of low-calorie, high-fiber, high-antioxidant vegetables and fruit.

The cornerstone of the diet is a bottomless pot of cabbage soup, which can be consumed anytime in any quantity. Aside from the soup, the eating plan is very restrictive.

Although there are several versions of the Cabbage Soup Diet—including some that add protein shakes to the mix—this is the diet most often circulated. At the end of the week, dieters have reported losing seven to fifteen pounds.

The Cabbage Soup Diet

Cabbage Soup Recipe

INGREDIENTS | SERVES 12–14

6 green onions, trimmed and sliced

2 green bell peppers, cored and diced

2 (16-ounce) cans diced tomatoes

1 (10-ounce) can Ro-Tel tomatoes (optional)

3 carrots, trimmed and sliced

8 ounces mushrooms, sliced

3 ribs celery, trimmed and sliced

½ head cabbage, trimmed and chopped

1 package Lipton Onion Soup Mix

2 bouillon cubes (optional)

12 cups water (or 8 cups water and 4 cups V-8 juice)

Herbs and seasonings as desired

Combine all ingredients in a large soup pot. Bring to a boil over high heat; reduce heat to medium low. Simmer 2 hours. Cool slightly before serving. Refrigerate or freeze any unused portions.

The Seven-Day Diet

DAY ONE
All the fruit you want, except bananas. All the cabbage soup you want.

DAY TWO
All the raw or cooked vegetables you want, with emphasis on leafy greens. Avoid dry beans, peas, and corn. All the cabbage soup you want. You may have 1 baked potato with butter for dinner.

DAY THREE
All the fruit you want, except bananas. All the vegetables you want, except potatoes, dry beans, peas, and corn. All the cabbage soup you want.

DAY FOUR
Up to 8 bananas and all the skim milk you want. All the cabbage soup you want. No other foods.

DAY FIVE
Ten to twenty ounces of lean beef, skinless chicken breast, or fish and up to 6 tomatoes. All the cabbage soup you want. At least 8 glasses of water.

DAY SIX
Up to 20 ounces of steak or skinless chicken (no fish) plus leafy green vegetables. At least 1 serving of cabbage soup.

DAY SEVEN
Brown rice, unsweetened fruit juices, and nonstarchy vegetables. All the cabbage soup you want.

Tips for Success

1. Follow the diet exactly.
2. Drink 4–6 glasses of water daily, as well as unsweetened tea and no-sugar-added cranberry juice. Do not drink any sugar-sweetened beverages.
3. Take a multivitamin tablet daily.
4. Eat plenty of soup to stave off hunger.
5. Follow the diet for only seven days at a time. If you have more weight to lose, allow two weeks of moderate eating between Cabbage Soup Diet weeks.

Index